Fluency in Number Facts Teacher's Guide

Years 1 & 2

Peter Clarke

William Collins' dream of knowledge for all began with the publication of his first book in 1819. A self-educated mill worker, he not only enriched millions of lives, but also founded a flourishing publishing house. Today, staying true to this spirit, Collins books are packed with inspiration, innovation and practical expertise. They place you at the centre of a world of possibility and give you exactly what you need to explore it.

Collins. Freedom to teach.

Published by Collins

An imprint of HarperCollins*Publishers*
77 – 85 Fulham Palace Road
Hammersmith
London
W6 8JB

Browse the complete Collins catalogue at
www.collins.co.uk

10 9 8 7 6 5 4 3 2 1

ISBN-978-0-00-753127-1

British Library Cataloguing in Publication Data
A Catalogue record for this publication is available from the British Library

Edited by Gaynor Spry
Cover design by Nikki Kenwood
Cover artwork by Gwyneth Williams
Internal design by Nikki Kenwood
Illustrations by Andy Robb and Jouve
Typeset by Jouve

Printed by Martins the Printers Ltd, Berwick upon Tweed

Acknowledgement
The author wishes to thank Brian Molyneaux for his valuable contribution to this publication.

Contents

Introduction

The first aim of The National Curriculum for Mathematics (2014) is to ensure that all pupils:

> *'become* ***fluent*** *in the fundamentals of mathematics, including through varied and frequent practice with increasingly complex problems over time, so that pupils have conceptual understanding and are able to recall and apply their knowledge rapidly and accurately to problems'.*

Mathematical fluency involves being able to reason mathematically and calculate accurately, efficiently and flexibly.

It is acquired by mastering the following knowledge and skills:

- a thorough conceptual understanding of number, including place value, addition, subtraction, multiplication and division
- the ability to identify patterns and relationships
- the development of strategic approaches to recall and derive number facts.

Essential to mastering these is:

- purposeful dialogue in pairs and as a group
- effective activities to practise and consolidate numerical skills and the recall of number facts
- meaningful and informative assessment, including self-assessment.

Fluency in Number Facts aims to support conceptual understanding, and the development of mental fluency, in basic numerical skills through whole-class, paired and individual games and activities, and assessment.

The series is divided into Key Stage 1 (Years 1 and 2), Lower Key Stage 2 (Years 3 and 4) and Upper Key Stage 2 (Years 5 and 6). It consists of three *Teacher's Guides*, accompanying *Facts and Games* books and *CD-ROMs* containing all of the resources needed for the games and activities in downloadable form.

Teacher's Guide

Containing Teacher's Notes on:
- whole-class games and activities
- paired games and activities
- individual activities

Facts and Games book

Containing:
- Maths Facts
- paired games

CD-ROM

Containing:
- Maths Facts from the *Facts and Games* books
- resources for the whole-class games and activities, including PowerPoint slides
- paired games from the *Facts and Games* books as well as additional paired activities
- individual activities
- Mental fluency challenges
- number cards
- assessment and record-keeping formats

Each *Teacher's Guide* and *Facts and Games* book covers three Key domains of becoming fluent in number, and are based on the expectations of The National Curriculum for Mathematics (2014).

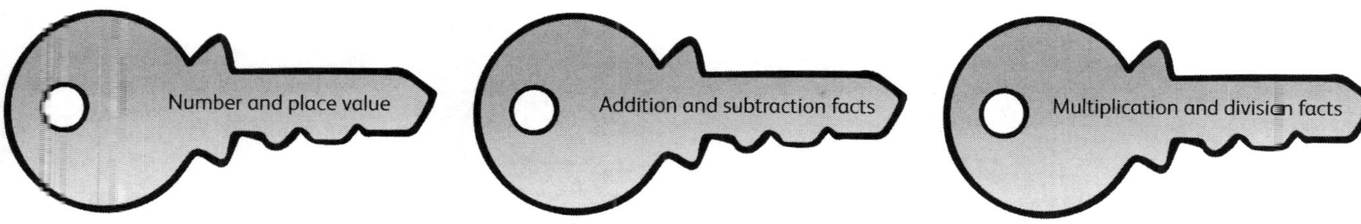

How to use *Fluency in Number Facts*

Fluency in Number Facts is a flexible 'dip in' resource that is designed to be used in many different ways to meet the needs of individual children, and different classroom and school organisational arrangements.

Each of the games and activities is intended to be used for approximately 10 minutes as a way of sharpening children's memory and recall of the basic number facts. Use them either at the start or end of a mathematics lesson or as a quick filler activity at any time throughout the day – a '10 minutes memory maths' session.

The following is a suggested approach to choosing a suitable game or activity:

Decide which Key domain you want to develop fluency in:
- Number and place value
- Addition and subtraction facts
- Multiplication and division facts

Refer to the *Fluency in Number Facts: Teacher's Guide*

↓

Decide whether you want the children to practise and consolidate their fluency in this Key domain:
as a whole class   in pairs   individually

Refer to the *Fluency in Number Facts: Teacher's Guide*

↓

Choose an appropriate game or activity.

Refer to the *Fluency in Number Facts: Teacher's Guide*

↓

Locate the necessary resources.

Refer to the *Fluency in Number Facts: Facts and Games book and/or the accompanying CD-ROM*

Curriculum information

The games and activities in this pack practise and consolidate the following Key Stage 1 (Years 1 and 2) National Curriculum for Mathematics (2014) Programme of Study:

Year 1

Number and place value

Pupils should be taught to:

- count to and across 100, forwards and backwards, beginning with 0 or 1, or from any given number
- count, read and write numbers to 100 in numerals; count in multiples of twos, fives and tens
- given a number, identify one more and one less
- identify and represent numbers using objects and pictorial representations including the number line, and use the language of: equal to, more than, less than (fewer), most, least
- read and write numbers from 1 to 20 in numerals and words.

Addition and subtraction

Pupils should be taught to:

- read, write and interpret mathematical statements involving addition (+), subtraction (–) and equals (=) signs
- represent and use number bonds and related subtraction facts within 20
- add and subtract 1-digit and 2-digit numbers to 20, including zero.
- solve one-step problems that involve addition and subtraction, using concrete objects and pictorial representations, and missing number problems such as $7 = \square - 9$.

Multiplication and division

Pupils should be taught to:

- solve one-step problems involving multiplication and division, by calculating the answer using concrete objects, pictorial representations and arrays with the support of the teacher.

Year 2

Number and place value

Pupils should be taught to:

- count in steps of 2, 3 and 5 from 0, and in tens from any number, forward or backward
- recognise the place value of each digit in a 2-digit number (tens, ones)
- identify, represent and estimate numbers using different representations, including the number line
- compare and order numbers from 0 up to 100; use <, > and = signs
- read and write numbers to at least 100 in numerals and in words.
- use place value and number facts to solve problems

Addition and subtraction

Pupils should be taught to:

- solve problems with addition and subtraction:
  - using concrete objects and pictorial representations, including those involving numbers, quantities and measures
  - applying their increasing knowledge of mental and written methods
- recall and use addition and subtraction facts to 20 fluently, and derive and use related facts up to 100
- add and subtract numbers using concrete objects, pictorial representations, and mentally, including:
  - a 2-digit number and ones
  - a 2-digit number and tens
  - two 2-digit numbers
  - adding three 1-digit numbers
- show that addition of two numbers can be done in any order (commutative) and subtraction of one number from another cannot
- recognise and use the inverse relationship between addition and subtraction and use this to check calculations and missing number problems.

Multiplication and division

Pupils should be taught to:

- recall and use multiplication and division facts for the 2, 5 and 10 multiplication tables, including recognising odd and even numbers
- calculate mathematical statements for multiplication and division within the multiplication tables and write them using the multiplication (×), division (÷) and equals (=) signs
- show that multiplication of two numbers can be done in any order (commutative) and division of one number by another cannot
- solve problems involving multiplication and division, using materials, arrays, repeated addition, mental methods, and multiplication and division facts, including problems in contexts.

Features of the *Fluency in Number Facts: Teacher's Guide*

The games and activities in the *Fluency in Number Facts: Teacher's Guide* are arranged according to the three Key domains. Within each of these Key domains the games and activities are further organised into whole-class, paired or individual games and activities. They are all designed to be used at any time throughout Years 1 & 2.

Whole-class games and activities

This section provides a series of teacher-led games and activities aimed at ensuring the whole class practise and consolidate their fluency in each of the three Key domains.

Each game and activity includes a list of the teacher and pupil resources required as well as instructions and, where appropriate, any variations.

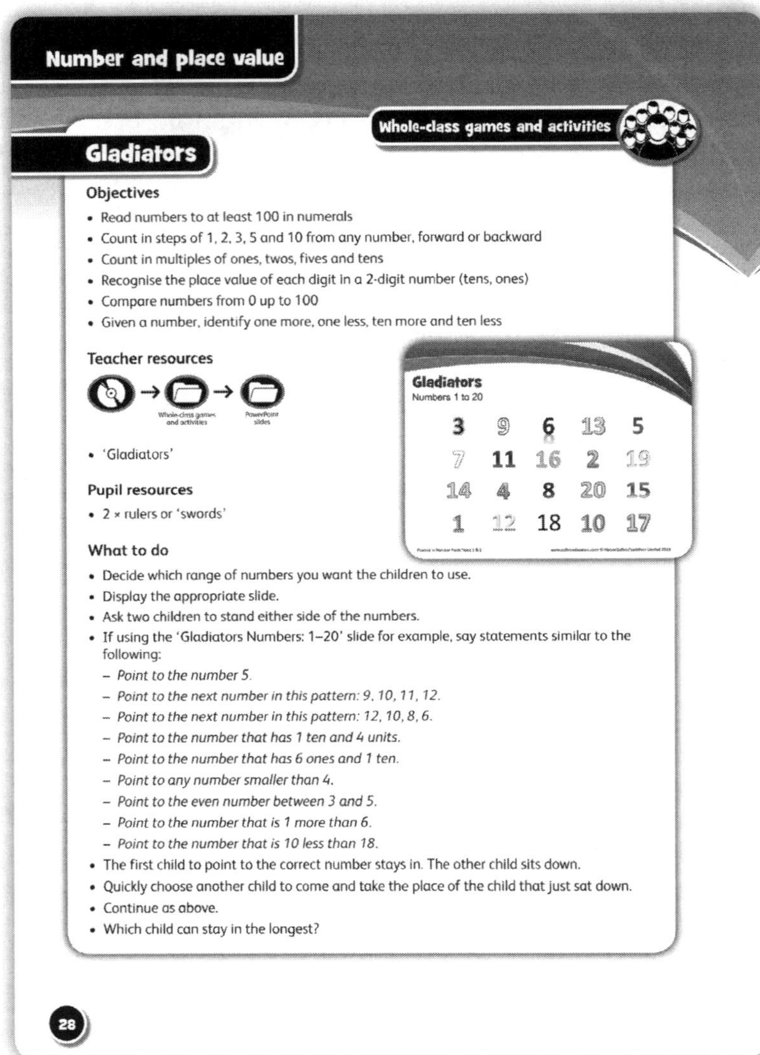

Number and place value

Whole-class games and activities

Gladiators

Objectives

- Read numbers to at least 100 in numerals
- Count in steps of 1, 2, 3, 5 and 10 from any number, forward or backward
- Count in multiples of ones, twos, fives and tens
- Recognise the place value of each digit in a 2-digit number (tens, ones)
- Compare numbers from 0 up to 100
- Given a number, identify one more, one less, ten more and ten less

Teacher resources

- 'Gladiators'

Pupil resources

- 2 × rulers or 'swords'

What to do

- Decide which range of numbers you want the children to use.
- Display the appropriate slide.
- Ask two children to stand either side of the numbers.
- If using the 'Gladiators Numbers: 1–20' slide for example, say statements similar to the following:
  - *Point to the number 5.*
  - *Point to the next number in this pattern: 9, 10, 11, 12.*
  - *Point to the next number in this pattern: 12, 10, 8, 6.*
  - *Point to the number that has 1 ten and 4 units.*
  - *Point to the number that has 6 ones and 1 ten.*
  - *Point to any number smaller than 4.*
  - *Point to the even number between 3 and 5.*
  - *Point to the number that is 1 more than 6.*
  - *Point to the number that is 10 less than 18.*
- The first child to point to the correct number stays in. The other child sits down.
- Quickly choose another child to come and take the place of the child that just sat down.
- Continue as above.
- Which child can stay in the longest?

PowerPoint slides required for some of the whole-class games and activities are located on the accompanying CD-ROM.

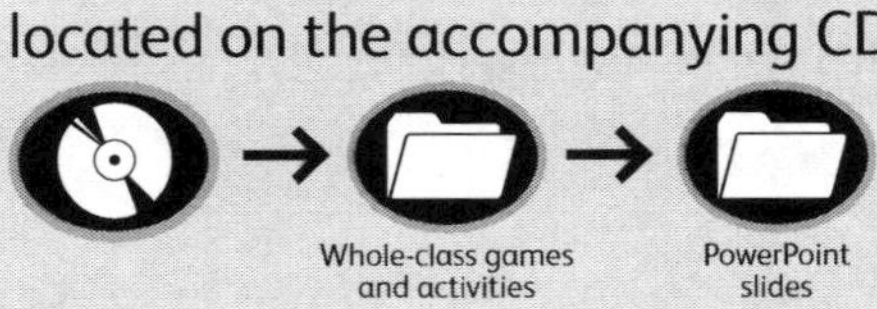

PDF files required for some of the whole-class games and activities are located on the accompanying CD-ROM.

Paired games and activities

Games and activities are provided which children undertake in pairs to practise and consolidate their fluency in each of the three Key domains.

Each game and activity includes a list of the resources required as well as instructions and, where appropriate, any variations.

PDF files required for some of the paired games and activities are located on the accompanying CD-ROM.

→ Paired games and activities

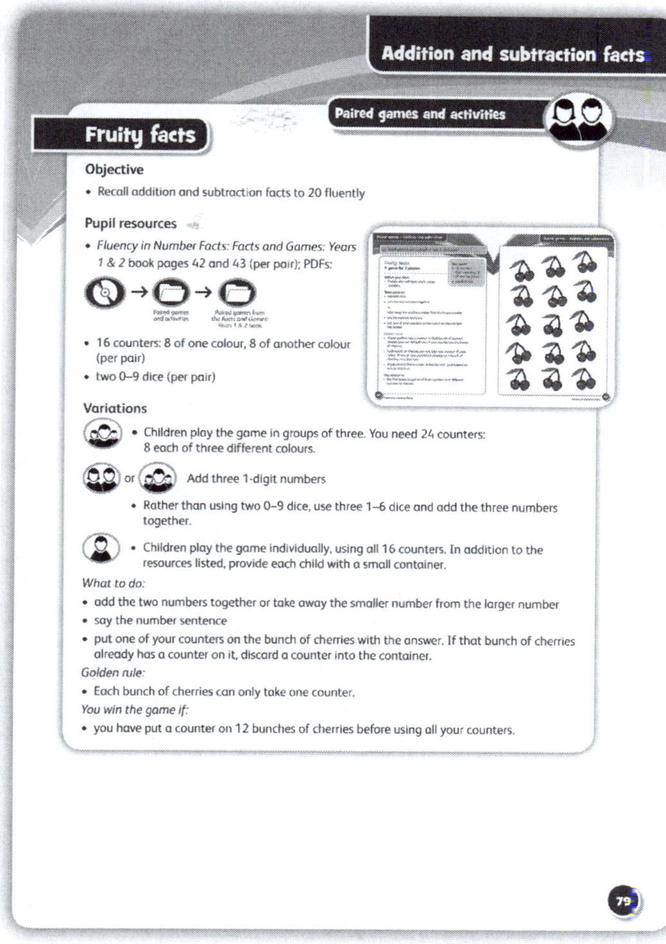
Addition and subtraction facts

Paired games and activities

Fruity facts

Objective

- Recall addition and subtraction facts to 20 fluently

Pupil resources

- *Fluency in Number Facts: Facts and Games: Years 1 & 2* book pages 42 and 43 (per pair); PDFs:

→ Paired games and activities → Paired games from the Facts and Games Years 1 & 2 book

- 16 counters: 8 of one colour, 8 of another colour (per pair)
- two 0–9 dice (per pair)

Variations

- Children play the game in groups of three. You need 24 counters: 8 each of three different colours.

or Add three 1-digit numbers

- Rather than using two 0–9 dice, use three 1–6 dice and add the three numbers together.

- Children play the game individually, using all 16 counters. In addition to the resources listed, provide each child with a small container.

What to do:

- add the two numbers together or take away the smaller number from the larger number
- say the number sentence
- put one of your counters on the bunch of cherries with the answer. If that bunch of cherries already has a counter on it, discard a counter into the container.

Golden rule:

- Each bunch of cherries can only take one counter.

You win the game if:

- you have put a counter on 12 bunches of cherries before using all your counters.

79

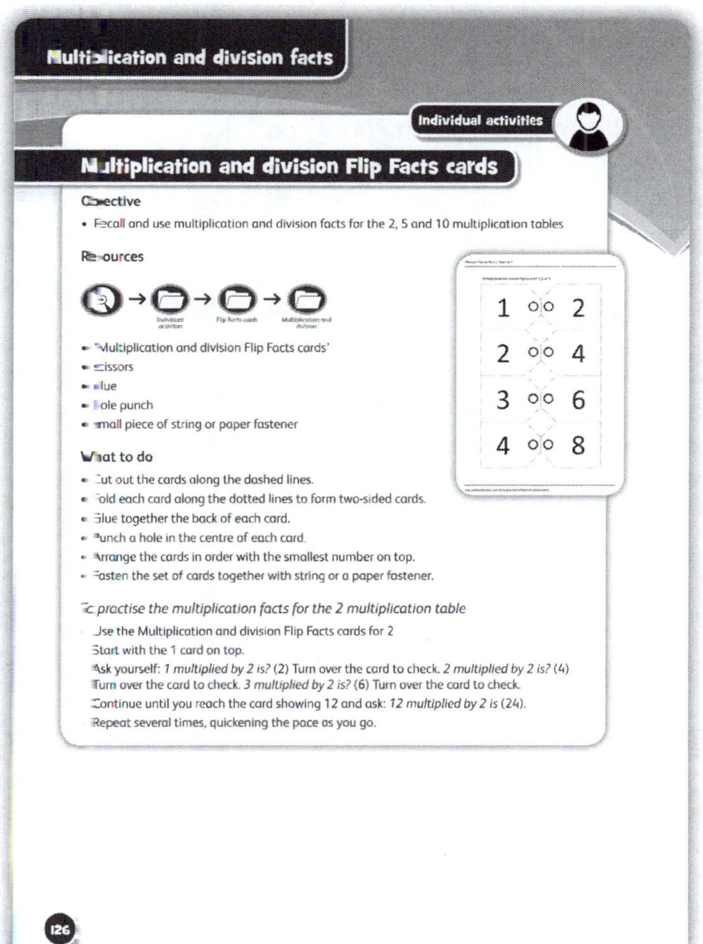
Multiplication and division facts

Individual activities

Multiplication and division Flip Facts cards

Objective

- Recall and use multiplication and division facts for the 2, 5 and 10 multiplication tables

Resources

→ Individual activities → Flip Facts cards → Multiplication and division

- 'Multiplication and division Flip Facts cards'
- scissors
- glue
- hole punch
- small piece of string or paper fastener

What to do

- Cut out the cards along the dashed lines.
- Fold each card along the dotted lines to form two-sided cards.
- Glue together the back of each card.
- Punch a hole in the centre of each card.
- Arrange the cards in order with the smallest number on top.
- Fasten the set of cards together with string or a paper fastener.

To practise the multiplication facts for the 2 multiplication table

Use the Multiplication and division Flip Facts cards for 2
Start with the 1 card on top.
Ask yourself: *1 multiplied by 2 is?* (2) Turn over the card to check. *2 multiplied by 2 is?* (4) Turn over the card to check. *3 multiplied by 2 is?* (6) Turn over the card to check.
Continue until you reach the card showing 12 and ask: *12 multiplied by 2 is* (24).
Repeat several times, quickening the pace as you go.

126

Individual activities

Individual activities are provided which children use, as and when required, to practise and consolidate their fluency in the Key domains of Addition and subtraction, and Multiplication and division.

PDF files required for the individual activities are located on the accompanying CD-ROM.

→ Individual activities

Features of the *Fluency in Number Facts: Facts and Games* book

Maths Facts

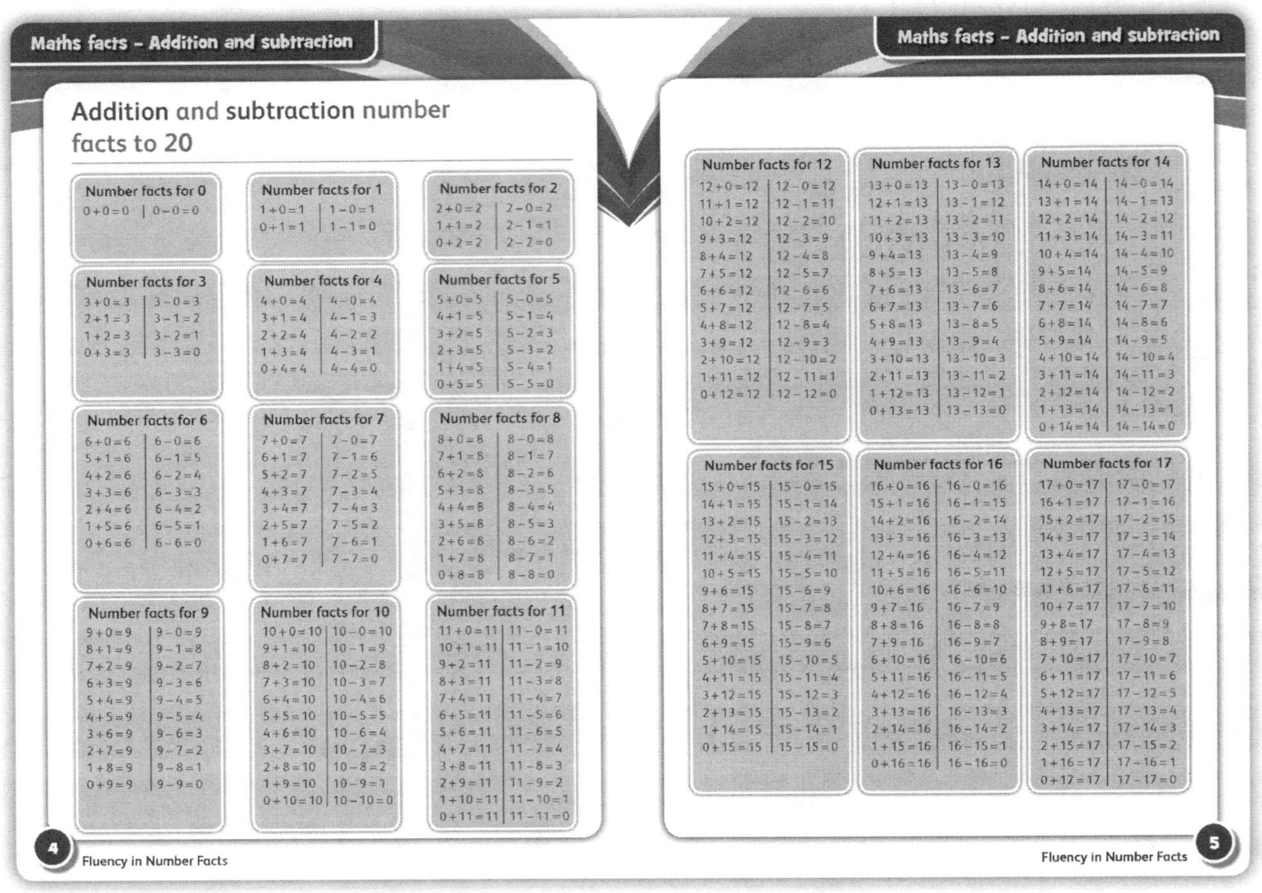
Maths facts – Addition and subtraction

Addition and subtraction number facts to 20

Number facts for 0

0+0=0	0−0=0

Number facts for 1

1+0=1	1−0=1
0+1=1	1−1=0

Number facts for 2

2+0=2	2−0=2
1+1=2	2−1=1
0+2=2	2−2=0

Number facts for 3

3+0=3	3−0=3
2+1=3	3−1=2
1+2=3	3−2=1
0+3=3	3−3=0

Number facts for 4

4+0=4	4−0=4
3+1=4	4−1=3
2+2=4	4−2=2
1+3=4	4−3=1
0+4=4	4−4=0

Number facts for 5

5+0=5	5−0=5
4+1=5	5−1=4
3+2=5	5−2=3
2+3=5	5−3=2
1+4=5	5−4=1
0+5=5	5−5=0

Number facts for 6

6+0=6	6−0=6
5+1=6	6−1=5
4+2=6	6−2=4
3+3=6	6−3=3
2+4=6	6−4=2
1+5=6	6−5=1
0+6=6	6−6=0

Number facts for 7

7+0=7	7−0=7
6+1=7	7−1=6
5+2=7	7−2=5
4+3=7	7−3=4
3+4=7	7−4=3
2+5=7	7−5=2
1+6=7	7−6=1
0+7=7	7−7=0

Number facts for 8

8+0=8	8−0=8
7+1=8	8−1=7
6+2=8	8−2=6
5+3=8	8−3=5
4+4=8	8−4=4
3+5=8	8−5=3
2+6=8	8−6=2
1+7=8	8−7=1
0+8=8	8−8=0

Number facts for 9

9+0=9	9−0=9
8+1=9	9−1=8
7+2=9	9−2=7
6+3=9	9−3=6
5+4=9	9−4=5
4+5=9	9−5=4
3+6=9	9−6=3
2+7=9	9−7=2
1+8=9	9−8=1
0+9=9	9−9=0

Number facts for 10

10+0=10	10−0=10
9+1=10	10−1=9
8+2=10	10−2=8
7+3=10	10−3=7
6+4=10	10−4=6
5+5=10	10−5=5
4+6=10	10−6=4
3+7=10	10−7=3
2+8=10	10−8=2
1+9=10	10−9=1
0+10=10	10−10=0

Number facts for 11

11+0=11	11−0=11
10+1=11	11−1=10
9+2=11	11−2=9
8+3=11	11−3=8
7+4=11	11−4=7
6+5=11	11−5=6
5+6=11	11−6=5
4+7=11	11−7=4
3+8=11	11−8=3
2+9=11	11−9=2
1+10=11	11−10=1
0+11=11	11−11=0

4 Fluency in Number Facts

Maths facts – Addition and subtraction

Number facts for 12

12+0=12	12−0=12
11+1=12	12−1=11
10+2=12	12−2=10
9+3=12	12−3=9
8+4=12	12−4=8
7+5=12	12−5=7
6+6=12	12−6=6
5+7=12	12−7=5
4+8=12	12−8=4
3+9=12	12−9=3
2+10=12	12−10=2
1+11=12	12−11=1
0+12=12	12−12=0

Number facts for 13

13+0=13	13−0=13
12+1=13	13−1=12
11+2=13	13−2=11
10+3=13	13−3=10
9+4=13	13−4=9
8+5=13	13−5=8
7+6=13	13−6=7
6+7=13	13−7=6
5+8=13	13−8=5
4+9=13	13−9=4
3+10=13	13−10=3
2+11=13	13−11=2
1+12=13	13−12=1
0+13=13	13−13=0

Number facts for 14

14+0=14	14−0=14
13+1=14	14−1=13
12+2=14	14−2=12
11+3=14	14−3=11
10+4=14	14−4=10
9+5=14	14−5=9
8+6=14	14−6=8
7+7=14	14−7=7
6+8=14	14−8=6
5+9=14	14−9=5
4+10=14	14−10=4
3+11=14	14−11=3
2+12=14	14−12=2
1+13=14	14−13=1
0+14=14	14−14=0

Number facts for 15

15+0=15	15−0=15
14+1=15	15−1=14
13+2=15	15−2=13
12+3=15	15−3=12
11+4=15	15−4=11
10+5=15	15−5=10
9+6=15	15−6=9
8+7=15	15−7=8
7+8=15	15−8=7
6+9=15	15−9=6
5+10=15	15−10=5
4+11=15	15−11=4
3+12=15	15−12=3
2+13=15	15−13=2
1+14=15	15−14=1
0+15=15	15−15=0

Number facts for 16

16+0=16	16−0=16
15+1=16	16−1=15
14+2=16	16−2=14
13+3=16	16−3=13
12+4=16	16−4=12
11+5=16	16−5=11
10+6=16	16−6=10
9+7=16	16−7=9
8+8=16	16−8=8
7+9=16	16−9=7
6+10=16	16−10=6
5+11=16	16−11=5
4+12=16	16−12=4
3+13=16	16−13=3
2+14=16	16−14=2
1+15=16	16−15=1
0+16=16	16−16=0

Number facts for 17

17+0=17	17−0=17
16+1=17	17−1=16
15+2=17	17−2=15
14+3=17	17−3=14
13+4=17	17−4=13
12+5=17	17−5=12
11+6=17	17−6=11
10+7=17	17−7=10
9+8=17	17−8=9
8+9=17	17−9=8
7+10=17	17−10=7
6+11=17	17−11=6
5+12=17	17−12=5
4+13=17	17−13=4
3+14=17	17−14=3
2+15=17	17−15=2
1+16=17	17−16=1
0+17=17	17−17=0

Fluency in Number Facts 5

Each *Fluency in Number Facts: Facts and Games* book contains lists of the key addition, subtraction, multiplication and division number facts that children need to be able to recall instantly. These facts are presented in different ways to assist children in developing a deeper understanding, and quick recall, of the facts.

Activities are provided in the *Fluency in Number Facts: Teacher's Guide* which suggest how best to make use of these Maths Facts.

PDF files of the Maths Facts pages from the *Fluency in Number Facts: Facts and Games: Years 1 & 2* book can also be found on the accompanying CD-ROM.

Maths Facts

Paired games

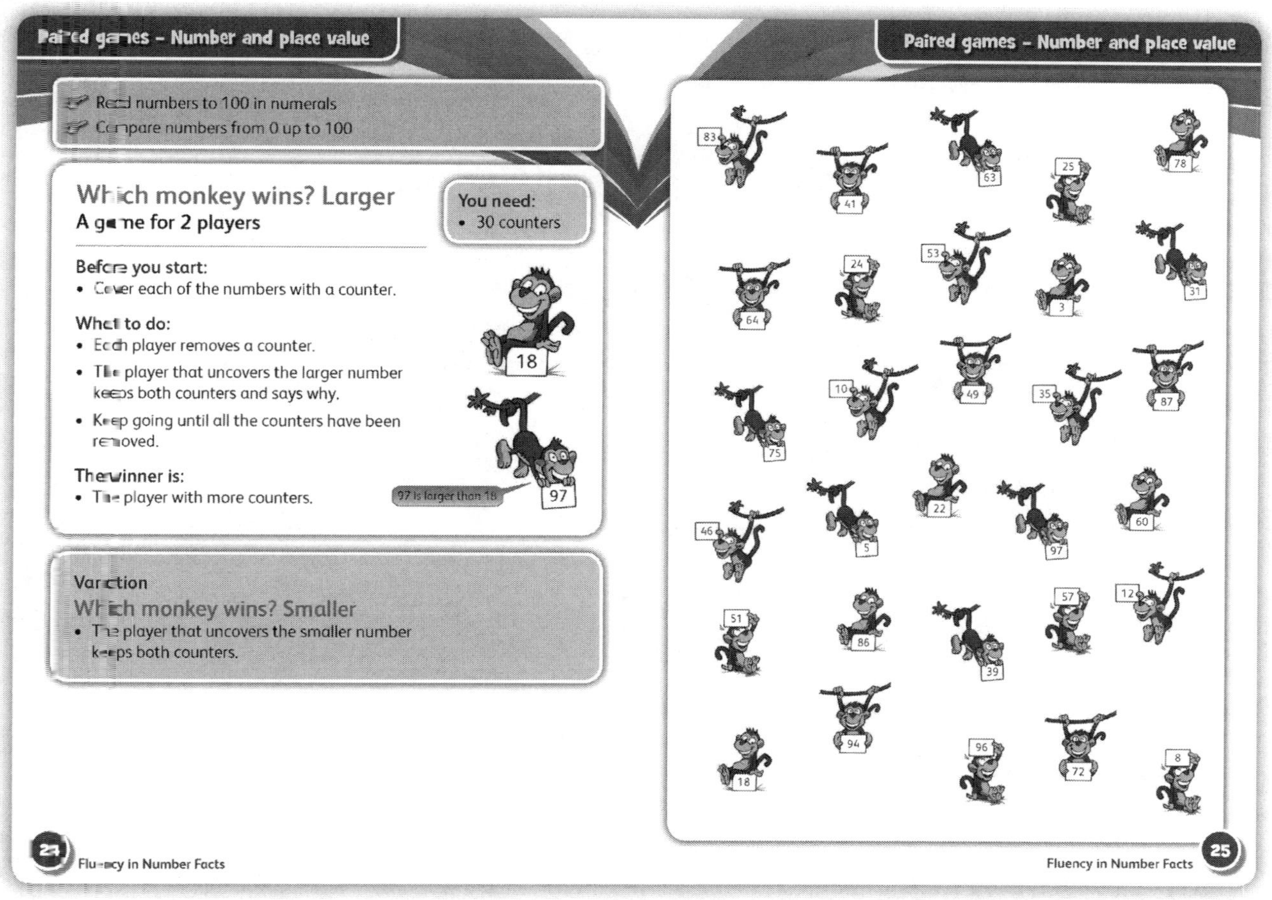

Paired games – Number and place value

- Read numbers to 100 in numerals
- Compare numbers from 0 up to 100

Which monkey wins? Larger
A game for 2 players

You need:
- 30 counters

Before you start:
- Cover each of the numbers with a counter.

What to do:
- Each player removes a counter.
- The player that uncovers the larger number keeps both counters and says why.
- Keep going until all the counters have been removed.

The winner is:
- The player with more counters.

97 is larger than 18

Variation
Which monkey wins? Smaller
- The player that uncovers the smaller number keeps both counters.

24 Fluency in Number Facts

Paired games – Number and place value

83, 41, 63, 25, 78, 64, 24, 53, 3, 31, 75, 10, 49, 35, 87, 46, 5, 22, 97, 60, 51, 86, 39, 57, 12, 18, 94, 96, 72, 8

Fluency in Number Facts 25

Each *Fluency in Number Facts: Facts and Games* book also includes a bank of paired games to help children become fluent in each of the three Key domains.

The games are organised according to the three Key domains and include a list of the resources required as well as instructions and, where appropriate, any variations.

Additional guidance on how to play the games, along with further variations, can be found in the *Fluency in Number Facts: Teacher's Guide*.

Each game is designed to last approximately 10 minutes.

PDF files of the paired games from the *Fluency in Number Facts: Facts and Games: Years 1 & 2* book can also be found on the accompanying CD-ROM.

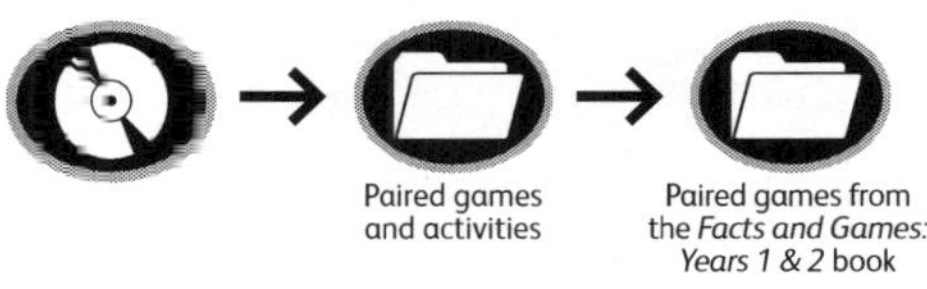

Features of the *Fluency in Number Facts*: CD-ROM

The following resources are available to download from the accompanying CD-ROM.

Maths Facts

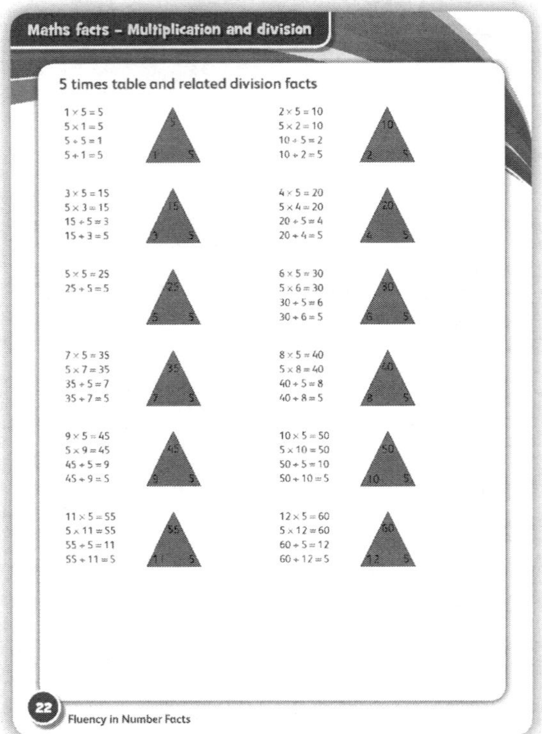

Maths facts – Multiplication and division

5 times table and related division facts

1 × 5 = 5
5 × 1 = 5
5 ÷ 5 = 1
5 ÷ 1 = 5

2 × 5 = 10
5 × 2 = 10
10 ÷ 5 = 2
10 ÷ 2 = 5

3 × 5 = 15
5 × 3 = 15
15 ÷ 5 = 3
15 ÷ 3 = 5

4 × 5 = 20
5 × 4 = 20
20 ÷ 5 = 4
20 ÷ 4 = 5

5 × 5 = 25
25 ÷ 5 = 5

6 × 5 = 30
5 × 6 = 30
30 ÷ 5 = 6
30 ÷ 6 = 5

7 × 5 = 35
5 × 7 = 35
35 ÷ 5 = 7
35 ÷ 7 = 5

8 × 5 = 40
5 × 8 = 40
40 ÷ 5 = 8
40 ÷ 8 = 5

9 × 5 = 45
5 × 9 = 45
45 ÷ 5 = 9
45 ÷ 9 = 5

10 × 5 = 50
5 × 10 = 50
50 ÷ 5 = 10
50 ÷ 10 = 5

11 × 5 = 55
5 × 11 = 55
55 ÷ 5 = 11
55 ÷ 11 = 5

12 × 5 = 60
5 × 12 = 60
60 ÷ 5 = 12
60 ÷ 12 = 5

22 Fluency in Number Facts

PDF files of the *Fluency in Number Facts: Facts and Games: Years 1 & 2* book Maths Facts pages.

Whole-class games and activities

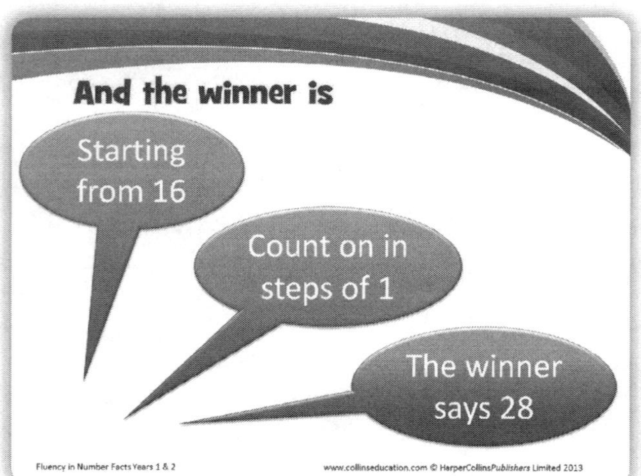

PowerPoint slides required for some of the whole-class games and activities. The slides are also provided as PDF files.

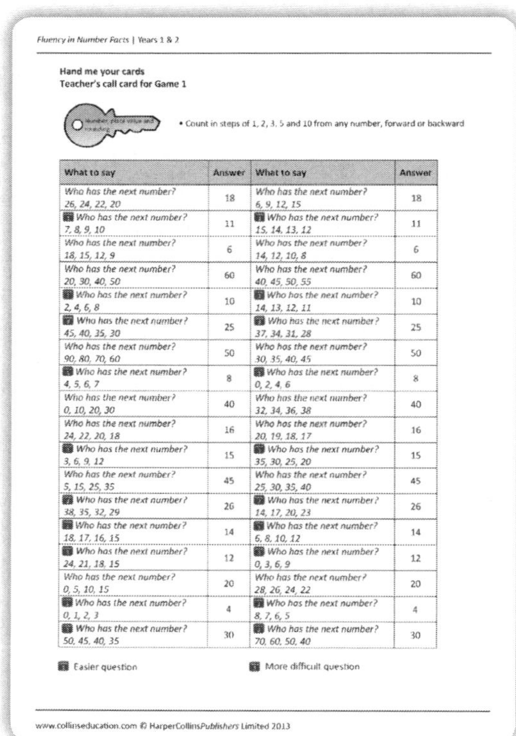

Fluency in Number Facts | Years 1 & 2

Hand me your cards
Teacher's call card for Game 1

• Count in steps of 1, 2, 3, 5 and 10 from any number, forward or backward

What to say	Answer	What to say	Answer
Who has the next number? 26, 24, 22, 20	18	*Who has the next number? 6, 9, 12, 15*	18
Who has the next number? 7, 8, 9, 10	11	*Who has the next number? 15, 14, 13, 12*	11
Who has the next number? 18, 15, 12, 9	6	*Who has the next number? 14, 12, 10, 8*	6
Who has the next number? 20, 30, 40, 50	60	*Who has the next number? 40, 45, 50, 55*	60
Who has the next number? 2, 4, 6, 8	10	*Who has the next number? 14, 13, 12, 11*	10
Who has the next number? 45, 40, 35, 30	25	*Who has the next number? 37, 34, 31, 28*	25
Who has the next number? 90, 80, 70, 60	50	*Who has the next number? 30, 35, 40, 45*	50
Who has the next number? 4, 5, 6, 7	8	*Who has the next number? 0, 2, 4, 6*	8
Who has the next number? 0, 10, 20, 30	40	*Who has the next number? 32, 34, 36, 38*	40
Who has the next number? 24, 22, 20, 18	16	*Who has the next number? 20, 19, 18, 17*	16
Who has the next number? 3, 6, 9, 12	15	*Who has the next number? 35, 30, 25, 20*	15
Who has the next number? 5, 15, 25, 35	45	*Who has the next number? 25, 30, 35, 40*	45
Who has the next number? 38, 35, 32, 29	26	*Who has the next number? 14, 17, 20, 23*	26
Who has the next number? 18, 17, 16, 15	14	*Who has the next number? 6, 8, 10, 12*	14
Who has the next number? 24, 21, 18, 15	12	*Who has the next number? 0, 3, 6, 9*	12
Who has the next number? 0, 5, 10, 15	20	*Who has the next number? 28, 26, 24, 22*	20
Who has the next number? 0, 1, 2, 3	4	*Who has the next number? 8, 7, 6, 5*	4
Who has the next number? 50, 45, 40, 35	30	*Who has the next number? 70, 60, 50, 40*	30

Easier question   More difficult question

www.collinseducation.com © HarperCollins*Publishers* Limited 2013

PDF files required for some of the whole-class games and activities.

Paired games and activities

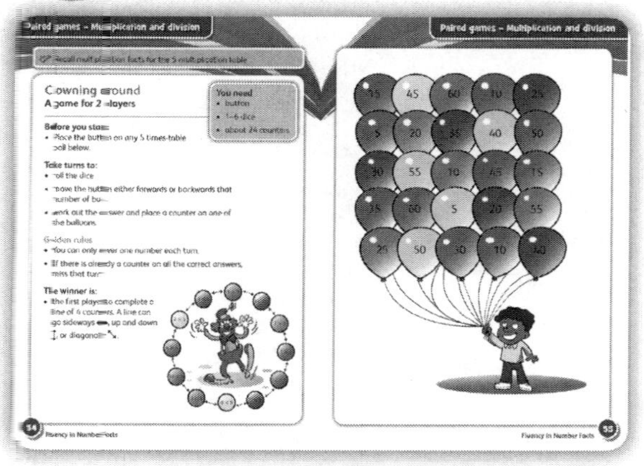

PDF files of the *Fluency in Number Facts: Facts and Games: Years 1 & 2* book paired games.

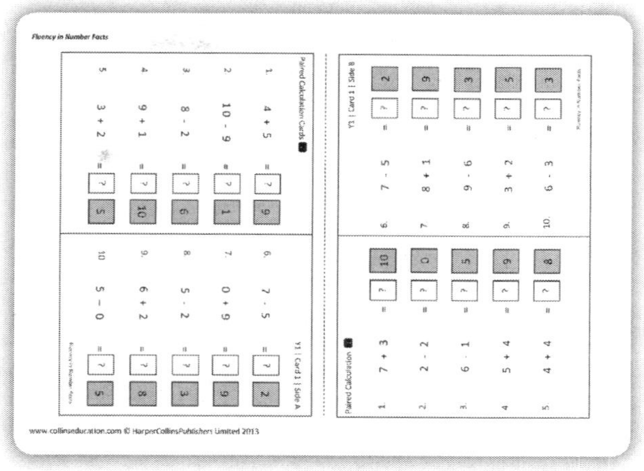

PDF files required for some of the paired games and activities.

Individual activities

PDF files required for some of the individual activities.

Written activities

Refer to pages 140–161 of the *Fluency in Number Facts: Teacher's Guide: Years 1 & 2* book for an explanation as to how to use each of the written activities.

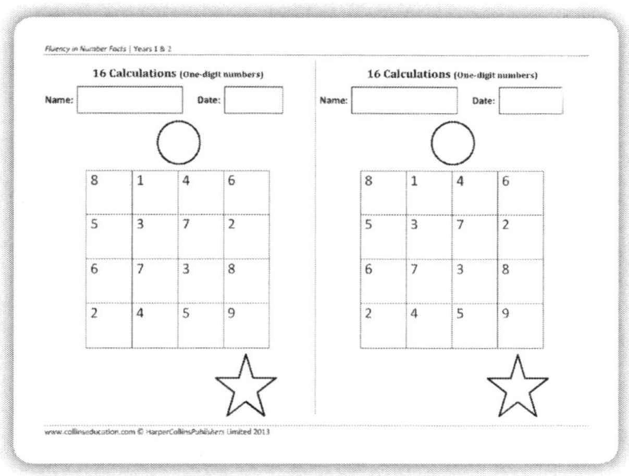

WORD files required for the written activities.

Mental fluency challenges

Fluency in Number Facts includes 36 graded Mental fluency challenges (18 for Year 1, and 18 for Year 2).

These challenges are aimed at providing children with further practice and consolidation and also at offering teachers a means of assessing individual children's proficiency in the mental recall of number facts.

Each challenge covers the key addition, subtraction, multiplication and division number facts that children need to be able to recall instantly by the end of Key Stage 1.

Careful consideration has been given to the progression of the Key Stage 1 curriculum, and for each year group the 18 challenges have been arranged into three different ability levels, with six exercises at each level: easy Challenge 1, average Challenge 2 and challenging Challenge 3.

It is recommended that children do the same exercise on two or three consecutive days. This way, the majority of children will see themselves making progress over the two or three days, thus providing greater encouragement and self-motivation.

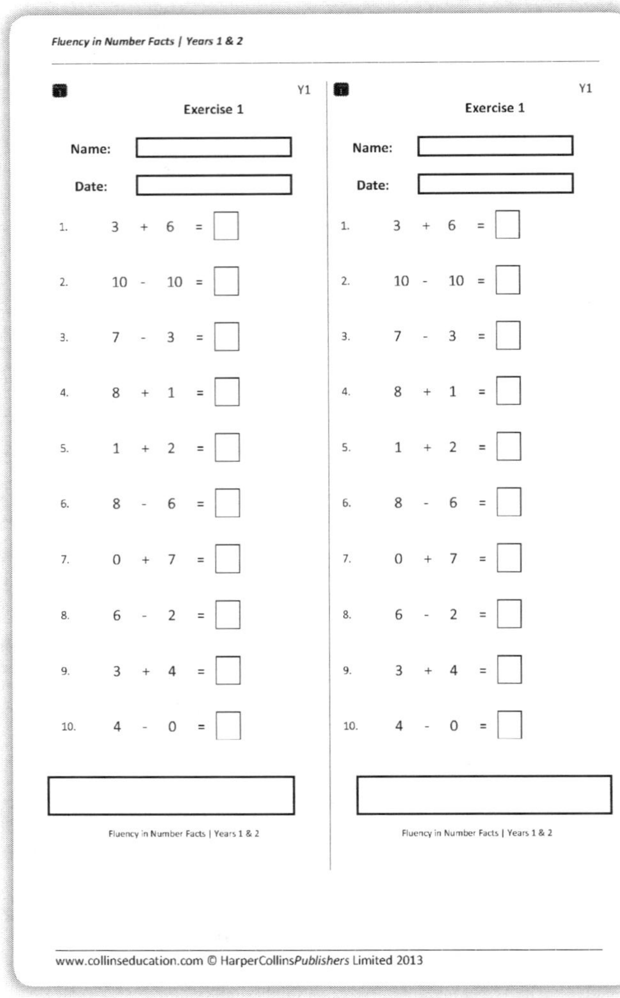
Fluency in Number Facts | Years 1 & 2

Y1 Exercise 1		Y1 Exercise 1	
Name:		Name:	
Date:		Date:	
1.	3 + 6 =	1.	3 + 6 =
2.	10 - 10 =	2.	10 - 10 =
3.	7 - 3 =	3.	7 - 3 =
4.	8 + 1 =	4.	8 + 1 =
5.	1 + 2 =	5.	1 + 2 =
6.	8 - 6 =	6.	8 - 6 =
7.	0 + 7 =	7.	0 + 7 =
8.	6 - 2 =	8.	6 - 2 =
9.	3 + 4 =	9.	3 + 4 =
10.	4 - 0 =	10.	4 - 0 =

Fluency in Number Facts | Years 1 & 2   Fluency in Number Facts | Years 1 & 2

www.collinseducation.com © HarperCollins*Publishers* Limited 2013

It is envisaged that these exercises could be given to the children either where they take as long as they need to answer all ten questions, or as a timed activity (for example: *I want you to answer as many of these questions as you can in eight minutes. Ready? Go!*). Alternatively, to encourage speed and recall, set the children to work and as they finish the exercise they raise their hand and you tell them how long it took them to complete it.

Both PDF and WORD versions of the Mental fluency challenges are provided.

The WORD version is provided so that individual schools or classes can, if they perceive it necessary, modify the content of the challenges to better suit the needs of their children. However, it is important to be aware that if changes are made to the content, that the continuity and progression of the challenges will be affected.

As well as the WORD and PDF versions of the Mental fluency challenges, there is also an audio file of each challenge.

A Mental fluency challenge answer sheet is also provided for children to use to record their answers when using the auditory version of the exercises.

Refer to pages 162–164 of the *Fluency in Number Facts: Teacher's Guide: Years 1 & 2* book for a more detailed explanation as to how to use the Mental fluency challenges.

Number cards

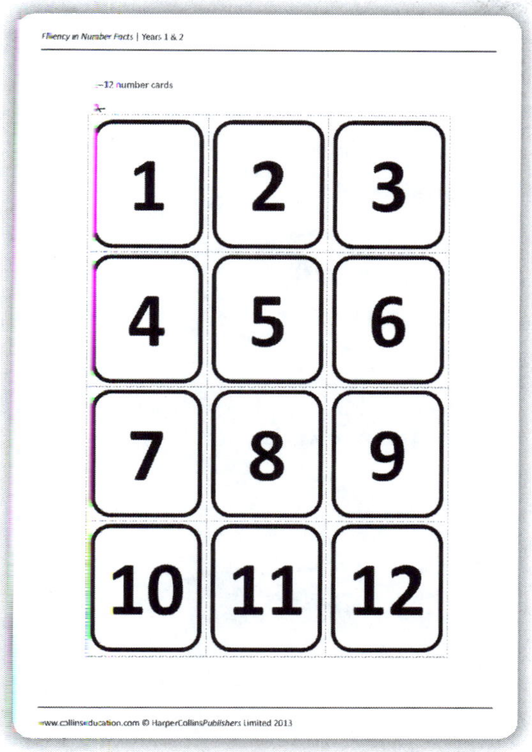

Fluency in Number Facts | Years 1 & 2

1–12 number cards

1	2	3
4	5	6
7	8	9
10	11	12

www.collinseducation.com © HarperCollins*Publishers* Limited 2013

PDF files of the number cards required for some of the games and activities.

Assessment and record-keeping formats

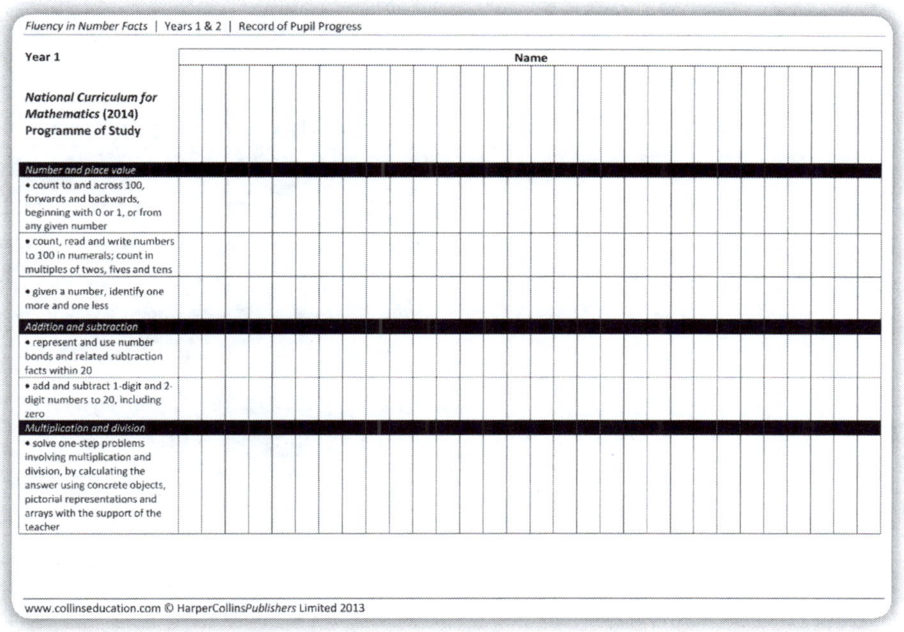

Fluency in Number Facts | Years 1 & 2 | Record of Pupil Progress

Year 1 ***National Curriculum for Mathematics* (2014) Programme of Study**	Name
Number and place value	
• count to and across 100, forwards and backwards, beginning with 0 or 1, or from any given number	
• count, read and write numbers to 100 in numerals; count in multiples of twos, fives and tens	
• given a number, identify one more and one less	
Addition and subtraction	
• represent and use number bonds and related subtraction facts within 20	
• add and subtract 1-digit and 2-digit numbers to 20, including zero	
Multiplication and division	
• solve one-step problems involving multiplication and division, by calculating the answer using concrete objects, pictorial representations and arrays with the support of the teacher	

www.collinseducation.com © HarperCollins*Publishers* Limited 2013

WORD files are provided for each of the following assessment and record-keeping formats:

- Record of Pupil Progress
  – Year 1
  – Year 2

These charts are designed to enable teachers to keep a record of the level of mastery that individual children have achieved in the Number and place value, Addition and subtraction, and Multiplication and division National Curriculum for Mathematics (2014) Programmes of Study. The assessment criteria provided on each chart can be modified to better suit the requirements of individual schools and classes.

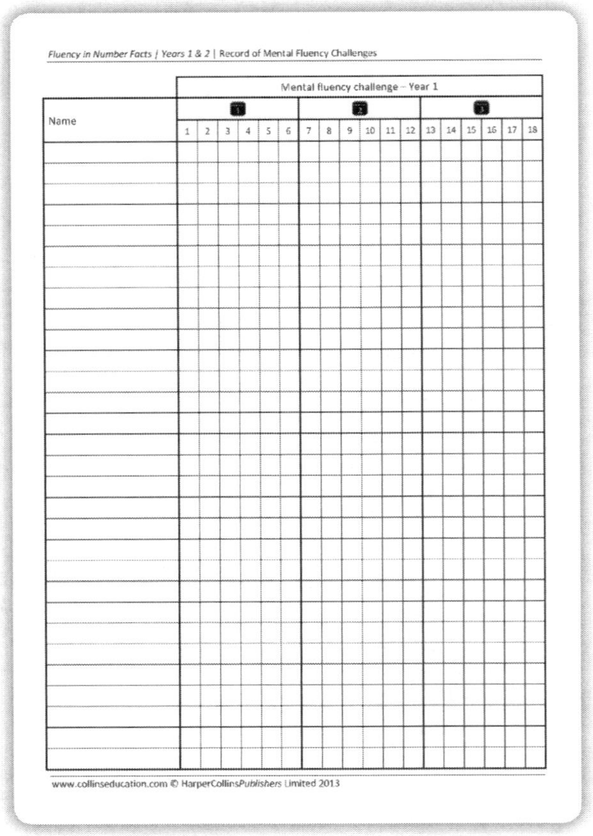

Fluency in Number Facts | Years 1 & 2 | Record of Mental Fluency Challenges

Name	1	2	3	4	5	6	7	8	9	10	11	12	13	14	15	16	17	18
	Mental fluency challenge – Year 1																	

www.collinseducation.com © HarperCollins*Publishers* Limited 2013

- Record of Mental fluency challenges:
  - Year 1
  - Year 2
- Record of Function machine strips:
  - Year 1
  - Year 2
- Record of Paired calculations cards:
  - Year 1
  - Year 2

These charts are designed to enable teachers to keep a record of which activity individual children have completed.

Record of Mental fluency challenges can also be used to record children's scores.

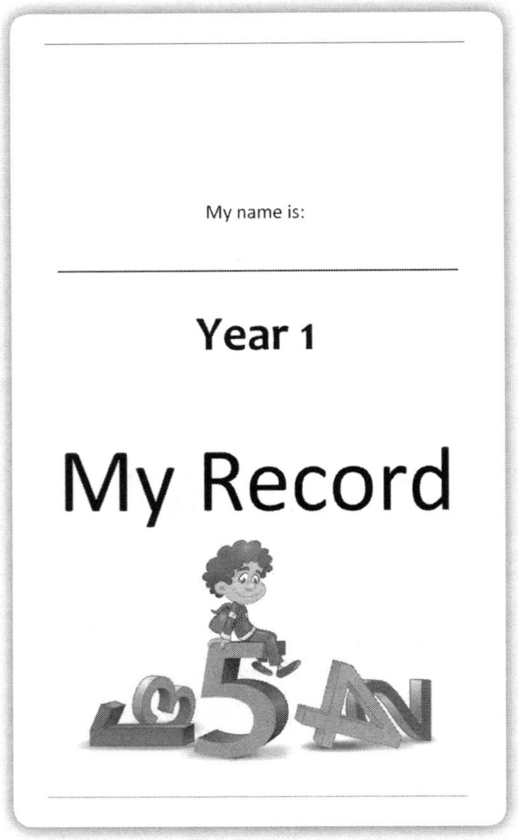

My name is:

Year 1

My Record

- Pupil self-assessment booklet:
  - Year 1
  - Year 2

These booklets are designed to be completed by individual children at the end of each term to assist them in gauging their own level of proficiency in each of the three Key domains. The assessment criteria provided on each booklet can be modified to better suit the requirements of individual classes and children. Also make sure that you print the Word files as a booklet as shown.

CD-ROM flowchart

The flowchart below has been included to assist teachers in locating the resources found on the accompanying *Fluency in Number Facts*: CD-ROM.

- **Homepage: Years 1 & 2**
  - **Maths Facts**
    - Addition and subtraction
    - Multiplication and division
  - **Whole-class games and activities**
    - Hand me your cards
      - Number and place value
      - Addition and subtraction
      - Multiplication and division
    - Loop cards
      - Number and place value
      - Addition and subtraction
      - Multiplication and division
    - Hands-on game boards
    - PowerPoint slides
  - **Paired games and activities**
    - Paired games from the *Facts and Games: Years 1 & 2* book
      - Number and place value
      - Addition and subtraction
      - Multiplication and division
    - Paired calculations cards
      - Year 1
      - Year 2
  - **Individual activities**
    - Flip Facts cards
      - Addition and subtraction
      - Multiplication and division
    - Function machine strips
      - Year 1
      - Year 2
  - **Written activities**
  - **Mental fluency challenges**
    - Year 1
      - Written versions
      - Written version answers
      - Audio version
    - Year 2
      - Written versions
      - Written version answers
      - Audio version
  - **Number cards**
  - **Assessment and record-keeping formats**

Say the target number

Objective

- Count in steps of 1, 2, 3, 5 and 10 from any number, forward or backward

Teacher resources

- none

Pupil resources

- none

What to do

- Arrange the children in a circle.
- Tell the children a start number, for example, 5; an end number, for example, 26; and a target number between the start and end numbers, for example, 18.
- Children take turns to count round the circle, starting from the start number.
- When a child says the target number, they stand up.
- Children continue the count until the end number is reached.
- The next child to count then goes back to the start number.
- Continue counting in this way until five children are standing.

Variations

- When the end number is said, rather than going back to the start number, the children continue the count backward from the end number to the start number.
- Ask the children to count in steps of 2, 3, 5 or 10.

And the winner is...

Objective

- Count in steps of 1, 2, 3, 5 and 10 from any number, forward or backward

Teacher resources

- 'And the winner is…'

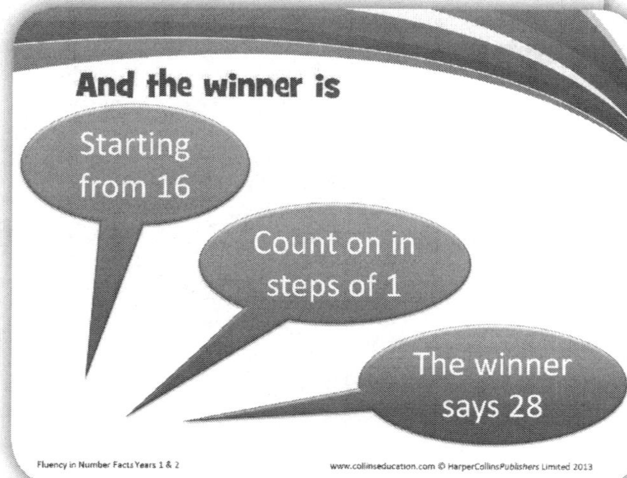

Pupil resources

- none

What to do

- Arrange the children into pairs.
- Display one of the 'And the winner is…' slides.
- Demonstrate with a child how to play the game:
  - decide who will start the count at the 'Starting from…' number, for example, 'Starting from 16
  - take turns to count in the steps shown, for example, 'Count on in steps of 1'
  - the winner is the player that says the winning number, i.e. 28.
- Children play the games in pairs.
- Use other 'And the winner is…' slides, to play several rounds.

Variation

- Change the start number, step and winning number on the slides.

Counting stick

Objectives

- Count in steps of 1, 2, 3, 5 and 10 from any number, forward or backward
- Count in multiples of ones, twos, fives and tens

Teacher resources

- counting stick, i.e. a stick ideally 1 metre in length, marked off in ten equal divisions. If possible, add pieces of Velcro at each divider in order to attach labels to the stick.

- small labels showing numbers 0–10, multiples of 2, 3, 5 and 10 to the 10th multiple (if appropriate). Alternatively, use Post-it Notes for the labels.

Pupil resources

- none

What to do

- Decide which multiple you want the children to practise, i.e. count in multiples of 1 from any number, forward or backward.
- Name one end of the stick 0 and the other 10. Count in steps of 1 forward and when confident, backward.
- Randomly point to divisions and ask questions such as: *Which number belongs here?* If appropriate, stick the corresponding label on the stick.
- When confident, name one end of the stick a number other than 0, for example, 14. Children count on from this number.

Variation

- Count in multiples of 2, 3, 5 or 10 from any number, forward or backward. Name one end of the stick 0 and the other end the 10th multiple. When confident, name one end of the stick a multiple other than 0.

Fizz / Fizz Buzz

Objective

- Count in multiples of twos, fives and tens

Teacher resources

- none

Pupil resources

- none

What to do

- Decide which multiples you want the children to practise, for example, multiples of 2.
- Recite the multiples of 2 from 2 to 24 with the class, i.e. *2, 4, 6, 8…*
- Ask the children to stand.
- Count forward round the class in steps of 1, from 1 to at least 24.
- When a multiple of 2 is reached, instead of saying the number the child says *Fizz*, i.e. 1st child says *1*, 2nd child says *Fizz*, 3rd child says *3*, 4th child says *Fizz*… (the 25th child starts from 1 again).
- Continue counting round the class for as long as is appropriate.

Variations

- Play 'Fizz' for the multiples of 5 or 10, counting forward to the 12th multiple.
- Play 'Fizz Buzz'. For example, for any multiple of 2 say *Fizz* and for any multiple of 5 say *Buzz*. If the number is a multiple of both 2 and 5, for example, 10, say *Fizz Buzz*.

Say it and you're out

Objective

- Count in multiples of ones, twos, fives and tens

Teacher resources

- none

Pupil resources

- none

What to do

- Decide which multiple you want children to practice, e.g. multiples of 2
- Recite the multiples of 2 from 2 to 24 with the class, i.e. *2, 4, 6, 8…*
- Write any three of these multiples of 2 on the board, for example, 6, 10 and 18.
- Ask the children to stand.
- Count forward round the class reciting the multiples of 2 from 2 to 24, i.e. 1st child says *2*, 2nd child says *4*, 3rd child says *6…* (the 13th child starts from 2 again).
- When a child says one of the multiples of 2 written on the board, that child has to sit down and is out.
- Continue counting round the class until one child is left standing. This child is the winner.

Variations

- Count forward and backward round the class reciting the multiples of 2 from 2 to 24, i.e. 1st child says *2*, 2nd child says *4*, 3rd child says *6…* 12th child says *24*, 13th child says *22*, 14th child says 20…
- When there are only four or five children left standing, ask the rest of the class if they can work out who will be the winner.
- Play 'Say it and you're out' counting in multiples of ones, fives and tens.

Remember the numbers

Objectives

- Read numbers to at least 100 in numerals
- Recognise the place value of each digit in a 2-digit number (tens, ones)
- Compare and order numbers from 0 up to 100

Teacher resources

- 'Remember the numbers'

Pupil resources

- none

What to do

- Say: *I'm going to show you a slide with some numbers on it. I'm then going to hide the numbers and ask you some questions about them. You need to try and remember the numbers before I hide them. Ready?*
- Display one of the 'Remember the numbers' slides for about 10 seconds.
- Hide the slide, pause, then ask questions similar to the following:
  - *What is the largest number?*
  - *What is the smallest number?*
  - *Which numbers are odd?*
  - *Which numbers are even?*
  - *Which numbers are less than 10?*
  - *Which numbers are greater than 10?*
  - *Which numbers have 1 ten?*

Variations

- Repeat using other 'Remember the numbers' slides.
- Change the numbers on the 'Remember the numbers' slides.

Point to it

Objective

- Recognise the place value of each digit in a 2-digit number (tens, ones)

Teacher resources

- 'Point to it'

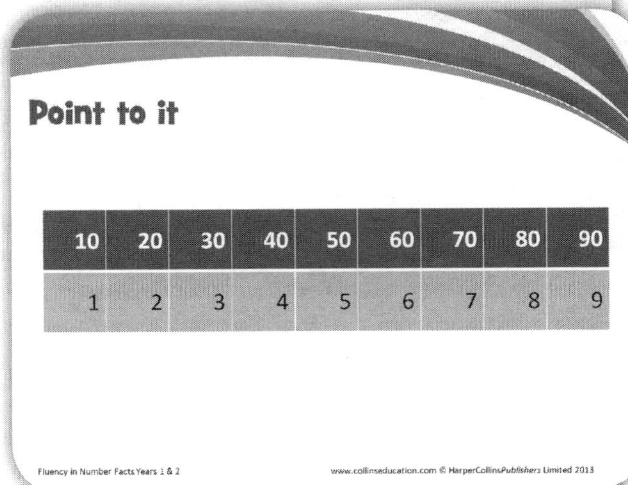

Pupil resources

- pencil and paper (per child)

What to do

- Ask each child to write down three 2-digit numbers, for example, 89, 71, 53.
- Display the first slide and point to a number on the slide, for example, 70.
- If a child has a number with the same place value, they cross it out, i.e. 71.
- If they don't, they do nothing.
- The winner is the first child to cross out all six digits in their three numbers.

(**Note:** Be sure to keep a record of the numbers pointed to for checking purposes.)

Variation

- Display the second slide and ask each child to write down three 3-digit numbers, e.g. 948, 614, 572.

Guess the number

Objectives

- Recognise the place value of each digit in a 2-digit number (tens, ones)
- Compare numbers from 0 up to 100

Teacher resources

- small pieces of paper or card
- hat
- something to fasten the paper or card onto the hat (for example, a paperclip)

Pupil resources

- none

What to do

- Write a 2-digit number on a small piece of paper or card, for example, 43, and fasten it to the hat.
- Ask a child to come to the front and, keeping the number a secret from this child, put the hat on them.
- This child then asks questions to the rest of the class to find out the number on the hat. However, they can only ask questions that will give a 'yes' or 'no' response, for example: *Is the number less than 50? Does the number have more than 5 tens?*
- Repeat using different numbers with other children.
- Who can guess the secret number asking the fewest questions?

Variation

- Write a 3-digit number on a small piece of paper or card.

Place value bingo

Objectives

- Read and write numbers to at least 100 in numerals
- Recognise the place value of each digit in a 2-digit number (tens, ones)

Teacher resources

→ Whole-class games and activities → PowerPoint slides

- 'Bingo'

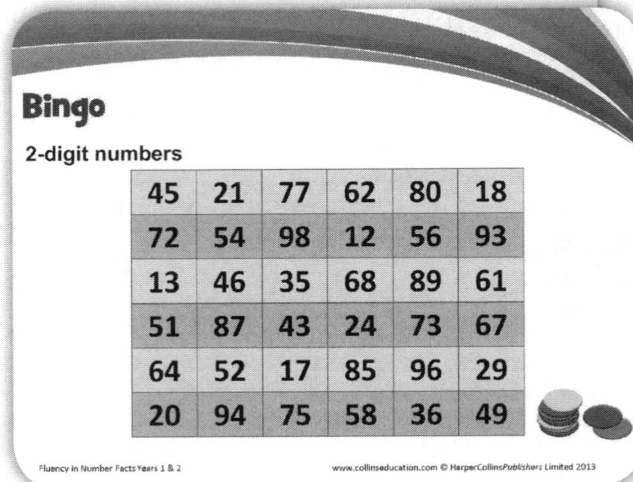

45	21	77	62	80	18
72	54	98	12	56	93
13	46	35	68	89	61
51	87	43	24	73	67
64	52	17	85	96	29
20	94	75	58	36	49

Pupil resources

- pencil and paper or small individual whiteboard and pen (per child)

What to do

- Display the 'Bingo: 2-digit numbers' slide.
- Ask each child to write down any five numbers from the slide.
- Ask questions similar to the following:
  - *Cross out any number that has 7 tens.*
  - *Cross out any number that has 6 ones.*
  - *Cross out any number that has 3 units.*
  - *Cross out the number that has 5 tens and 4 units.*
  - *Cross out the number that has 3 ones and 7 tens.*
- Children see if any of their five numbers match the description.
- If a child has a match, they cross out that number.
- The winner is the first child to cross out all five of their numbers and call out 'Bingo!'

(**Note:** Be sure to keep a record of the numbers for checking purposes.)

Variations

- Ask the children to write down more or fewer than five numbers from the slide.
- Use the 'Bingo: 3-digit numbers' slide.

Higher or lower?

Objectives

- Read numbers to at least 100 in numerals
- Recognise the place value of each digit in a 2-digit number (tens, ones)
- Compare and order numbers from 0 up to 100

Teacher resources

- 'Higher or Lower: 1–10'
- 'Higher or Lower: 1–20'
- 'Higher or Lower: 2-digit numbers'

Pupil resources

- none

What to do

- Decide which range of numbers you want the children to use and choose the appropriate set of slides.
- Display the first slide. For example, if using the 'Higher or lower: 2-digit numbers', the number 25.
- Tell the children that there are ten slides altogether, and that each slide has a number on it from 11–100 (or 1–10 / 1–20, depending on which set of slides you have chosen to use).
- Ask the children to decide whether they think the next number will be higher or lower than the current number, i.e. 25.
- If they think the number is going to be larger, they put their hands in the air.
- If they think the number is going to be smaller, they put their hands on their head.
- Display the second slide, i.e. 14.
- Keep going until all ten slides are revealed.

(**Note:** The question mark at the side of the second to last slide is to indicate that the next slide is the last slide.)

Variations

- Re-arrange the order of the slides. Ensure that the second to last slide has the question mark on it and that the last slide has a 'glow' around the number.
- Change the numbers on the slides.

Gladiators

Objectives

- Read numbers to at least 100 in numerals
- Count in steps of 1, 2, 3, 5 and 10 from any number, forward or backward
- Count in multiples of ones, twos, fives and tens
- Recognise the place value of each digit in a 2-digit number (tens, ones)
- Compare numbers from 0 up to 100
- Given a number, identify one more, one less, ten more and ten less

Teacher resources

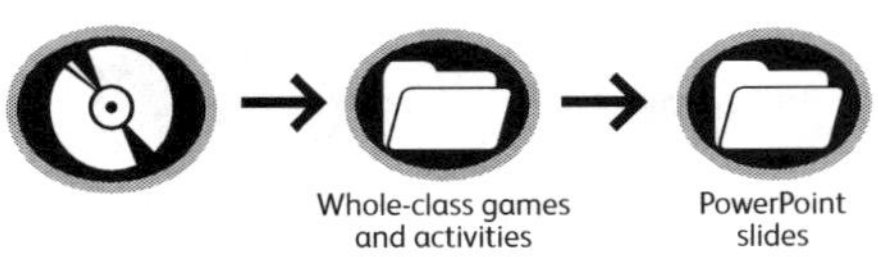

- 'Gladiators'

Pupil resources

- 2 × rulers or 'swords'

What to do

- Decide which range of numbers you want the children to use.
- Display the appropriate slide.
- Ask two children to stand either side of the numbers.
- If using the 'Gladiators Numbers: 1–20' slide for example, say statements similar to the following:
  - *Point to the number 5.*
  - *Point to the next number in this pattern: 9, 10, 11, 12.*
  - *Point to the next number in this pattern: 12, 10, 8, 6.*
  - *Point to the number that has 1 ten and 4 units.*
  - *Point to the number that has 6 ones and 1 ten.*
  - *Point to any number smaller than 4.*
  - *Point to the even number between 3 and 5.*
  - *Point to the number that is 1 more than 6.*
  - *Point to the number that is 10 less than 18.*
- The first child to point to the correct number stays in. The other child sits down.
- Quickly choose another child to come and take the place of the child that just sat down.
- Continue as above.
- Which child can stay in the longest?

Variations

- The children sitting down ask the two children standing by the numbers a question where the answer is on the slide.
- To quicken the game, have two children standing either side of the numbers, one behind the other. When a child loses and has to sit down, there is an immediate replacement.
- Use the 'Gladiators Numbers: 1–10' or 'Gladiators: 2-digit numbers' slide.
- Use the 'Gladiators: 2 times table' slide. Say statements similar to the following:
  - *Point to the next number in this pattern: 0, 2, 4, 6.*
  - *Point to the next number in this pattern: 18, 16, 14, 12.*
- Use the following slides in a similar way: 'Gladiators: 5 times table' and 'Gladiators: 10 times table'.
- To consolidate children's understanding use the 'Gladiators: 2, 5 and 10 times tables' slide, and say statements similar to the following:
  - *Point to the next number in this pattern: 0, 5, 10, 15.*
  - *Point to the next number in this pattern: 20, 18, 16, 14.*
  - *Point to the next number in this pattern: 20, 30, 40, 50.*

Hands-on

Objectives

- Read and write numbers to at least 100 in numerals
- Count in steps of 1, 2, 3, 5 and 10 from any number, forward or backward
- Count in multiples of ones, twos, fives and tens
- Recognise the place value of each digit in a 2-digit number (tens, ones)
- Compare numbers from 0 up to 100
- Given a number, identify one more, one less, ten more and ten less

Teacher resources

- none

Pupil resources

- 'Hands-on' game board (per pair)

What to do

- Decide which range of numbers you want the children to use.
- Arrange the children into pairs and provide each pair with a copy of the appropriate 'Hands-on' game board.
- Tell the children to put the game board between them, and for both children to put their index finger on a hand at the bottom of the game board.
- If using the 'Hands-on: Numbers 1–20' game board, say statements similar to the following:
  - *Point to the number 17.*
  - *Point to the next number in this pattern: 17, 16, 15, 14.*
  - *Point to the next number in this pattern: 4, 6, 8, 10.*
  - *Point to the number that has 1 ten and 7 units.*
  - *Point to the number that has 2 ones and 1 ten.*
  - *Point to any number larger than 12.*
  - *Point to the odd number between 12 and 14.*
  - *Point to the number that is 1 more than 7.*
  - *Point to the number that is 10 less than 19.*
- The first child to point to the correct number wins.
- Children keep count of how many rounds they win.
- Play for as long as is appropriate.
- The winner in each pair is the child who wins more rounds.

Variations

- Provide each pair with a pile of counters. As a child wins a game they take a counter. The winner in each pair is the child who wins more counters.
- Use the 'Hands-on: Numbers 1–10' game board, Hands-on: 'Numbers 1–12' game board, or 'Hands-on: 2-digit numbers' game board.
- Use the 'Hands-on: Multiples of 2' game board. Say statements similar to the following:
  – *Point to the next number in this pattern: 2, 4, 6, 8.*
  – *Point to the next number in this pattern: 14, 12, 10, 8.*
- Use the 'Hands-on: Multiples of 5' game board and 'Hands-on: Multiples of 10' game board in a similar way.

Who's left standing?

Objectives

- Read numbers to at least 100 in numerals
- Count in steps of 1, 2, 3, and 5 from 0, and count in tens from any number, forward or backward
- Count in multiples of ones, twos, fives and tens
- Recognise the place value of each digit in a 2-digit number (tens, ones)
- Compare and order numbers from 0 up to 100
- Given a number, identify one more, one less, ten more and ten less

Teacher resources

- none

Pupil resources

Number cards

- '1–12 number cards': (one card per child, but only use the 2–9 number cards) or
- '1–20 number cards': (one card per child) or
- '2-digit number cards': (one card per child)

What to do

Game 1: Count in steps of 1, 2, 3 and 5

- Provide each child with a 2–9 number card.
- Say: *Everyone stand up. Look at the number on your card. Sit down if the number on your card is the next number in the pattern:*
  - *3, 4, 5, 6…* (7)
  - *10, 8, 6, 4…* (2)
  - *14, 12, 10, 8…* (6)
  - *30, 25, 20, 15, 10…* (5)
  - *0, 1, 2, 3…* (4)
  - *0, 2, 4, 6…* (8)
  - *15, 12, 9, 6…* (3)

The winners are the children still standing with 9 on their cards.

Who's left standing?

(continued)

Game 2: Count in steps of 1, 2, 3, 5 and 10

- Provide each child with a 1–20 number card.
- Say: *Everyone stand up. Look at the number on your card. Sit down if the number on your card is the next number in the pattern:*
  - *6, 8, 10, 12…* (14)
  - *12, 11, 10, 9…* (8)
  - *5, 7, 9, 11…* (13)
  - *4, 7, 10, 13…* (16)
  - *5, 4, 3, 2…* (1)
  - *6, 9, 12, 15…* (18)
  - *0, 5, 10…* (15)
  - *4, 6, 8, 10…* (12)
  - *18, 15, 12, 9…* (6)
  - *0, 5, 10, 15…* (20)
  - *1, 2, 3, 4…* (5)
  - *5, 6, 7, 8…* (9)
  - *12, 10, 8, 6…* (4)
  - *42, 32, 22, 12…* (2)
  - *50, 40, 30, 20…* (10)
  - *7, 10, 13, 16…* (19)
  - *7, 8, 9, 10…* (11)
  - *15, 12, 9, 6…* (3)
  - *47, 37, 27, 17…* (7)

The winners are the children still standing with 17 on their cards.

Game 3: Compare and order numbers to 10

- Provide each child with a 2–9 number card.
- Say: *Everyone stand up. Look at the number on your card. Sit down if the number on your card is:*
  - *between 4 and 7* (5 and 6)
  - *between 2 and 5* (3 and 4)
  - *more than 7* (8 and 9)
  - *less than 3* (2)

The winners are the children still standing with 7 on their cards.

Game 4: Compare and order numbers to 20

- Provide each child with a 1–20 number card.
- Say: *Everyone stand up. Look at the number on your card. Sit down if the number on your card is:*
  - *between 6 and 10* (7, 8, 9)
  - *between 9 and 12* (10, 11)
  - *more than 16* (17, 18, 19, 20)
  - *between 11 and 14* (12, 13)
  - *between 3 and 7* (4, 5, 6)
  - *less than 4* (1, 2, 3)

The winners are the children still standing with 14, 15 or 16 on their cards.

(*continued*)

Who's left standing?

(continued)

Game 5: Compare and order numbers to 100

- Provide each child with a number card from '2-digit number cards'. (**Note:** Ensure you use the 12 number cards provided on the CD-ROM.)
- Say: *Everyone stand up. Look at the number on your card. Sit down if the number on your card is:*
  - *between 42 and 46* (43, 45)
  - *between 62 and 65* (63)
  - *more than 77* (78)
  - *between 50 and 55* (52)
  - *between 55 and 60* (56)
  - *between 25 and 35* (27, 29, 30)
  - *between 60 and 62* (61)
  - *between 72 and 75* (74)

The winners are the children still standing with 38 on their cards.

Game 6: Recognise the place value of each digit in a 2-digit number (tens, ones)

- Provide each child with a number card from '2-digit number cards'. (**Note:** Ensure you use the 12 number cards provided on the CD-ROM.)
- Say: *Everyone stand up. Look at the number on your card. Sit down if the number on your card has:*
  - *2 tens* (27, 29)
  - *3 ones (or units)* (43, 63)
  - *5 tens* (52, 56)
  - *8 ones (or units)* (38, 78)
  - *3 tens* (30, 38)
  - *4 ones (or units)* (74)
  - *6 tens* (61, 63)
  - *7 tens* (74, 78)

The winners are the children still standing with 45 on their cards.

Game 7: Given a number less than 10, identify one more and one less

- Provide each child with a 2–9 number card.
- Say: *Everyone stand up. Look at the number on your card. Sit down if the number on your card is:*
  - *1 more than 2* (3)
  - *1 more than 5* (6)
  - *1 less than 10* (9)
  - *1 less than 3* (2)
  - *1 more than 4* (5)
  - *1 less than 9* (8)
  - *1 more than 6* (7)

The winners are the children still standing with 4 on their cards.

Who's left standing?

(continued)

Game 8: Given a number less than 20, identify one more and one less

- Provide each child with a 1–20 number card.
- Say: *Everyone stand up. Look at the number on your card. Sit down if the number on your card is:*
  - *1 more than 3* (4)
  - *1 more than 17* (18)
  - *1 less than 9* (8)
  - *1 less than 15* (14)
  - *1 more than 0* (1)
  - *1 less than 13* (12)
  - *1 less than 16* (15)
  - *1 more than 8* (9)
  - *1 less than 11* (10)
  - *1 more than 2* (3)
  - *1 more than 19* (20)
  - *1 less than 6* (5)
  - *1 more than 5* (6)
  - *1 less than 3* (2)
  - *1 more than 18* (19)
  - *1 less than 17* (16)
  - *1 more than 10* (11)
  - *1 more than 16* (17)
  - *1 less than 8* (7)

The winners are the children still standing with 13 on their cards.

Game 9: Given a number, identify ten more and ten less

- Provide each child with a number card from '2-digit number cards'. (**Note:** Ensure you use the 12 number cards provided on the CD-ROM.)
- Say: *Everyone stand up. Look at the number on your card. Sit down if the number on your card is:*
  - *10 more than 20* (30)
  - *10 less than 66* (56)
  - *10 more than 33* (43)
  - *10 less than 39* (29)
  - *10 more than 51* (61)
  - *10 less than 55* (45)
  - *10 more than 17* (27)
  - *10 less than 48* (38)
  - *10 more than 42* (52)
  - *10 less than 73* (63)
  - *10 more than 64* (74)

The winners are the children still standing with 78 on their cards.

Forming groups

Objectives

- Read numbers to at least 100 in numerals
- Recognise the place value of each digit in a 2-digit number (tens, ones)
- Compare and order numbers from 0 up to 100

Teacher resources

- none

Pupil resources

Number cards

- '2-digit number cards' (one card per child) or
- 'Multiples of 2 number cards' (one card per child) or
- 'Multiples of 5 number cards' (one card per child) or
- 'Multiples of 10 number cards' (one card per child)

What to do

Game 1: Recognise the place value of each digit in a 2-digit number (tens, ones)

- Using the '2-digit number cards', the 'Multiples of 2 number card's (2-digit number cards only), the 'Multiples of 5 number cards' (2-digit number cards only), and the 'Multiples of 10 number cards' (2-digit number cards only), provide each child with one card. Ensure that every child has a different 2-digit number card.
- Point and say: *Everyone stand up. Look at the number on your card. When I say 'Go!' I want everyone with 2 tens to move to this side of the room. Everyone with 8 units to move to this side of the room, and everyone else to move to the back of the room. Ready? Go!*
- Once the three groups have been formed, ask the members of each group in turn to call out their number.

Variation

- Use different criteria to sort the numbers, for example, 5 tens, 2 units, *neither* 5 tens *nor* 2 units.

Forming groups

(continued)

Game 2: Compare and order numbers from 0 up to 100

- Using the '2-digit number cards', the 'Multiples of 2 number cards', the 'Multiples of 5 number cards' and the 'Multiples of 10 number cards', provide each child with one card. Ensure that every child has a different number card.
- Point and say: *Everyone stand up. Look at the number on your card. When I say 'Go!' I want everyone with the number 50 or a number less than 50 to move to this side of the room, and everyone with a number that is more than 50 to move to this side of the room. Ready? Go!*
- Once the two groups have been formed, ask the members of each group in turn to call out their number. Point and say: *Everyone hold up your number card. This group, starting with Toby, call out your numbers. Now this group, starting with Naseem, tell us your numbers.*
- Then say: *As quick as you can I want each group to put yourselves in order, smallest number to largest number. Ready? Go!*
- Once the two groups have ordered their cards, ask the members of each group in turn to call out their number, starting with the smallest number.

Variation

- Use different criteria to compare and order the numbers, for example:

Three groups:
- less than 33
- between 33 and 66
- more than 66

Four groups:
- less than 26
- between 26 and 49
- between 50 and 76
- more than 76

Which monkey wins?

Larger

Smaller

Objectives

- Read numbers to 100 in numerals
- Compare numbers from 0 up to 100

Pupil resources

- *Fluency in Number Facts: Facts and Games: Years 1 & 2* book pages 24 and 25 (per pair); PDFs:

- 30 counters (per pair)

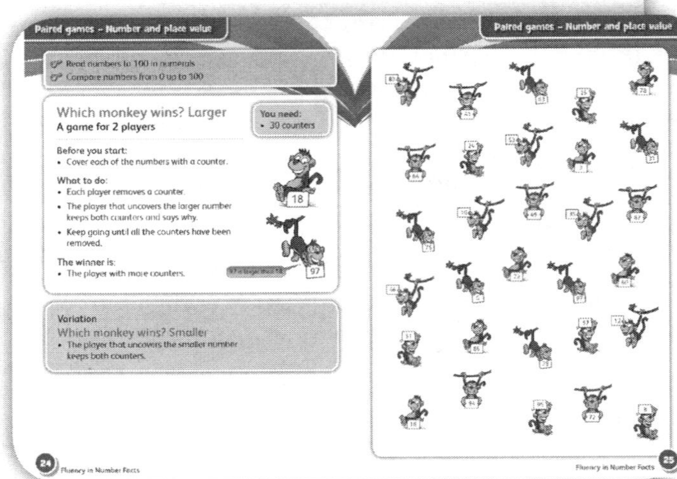
Paired games – Number and place value

Read numbers to 100 in numerals
Compare numbers from 0 up to 100

Which monkey wins? Larger
A game for 2 players

You need:
- 30 counters

Before you start:
- Cover each of the numbers with a counter.

What to do:
- Each player removes a counter.
- The player that uncovers the larger number keeps both counters and says why.
- Keep going until all the counters have been removed.

The winner is:
- The player with more counters.

Variation
Which monkey wins? Smaller
- The player that uncovers the smaller number keeps both counters.

24 Fluency in Number Facts

Paired games – Number and place value

Fluency in Number Facts 25

Variations

Order numbers from 0 up to 100

- Play *Largest monkey wins*: A game for three players
- Cover each of the numbers with a counter.
- Each player removes a counter.
- The player that uncovers the largest number keeps all three counters.
- Keep going until all the counters have been removed.

Order numbers from 0 up to 100

- Play *Smallest monkey wins*: A game for three players
- Cover each of the numbers with a counter.
- Each player removes a counter.
- The player that uncovers the smallest number keeps all three counters.
- Keep going until all the counters have been removed.

Order numbers from 0 up to 100

- Play *Number in-between wins*: A game for three players
- Cover each of the numbers with a counter.
- Each player removes a counter.
- The player that uncovers the number in the middle keeps all three counters.
- Keep going until all the counters have been removed.

- Children play the game individually, removing two counters at a time and saying to themselves the number that is larger (or smaller).

Balloon numbers

Objectives

- Read numbers to 100 in numerals
- Recognise the place value of each digit in a 2-digit number (tens, ones)
- Order numbers from 0 up to 100

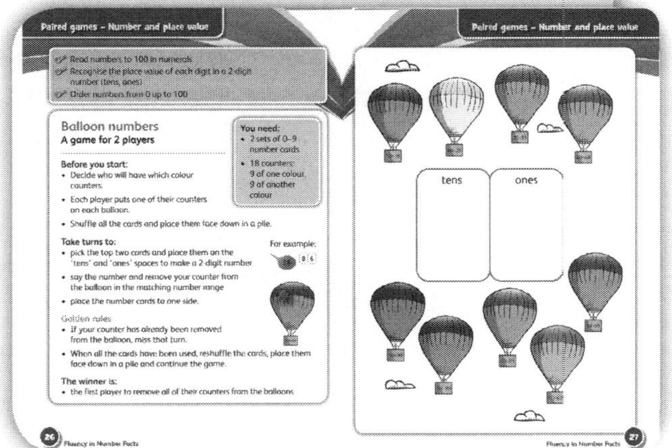

Pupil resources

- *Fluency in Number Facts: Facts and Games: Years 1 & 2* book pages 26 and 27 (per pair); PDFs:

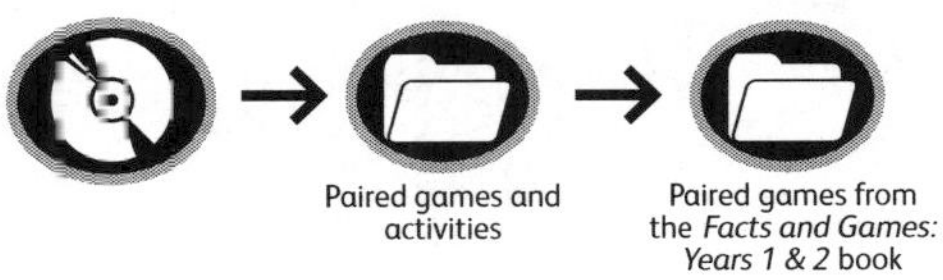

- 2 sets of 0–9 digit cards (per pair)
- 18 counters: 9 of one colour, 9 of another colour (per pair)

Notes

- If appropriate, discuss with the children how the number cards can be swapped around to create two different 2-digit numbers, for example:

Variations

- Children play the game in groups of three. You need 27 counters: 9 each of 3 different colours.

or *Before you start:*

- Decide who will have which colour counters.
- Shuffle all the cards and place them face down in a pile.

Take turns to:

- pick the top two cards and place them on the 'tens' and 'ones' cards to make a 2-digit number
- say the number and put one of your coloured counters on the balloon in the matching number range
- place the digit cards to one side.

Golden rules:

- If a balloon already has one of your coloured counters on it, miss that turn.
- When all the cards have been used, reshuffle the cards, place them face down in a pile and continue the game.

The winner is:

- the first player to put one of their counters on each of the balloons.

(**Note:** This variation can also be played with three players (see the first variation).)

- Children play the game individually, aiming to put a counter on each of the nine balloons.

Take the right path

Objectives

- Read numbers to 100 in numerals
- Compare numbers from 0 up to 100; use < and > signs

Pupil resources

- *Fluency in Number Facts: Facts and Games: Years 1 & 2* book pages 28 and 29 (per pair); PDFs:

→ Paired games and activities → Paired games from the *Facts and Games: Years 1 & 2* book

- pencil and paperclip (for the spinner) (per pair)
- 2 counters of different colours (per pair)

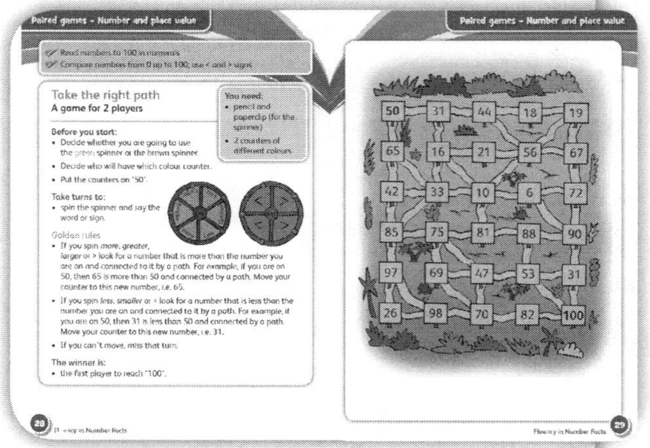

Notes

- The green spinner is the easier version and the brown spinner is the more difficult version.
- Before the children play the game, ensure that they are familiar with:
  - how to use the spinner (see *Facts and Games: Years 1 & 2* book page 64)
  - the terms 'more', 'greater', larger', 'less' and 'smaller' (for the green spinner)
  - the less than (<) and greater than (>) symbols (for the brown spinner).

Variations

- Children play the game in groups of three. You need three counters of different colours.

or

- Begin the game by putting the counters on '100'. The winner is the first player to reach '50'.

- Children play the game individually. How few spins do they take to reach 100?

Staircase counting

Objective

- Count in multiples of twos, fives and tens

Pupil resources

- *Fluency in Number Facts: Facts and Games: Years 1 & 2* book pages 30 and 31 (per pair); PDFs:

→ Paired games and activities → Paired games from the *Facts and Games: Years 1 & 2* book

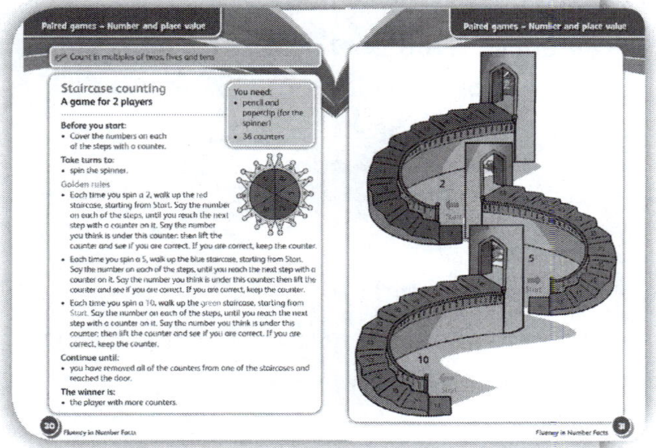

Paired games – Number and place value

Count in multiples of twos, fives and tens

Staircase counting
A game for 2 players

You need:
- pencil and paperclip (for the spinner)
- 36 counters

Before you start:
- Cover the numbers on each of the steps with a counter.

Take turns to:
- spin the spinner.

Golden rules
- Each time you spin a 2, walk up the red staircase, starting from Start. Say the number on each of the steps, until you reach the next step with a counter on it. Say the number you think is under this counter; then lift the counter and see if you are correct. If you are correct, keep the counter.
- Each time you spin a 5, walk up the blue staircase, starting from Start. Say the number on each of the steps, until you reach the next step with a counter on it. Say the number you think is under this counter; then lift the counter and see if you are correct. If you are correct, keep the counter.
- Each time you spin a 10, walk up the green staircase, starting from Start. Say the number on each of the steps, until you reach the next step with a counter on it. Say the number you think is under this counter; then lift the counter and see if you are correct. If you are correct, keep the counter.

Continue until:
- you have removed all of the counters from one of the staircases and reached the door.

The winner is:
- the player with more counters.

20 Fluency in Number Facts

Paired games – Number and place value

Fluency in Number Facts 21

- pencil and paper (for the spinner) (per pair)
- 36 counters (per pair)

Notes

- Before the children play the game, ensure that they are familiar with how to use the spinner (see *Facts and Games: Years 1 & 2* book page 64).

Variations

- Children play the game (and the two variations below) in groups of three.

or Count back in steps of 2, 5 and 10

- Rather than walking up the staircases from 'Start', children start at the top of each staircase and walk down, counting backwards. However, at the beginning of the game when covering the numbers on each step with a counter, children do not place a counter over the 12th multiple step, i.e. 24 on the red staircase, 60 on the blue staircase and 120 on the green staircase.

or Count on and back in steps of 2, 5 and 10

Before you start:

- Cover all but one of the numbers on each of the staircases with a counter, for example, do not cover: 12 on the staircase for 2, 15 on the staircase for 5, or 80 on the staircase for 10.
- Decide who will go first.

What to do:

- Choosing one of the staircases, the first player says either the number before, or the number after, the number that is not covered with a counter, for example, for the staircase for 2, either the number 10 or 14. They remove the counter covering that number and if their guess is correct they keep the counter. If not, they place the counter to one side.
- The next player repeats the above, choosing one of the staircases, saying either the number before, or the number after, the numbers that are not covered with a counter.
- The game continues until all the counters have been removed from each of the staircases.
- The winner is the player with more counters.

Courtyard counting

Objective

- Count in multiples of twos, fives and tens

Pupil resources

- *Fluency in Number Facts: Facts and Games: Years 1 & 2* book pages 32 and 33 (per pair); PDFs:

- button (per pair)
- 2 counters of different colours (per pair)
- 1–6 dice (per pair)

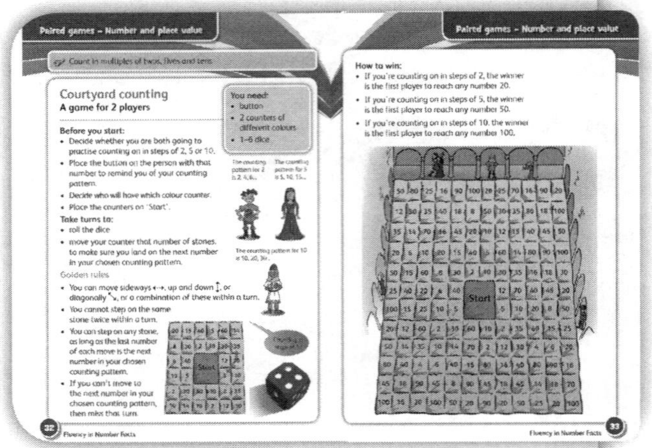
Paired games – Number and place value

Count in multiples of twos, fives and tens

Courtyard counting
A game for 2 players

You need:
- button
- 2 counters of different colours
- 1–6 dice

Before you start:
- Decide whether you are both going to practise counting on in steps of 2, 5 or 10.
- Place the button on the person with that number to remind you of your counting pattern.
- Decide who will have which colour counter.
- Place the counters on 'Start'.

Take turns to:
- roll the dice
- move your counter that number of stones, to make sure you land on the next number in your chosen counting pattern.

Golden rules
- You can move sideways, up and down, or diagonally, or a combination of these within a turn.
- You cannot step on the same stone twice within a turn.
- You can step on any stone, as long as the last number of each move is the next number in your chosen counting pattern.
- If you can't move to the next number in your chosen counting pattern, then miss that turn.

32 Fluency in Number Facts

Paired games – Number and place value

How to win:
- If you're counting on in steps of 2, the winner is the first player to reach any number 20.
- If you're counting on in steps of 5, the winner is the first player to reach any number 50.
- If you're counting on in steps of 10, the winner is the first player to reach any number 100.

Fluency in Number Facts 33

Notes

- Some children may have difficulty in understanding the rules of this game. Displaying the PDF of the game on the interactive whiteboard (IWB) and playing the game with the children will help clarify these rules.

Variations

- Children play the game in groups of three. You need three counters of different colours.

or Count back in steps of 2, 5 and 10

- Rather than placing their counters on 'Start', the children place their counters on any 20, any 50, or any 100, depending on whether they are counting in steps of 2, 5 or 10. They follow the same rules as described in the *Facts and Games* book, but rather than counting forwards, they count backwards. The winner is the first player to reach any paving stone with 2 or 5 or 10 on it (depending on which counting pattern they are practising).

  (**Note:** This variation can also be played with three players (see the first variation).)

- Children play the game individually. Can they complete their chosen counting sequence without missing a turn, for example, in ten moves?

Cover the boxes

1 more and 1 less
10 more and 10 less

Objectives

- Read numbers to 100 in numerals
- Recognise the place value of each digit in a 2-digit number (tens, ones)
- Given a number, identify one more and one less
- Given a number, identify 10 more and 10 less

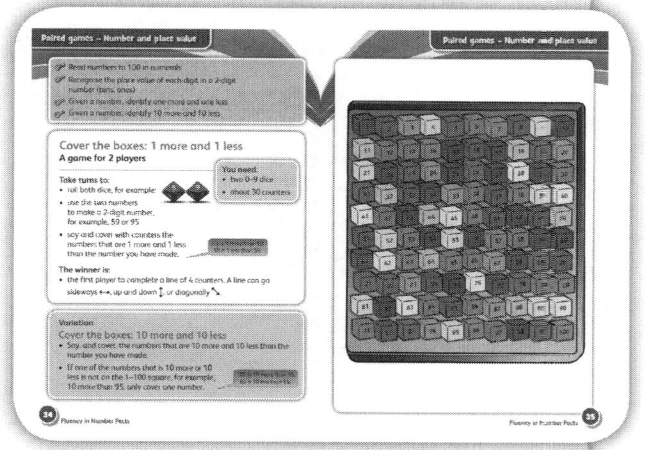

Paired games – Number and place value

- Read numbers to 100 in numerals
- Recognise the place value of each digit in a 2-digit number (tens, ones)
- Given a number, identify one more and one less
- Given a number, identify 10 more and 10 less

Cover the boxes: 1 more and 1 less
A game for 2 players

You need:
- two 0–9 dice
- about 30 counters

Take turns to:
- roll both dice, for example:
- use the two numbers to make a 2-digit number, for example, 59 or 95
- say and cover with counters the numbers that are 1 more and 1 less than the number you have made.

The winner is:
- the first player to complete a line of 4 counters. A line can go sideways ↔, up and down ↕, or diagonally ↘.

Variation
Cover the boxes: 10 more and 10 less
- Say and cover the numbers that are 10 more and 10 less than the number you have made.
- If one of the numbers that is 10 more or 10 less is not on the 1–100 square, for example, 10 more than 95, only cover one number.

34 Fluency in Number Facts

Paired games – Number and place value

Fluency in Number Facts 35

Pupil resources

- *Fluency in Number Facts: Facts and Games: Years 1 & 2* book pages 34 and 35 (per pair); PDFs:

Paired games and activities → Paired games from the *Facts and Games: Years 1 & 2* book

- 2 × 0–9 dice (per pair)
- about 30 counters (per pair)

Variations

- Children play the game in groups of three.

 or 

- Rather than using two 0–9 dice, children use two shuffled sets of 0–9 number cards.

- Children play the game individually. How few rolls of the dice do they take to complete a line of four counters?

Diamond grab

1 more and 1 less

10 more and 10 less

Objectives

- Read numbers to 100 in numerals
- Recognise the place value of each digit in a 2-digit number (tens, ones)
- Given a number, identify one more and one less
- Given a number, identify 10 more and 10 less

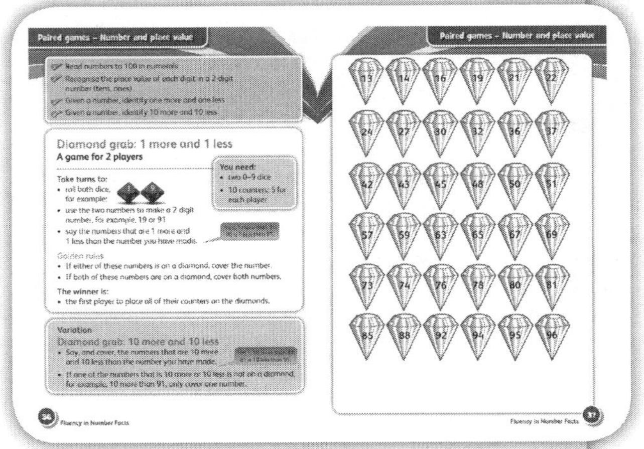

Pupil resources

- *Fluency in Number Facts: Facts and Games: Years 1 & 2* book Pages 36 and 37 (per pair); PDFs:

- 2 × 0–9 dice (per pair)
- 10 counters: 5 for each player (per pair)

Variations

- Children play the game in groups of three. You need 15 counters.

or

- Rather than using two 0–9 dice, children use two shuffled sets of 0–9 number cards.

- When playing *Diamond Grab: 1 more and 1 less*, provide each pair with 20 counters. The winner is the first player to complete a line of four counters. A line can go sideways, up and down or diagonally.

- When playing *Diamond Grab: 10 more and 10 less*, provide each pair with 20 counters. The winner is the first player to complete a line of three counters. A line can go sideways, up and down or diagonally.

- Children play the game individually. What is the longest line of counters made, once all 20 counters have been used?

Which is larger?

Objectives

- Read numbers to 100 in numerals
- Compare numbers from 0 up to 100

Pupil resources

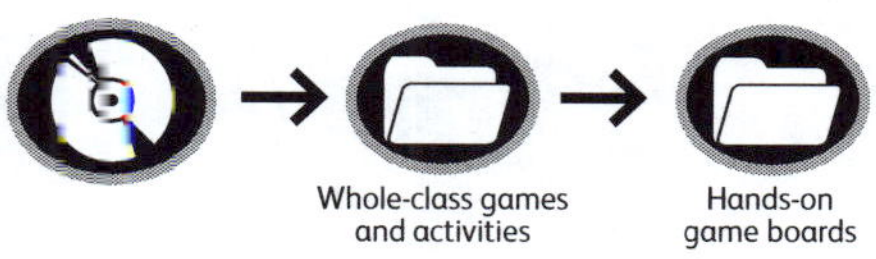

- 'Hands-on: Numbers 1–10' (per pair)
- 10 counters (per pair)

What to do

- Cover each of the numbers on the flags with a counter.
- Each child then removes one counter from the flags.
- The child who removes the counter from the larger number keeps both counters.
- The game continues until all the counters are removed from the flags.
- The winner is the child with more counters.
- Play three games.

Variations

Play 'Which is smaller?'

- The child who removes the counter from the smaller number keeps both counters.
- Use the 'Hands-on: Numbers 1–12' (per pair) and 12 counters (per pair).
- Use the 'Hands-on: Numbers 1–20' (per pair) and 20 counters (per pair).
- Use the 'Hands-on: 2-digit numbers' (per pair) and 10 counters (per pair).

More than

Objectives

- Read numbers to 100 in numerals
- Compare numbers from 0 up to 100

Pupil resources

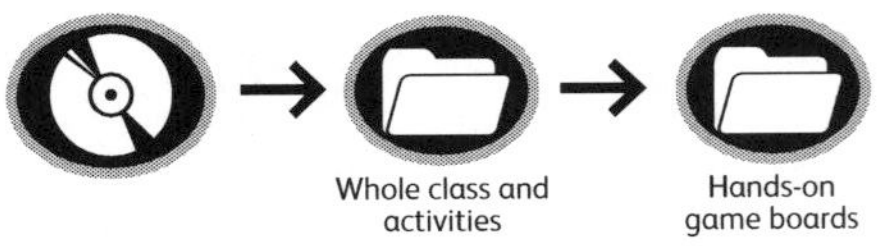

- 'Hands-on: Numbers 1–10' (per pair)
- 0–9 dice (per pair)
- 12 counters: 6 of one colour, 6 of another colour (per pair)

What to do

- Before you start decide who will have which colour counters.
- Take turns to:
  - roll the dice, for example, 4, and find a number on the grid that is more than the dice number, saying, for example, '8 is more than 4'
  - cover the number, i.e. 8, using one of your counters.
- You can only cover one number each turn.
- If no number can be covered, miss that turn.
- The winner is the player with more counters on the game board once all the numbers have a counter on them.

Variations

- Use the 'Hands-on: Numbers 1–20' (per pair) and 16 counters: 8 of one colour, 8 of another colour (per pair).
- Use the 'Hands-on: Numbers 1–12' (per pair); a 1–12 dice (per pair) and 20 counters (per pair). The winner is the first player to complete a line of 4 counters. A line can go sideways, up and down or diagonally.
- Children play 'Less than' using the three different 'Hands-on' game boards. If the children roll a 0 or 1, they roll the dice again.

One more

Objective

- Given a number to 100, identify one more and one less

Pupil resources

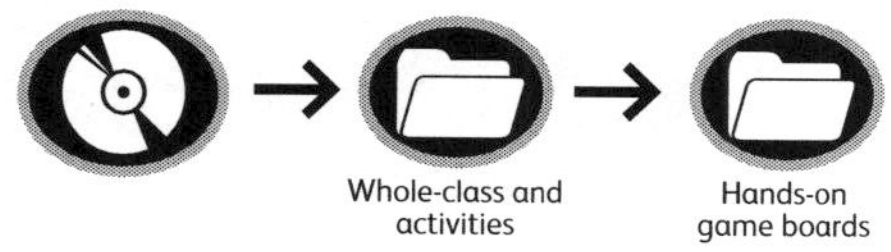

- 'Hands-on: Numbers 1–10' (per pair)
- 0–9 dice (per pair)
- 12 counters: 6 of one colour, 6 of another colour (per pair)

What to do

- Before you start decide who will have which colour counters.
- Take turns to:
  - roll the dice, for example, 6
  - say the number that is 1 more than the number rolled, i.e. 7
  - cover the number, i.e. 7, using one of your counters.
- If the number is already covered, miss that turn.
- The winner is the player with more counters on the game board once all the numbers have a counter on them.

Variations

- Use the 'Hands-on: Numbers 1–12' (per pair), a 1–12 dice (per pair) and 16 counters: 8 of one colour, 8 of another colour (per pair)
- Before you start decide who will have which colour counters.
- Take turns to:
  - roll the dice, for example, 9
  - say the number that is either 1 more or 1 less than the number rolled, i.e. 10 or 8
  - cover the number, for example, 10, using one of your counters.
- If the number is already covered, miss that turn.
- The winner is the player with more counters on the game board once all the numbers have a counter on them.

- Use the 'Hands-on: Numbers 1–20' (per pair), a 1–20 dice (per pair) and 24 counters: 12 of one colour, 12 of another colour (per pair)
- Before you start decide who will have which colour counters.
- Take turns to:
  - roll the dice, for example, 14
  - say the number that is either 1 more or 1 less than the number rolled, i.e. 15 or 13
  - cover the number, for example, 13, using one of your counters.
- If the number is already covered, miss that turn.
- The winner is the player with more counters on the game board once all the numbers have a counter on them.

Counters in a box

Objectives

- Recall and use addition and subtraction facts to 20 fluently
- Add and subtract numbers mentally, including adding three 1-digit numbers

Teacher resources

- small box or container
- some counters

Pupil resources

- none

What to do

- Show the children the empty box and the counters.
- Say: *I'm going to tell you to close your eyes. I'm then going to put different sets of counters into this box. As I put some counters into the box I'm going to tell you how many I'm putting in. You have to keep a count of how many counters are in the box. Don't open your eyes until I say so. Ready? Close your eyes.*
- Place some counters into the box, saying how many, for example: *two.*
- Place some more counters into the box, saying how many, for example: *three.*
- Place another set of counters into the box, again saying how many, for example: *five.*
- Say: *Open your eyes.*
- Ask: *How many counters did I put into the box? Is Jake right? Let's check.*
- Empty the counters from the box and count how many there are.
- Repeat several times.

Variations

- Don't say how many counters you are putting into the box each time, encourage the children to listen and count.
- As well as putting sets of counters into the box, take sets of counters out of the box.
- Use objects other than counters.
- Play 'Numbers in a box' using two sets of 0–9 number cards instead of counters.

Whole-class games and activities

Hold it up

Objectives

- Recall and use addition and subtraction facts to 20 fluently, and derive and use related facts up to 100
- Add and subtract numbers mentally, including a 2-digit number and ones, a 2-digit number and tens, two 2-digit numbers, and adding three 1-digit numbers

Teacher resources

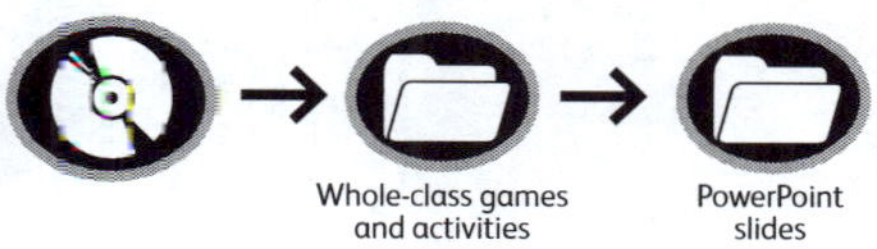

- 'Hold it up'

Pupil resources

- set of 0–9 number cards or small individual whiteboard and pen (per child)

What to do

- Using the 'Hold it up: Numbers 1–10' slide, write an addition or subtraction operation in the box at the top of the slide, for example, 7 +.
- Point to one of the coloured 1–10 numbers on the slide.
- Children work out the answer and hold up the appropriate number card(s).
- Repeat several times.

Variations

- Write different addition or subtraction operations in the box.
- Use the 'Hold it up: Numbers 1–12' slide.
- Use the 'Hold it up: Numbers 1–20' slide.
- Use the 'Hold it up: 2-digit numbers' slide.
- Change the numbers on the 'Hold it up' slides.

Gladiators

Objectives

- Recall and use addition and subtraction facts to 20 fluently, and derive and use related facts up to 100
- Add and subtract numbers mentally, including a 2-digit number and ones, a 2-digit number and tens, two 2-digit numbers, and adding three 1-digit numbers

Teacher resources

- 'Gladiators'

Pupil resources

- 2 × rulers or 'swords'

What to do

- Display the 'Gladiators Numbers: 1–10' slide.
- Ask two children to stand either side of the numbers.
- Ask an addition or subtraction calculation where the answer is on the board, for example: *4 add 3 is…*
- The first child to point to the correct answer stays in. The other child sits down.
- Quickly choose another child to come and take the place of the child that just sat down.
- Continue as above.
- Which child can stay in the longest?

Variations

- The children sitting down ask the two children standing by the numbers a question where the answer is on the slide.
- To quicken the game, have two children standing either side of the numbers, one behind the other. When a child loses and has to sit down, there is an immediate replacement.
- Use the 'Gladiators Numbers: 1–20' slide.
- Use the 'Gladiators: 2-digit numbers' slide

Hands-on

Objectives

- Recall and use addition and subtraction facts to 20 fluently, and derive and use related facts up to 100
- Add and subtract numbers mentally, including a 2-digit number and ones, a 2-digit number and tens, two 2-digit numbers, and adding three 1-digit numbers

Teacher resources

- none

Pupil resources

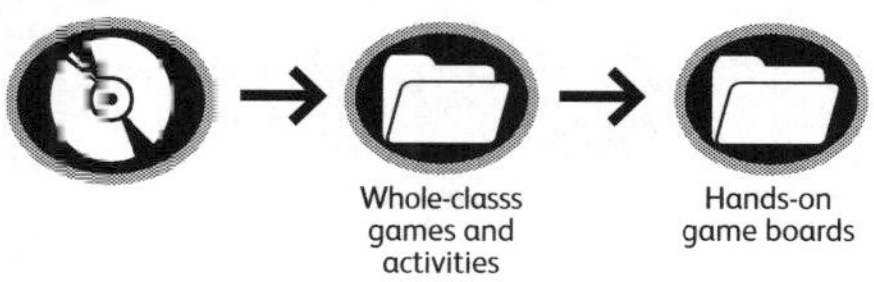

- 'Hands-on' game board (per pair)

What to do

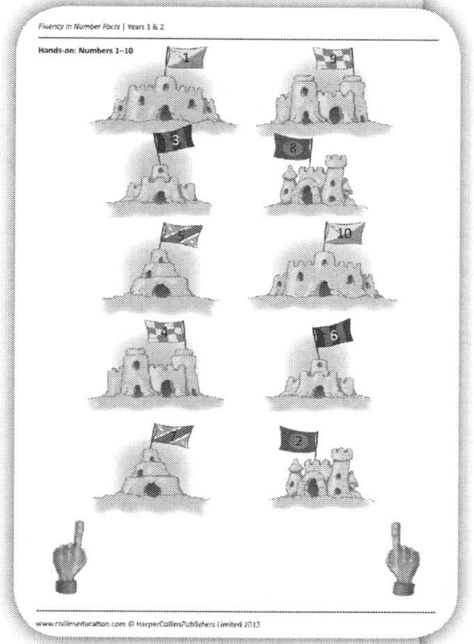

- Decide which range of numbers you want the children to use to practise and consolidate the addition and subtraction facts.
- Arrange the children into pairs and provide each pair with a copy of the appropriate Hands-on game board, for example, 'Hands-on: Numbers 1–10'.
- Ask the children to put the game board between them, and for each child to put their index finger on a hand at the bottom of the game board.
- Ask an appropriate addition or subtraction calculation that the children are practicing, for example: *5 add 4*.
- The first child to point to the correct answer wins.
- Children keep count of how many rounds they win.
- Play for as long as is appropriate.
- The winner in each pair is the child who wins more rounds.

Variation

- Provide each pair with a pile of counters. As a child wins a game they take a counter. The winner in each pair is the child who wins more counters.
- Use the 'Hands-on: Numbers 1–12' game board.
- Use the 'Hands-on: Numbers 1–20' game board.
- Use the 'Hands-on: 2-digit numbers' game board.

Bingo

Objectives

- Recall and use addition and subtraction facts to 20 fluently, and derive and use related facts up to 100
- Add and subtract numbers mentally, including a 2-digit number and ones, a 2-digit number and tens, two 2-digit numbers, and adding three 1-digit numbers

Teacher resources

- 'Bingo'

Pupil resources

- pencil and paper or small individual whiteboard and pen (per child)

What to do

- Display the 'Bingo: Numbers 1–20' slide.
- Ask each child to write down any five numbers from the slide.
- Ask questions involving addition and subtraction where the answer is from 1 to 20.
- Children look to find if any of their five numbers is the answer to the question.
- If a child has the answer, they cross out that number.
- The winner is the first child to cross out all five of their numbers and call out 'Bingo!'

(**Note**: Be sure to keep a record of the answers for checking purposes.)

Variations

- Ask the children to write down more or fewer than five numbers from the slide.
- Use the 'Bingo: 2-digit numbers' slide.

Four in a row

Objectives

- Recall and use addition and subtraction facts to 20 fluently, and derive and use related facts up to 100
- Add and subtract numbers mentally, including a 2-digit number and ones

Teacher resources

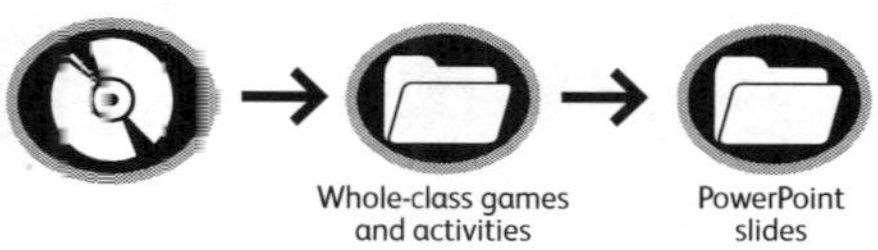

- 'Four in a row'
- 0–9 dice

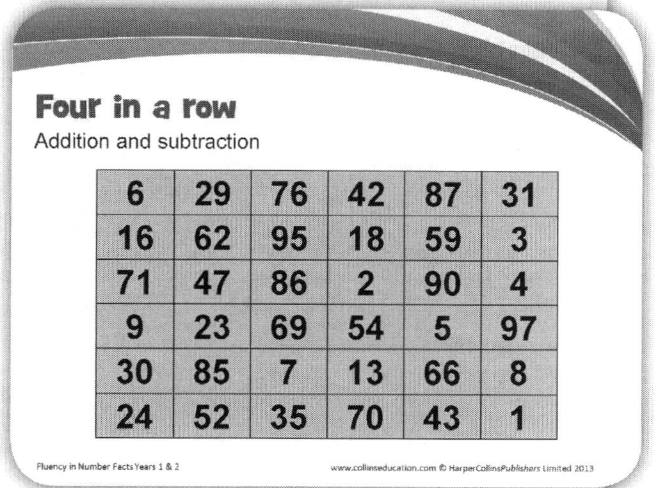

Four in a row

Addition and subtraction

6	29	76	42	87	31
16	62	95	18	59	3
71	47	86	2	90	4
9	23	69	54	5	97
30	85	7	13	66	8
24	52	35	70	43	1

Fluency in Number Facts Years 1 & 2 www.collinseducation.com © HarperCollinsPublishers Limited 2013

Pupil resources

- none

What to do

- Divide the class into two teams – a red team and a blue team.
- Display the 'Four in a row: Addition and subtraction' slide.
- Explain that the object of the game is for a team to highlight a row of four numbers: either side to side, up and down or diagonally.
- To highlight a number, a team must successfully answer an addition or subtraction question.
- Invite a child from the red team to roll the dice and say the number.
- Ask an addition or subtraction question that includes the number rolled and with an answer that is on the slide.
- Select a child from the red team to call out the answer.
- If correct, this number is highlighted in red on the slide. If incorrect, ask a child from the blue team to give the answer. If correct, this number is highlighted in blue.
- Next, invite a child from the blue team to roll the dice.
- Repeat the above, at a quick pace, until one team has highlighted a row of four numbers.

Variation

- The team that rolls the dice decides what number to add to, or subtract from, the dice number.

Tell me the facts

Objectives

- Recall and use addition and subtraction facts to 20 fluently, and derive and use related facts up to 100
- Add and subtract numbers mentally, including a 2-digit number and ones, a 2-digit number and tens, two 2-digit numbers, and adding three 1-digit numbers

Teacher resources

→ Whole-class games and activities → PowerPoint slides

- 'Tell me the facts'

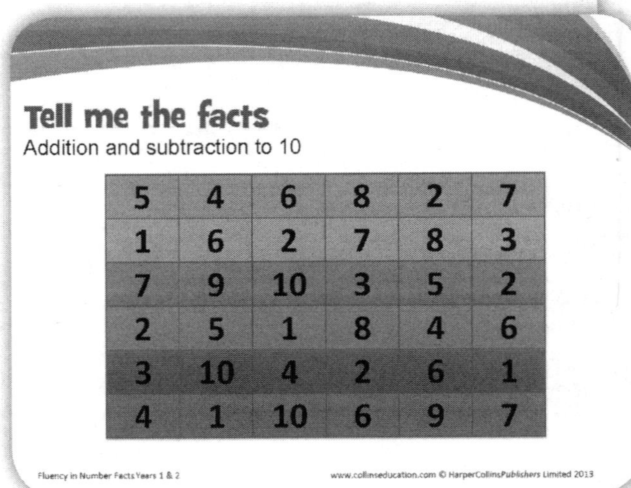

5	4	6	8	2	7
1	6	2	7	8	3
7	9	10	3	5	2
2	5	1	8	4	6
3	10	4	2	6	1
4	1	10	6	9	7

Pupil resources

- none

What to do

- Display the 'Tell me the facts: Addition and subtraction to 10' slide.
- Ask a child to highlight two numbers next to each other either side to side, up and down, or diagonally and say a known addition or subtraction number fact about these two numbers, i.e. *I know that the sum of 6 and 9 is 15.*
- Repeat, asking other children to come and highlight two other numbers, saying a known addition or subtraction number fact about the two numbers.

Variations

- Ask questions such as:
  - *Point to two numbers next to each other that have a total of 14.*
  - *Point to two numbers next to each other that have a difference of 3.*
- Use the 'Tell me the facts: Addition and subtraction to 20' slide.
- Use the 'Tell me the facts: Addition and subtraction to 100' slide.

Tell me your numbers

Objectives

- Recall and use addition and subtraction facts to 20 fluently, and derive and use related facts up to 100
- Add and subtract numbers mentally, including a 2-digit number and ones, a 2-digit number and tens, two 2-digit numbers, and adding three 1-digit numbers

Teacher resources

- none

Pupil resources

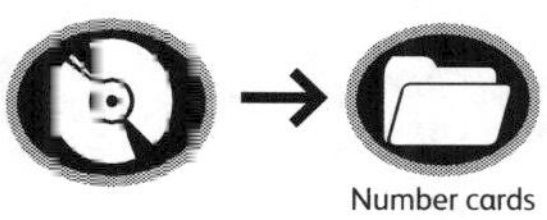

Number cards

- '1–12 number cards' (one card per child, but only use the 1–9 number cards) or
- 'Two-digit number cards' (one card per child)

What to do

- Provide each child with a 1–9 number card or 2-digit number card.
- Quickly call out two children's names.
- Both children stand and say the number on their card.
- Ask these two children an appropriate addition or subtraction question using the two numbers on the cards.
- The two children answer, then sit down.
- Repeat for other pairs of children, or groups of three.

Who's left standing?

Objectives

- Recall and use addition and subtraction facts to 20 fluently, and derive and use related facts up to 100
- Add and subtract numbers mentally, including a 2-digit number and ones, a 2-digit number and tens, two 2-digit numbers, and adding three 1-digit numbers

Teacher resources

- none

Pupil resources

Number cards

- '1–12 number cards' (one card per child, but only use the 1–9 number cards) or
- '1–20 number cards' (one card per child) or
- '2-digit number cards' (one card per child)

What to do

Game 1: Recall and use addition facts to 10

- Provide each child with a 1–9 number card.
- Say: *Everyone stand up. Look at the number on your card. Sit down if the number on your card is the answer to:*
  - *4 plus 2* (6)
  - *1 add zero* (1)
  - *2 more than 3* (5)
  - *1 plus 1* (2)
  - *5 plus 3* (8)
  - *4 add 5* (9)
  - *5 add 2* (7)
  - *1 more than 3* (4)

The winners are the children still standing with 3 on their cards.

Game 2: Recall and use subtraction facts to 10

- Provide each child with a 1–9 number card.
- Say: *Everyone stand up. Look at the number on your card. Sit down if the number on your card is the answer to:*
  - *10 subtract 3* (7)
  - *1 less than 10* (9)
  - *7 minus 3* (4)
  - *the difference between 8 and 6* (2)
  - *the difference between 5 and 4* (1)
  - *9 subtract 6* (3)
  - *10 minus 2* (8)
  - *7 take away 1* (6)

The winners are the children still standing with 5 on their cards.

Who's left standing?

(continued)

Game 3: Recall and use addition and subtraction facts to 10

- Provide each child with a 1–9 number card.
- Say: *Everyone stand up. Look at the number on your card. Sit down if the number on your card is the answer to:*
  - *5 plus 2* (7)
  - *2 more than 4* (6)
  - *the difference between 8 and 6* (2)
  - *10 subtract 9* (1)
  - *the sum of 3 and 6* (9)
  - *7 take away 2* (5)
  - *3 add 1* (4)
  - *8 minus 5* (3)

The winners are the children still standing with 8 on their cards.

Game 4: Recall and use addition facts to 20

- Provide each child with a 1–20 number card.
- Say: *Everyone stand up. Look at the number on your card. Sit down if the number on your card is the answer to:*
  - *6 add 4* (10)
  - *2 plus 5* (7)
  - *9 add 5* (14)
  - *3 plus 3* (6)
  - *2 more than 14* (16)
  - *1 add 1* (2)
  - *7 plus 4* (11)
  - *1 add zero* (1)
  - *12 plus 7* (19)
  - *5 plus 4* (9)
  - *2 more than 6* (8)
  - *10 add 10* (20)
  - *3 plus 2* (5)
  - *12 add 5* (17)
  - *9 plus 4* (13)
  - *3 plus 1* (4)
  - *10 add 5* (15)
  - *1 more than 2* (3)
  - *9 add 9* (18)

The winners are the children still standing with 12 on their cards.

(continued)

Who's left standing?

(continued)

Game 5: Recall and use subtraction facts to 20

- Provide each child with a 1–20 number card.
- Say: *Everyone stand up. Look at the number on your card. Sit down if the number on your card is the answer to:*
  - *15 take away 2* (13)
  - *13 subtract 9* (4)
  - *2 less than 17* (15)
  - *9 take away 6* (3)
  - *the difference between 20 and 2* (18)
  - *1 less than 10* (9)
  - *16 subtract 4* (12)
  - *20 minus zero* (20)
  - *the difference between 7 and 2* (5)
  - *20 minus 4* (16)
  - *8 minus 6* (2)
  - *the difference between 18 and 8* (10)
  - *17 minus 10* (7)
  - *18 subtract 4* (14)
  - *the difference between 10 and 4* (6)
  - *19 minus 8* (11)
  - *15 take away 14* (1)
  - *1 less than 20* (19)
  - *20 subtract 3* (17)

The winners are the children still standing with 8 on their cards.

Game 6: Recall and use addition and subtraction facts to 20

- Provide each child with a 1–20 number card.
- Say: *Everyone stand up. Look at the number on your card. Sit down if the number on your card is the answer to:*
  - *8 add 8* (16)
  - *7 take away 5* (2)
  - *6 plus 5* (11)
  - *5 plus 5* (10)
  - *13 minus 6* (7)
  - *2 less than 16* (14)
  - *4 plus 2* (6)
  - *9 subtract 8* (1)
  - *12 add 7* (19)
  - *8 add 4* (12)
  - *7 plus 6* (13)
  - *the difference between 16 and 12* (4)
  - *13 add 5* (18)
  - *16 minus 7* (9)
  - *14 subtract 6* (8)
  - *10 add 10* (20)
  - *the difference between 11 and 6* (5)
  - *7 plus 8* (15)
  - *15 subtract 12* (3)

The winners are the children still standing with 17 on their cards.

Who's left standing?

(continued)

Game 7: Add numbers mentally, including a 2-digit number and ones

- Provide each child with a number card from '2-digit number cards'. (**Note:** Ensure you use the 12 number cards provided on the CD-ROM.)
- Say: *Everyone stand up. Look at the number on your card. Sit down if the number on your card is the answer to:*
  - *37 add 6* (43)
  - *23 plus 4* (27)
  - *45 add 7* (52)
  - *the sum of 33 and 5* (38)
  - *3 more than 71* (74)
  - *58 plus 5* (63)
  - *3 more than 75* (78)
  - *37 add 8* (45)
  - *27 plus 2* (29)
  - *47 add 9* (56)
  - *24 plus 6* (30)

The winners are the children still standing with 61 on their cards.

Game 8: Subtract numbers mentally, including a 2-digit number and ones

- Provide each child with a number card from '2-digit number cards'. (**Note:** Ensure you use the 12 number cards provided on the CD-ROM.)
- Say: *Everyone stand up. Look at the number on your card. Sit down if the number on your card is the answer to:*
  - *61 subtract 5* (56)
  - *4 less than 34* (30)
  - *the difference between 69 and 6* (63)
  - *80 minus 2* (78)
  - *54 subtract 9* (45)
  - *the difference between 58 and 6* (52)
  - *48 minus 5* (43)
  - *the difference between 68 and 7* (61)
  - *4 less than 31* (27)
  - *41 minus 3* (38)
  - *76 take away 2* (74)

The winners are the children still standing with 29 on their cards.

(continued)

Who's left standing?

(continued)

- **Game 9:** Add and subtract numbers mentally, including a 2-digit number and ones
- Provide each child with a number card from '2-digit number cards'. (**Note:** Ensure you use the 12 number cards provided on the CD-ROM.)
- Say: *Everyone stand up. Look at the number on your card. Sit down if the number on your card is the answer to:*
  - *35 take away 8* (27)
  - *56 minus 4* (52)
  - *34 plus 4* (38)
  - *55 add 6* (61)
  - *the difference between 79 and 5* (74)
  - *51 subtract 6* (45)
  - *the sum of 22 and 7* (29)
  - *3 more than 53* (56)
  - *9 less than 39* (30)
  - *the sum of 55 and 8* (63)
  - *2 less than 80* (78)

The winners are the children still standing with 43 on their cards.

Game 10: Add numbers mentally, including a 2-digit number and tens

- Provide each child with a number card from '2-digit number cards'. (**Note:** Ensure you use the 12 number cards provided on the CD-ROM.)
- Say: *Everyone stand up. Look at the number on your card. Sit down if the number on your card is the answer to:*
  - *10 more than 19* (29)
  - *26 add 30* (56)
  - *20 plus 10* (30)
  - *23 add 20* (43)
  - *31 plus 30* (61)
  - *28 plus 10* (38)
  - *40 more than 34* (74)
  - *23 plus 40* (63)
  - *the total of 28 and 50* (78)
  - *25 add 20* (45)
  - *22 add 30* (52)

The winners are the children still standing with 27 on their cards.

Game 11: Subtract numbers mentally, including a 2-digit number and tens

- Provide each child with a number card from '2-digit number cards'. (**Note:** Ensure you use the 12 number cards provided on the CD-ROM.)
- Say: *Everyone stand up. Look at the number on your card. Sit down if the number on your card is the answer to:*
  - *73 minus 30* (43)
  - *94 take away 20* (74)
  - *the difference between 93 and 30* (63)
  - *88 minus 10* (78)
  - *89 take away 60* (29)
  - *88 minus 50* (38)
  - *85 subtract 40* (45)
  - *76 subtract 20* (56)
  - *the difference between 47 and 20* (27)
  - *10 less than 71* (61)
  - *50 less than 80* (30)

The winners are the children still standing with 52 on their cards.

Who's left standing?

(continued)

Game 12: Add and subtract numbers mentally, including a 2-digit number and tens

- Provide each child with a number card from '2-digit number cards'. (**Note:** Ensure you use the 12 number cards provided on the CD-ROM.)
- Say: *Everyone stand up. Look at the number on your card. Sit down if the number on your card is the answer to:*
  - *44 plus 30* (74)
  - *57 minus 30* (27)
  - *the difference between 79 and 50* (29)
  - *10 more than 35* (45)
  - *38 add 40* (78)
  - *10 less than 73* (63)
  - *96 take away 40* (56)
  - *10 more than 20* (30)
  - *32 plus 20* (52)
  - *83 subtract 40* (43)
  - *91 minus 30* (61)

The winners are the children still standing with 38 on their cards.

Game 13: Add numbers mentally, including two 2-digit numbers

- Provide each child with a number card from '2-digit number cards'. (**Note:** Ensure you use the 12 number cards provided on the CD-ROM.)
- Say: *Everyone stand up. Look at the number on your card. Sit down if the number on your card is the answer to:*
  - *35 plus 43* (78)
  - *11 add 34* (45)
  - *16 plus 13* (29)
  - *14 add 42* (56)
  - *15 plus 15* (30)
  - *31 add 21* (52)
  - *20 more than 41* (61)
  - *22 plus 16* (38)
  - *the sum of 15 and 12* (27)
  - *41 plus 22* (63)
  - *21 add 22* (43)

The winners are the children still standing with 74 on their cards.

Game 14: Subtract numbers mentally, including two 2-digit numbers

- Provide each child with a number card from '2-digit number cards'. (**Note:** Ensure you use the 12 number cards provided on the CD-ROM.)
- Say: *Everyone stand up. Look at the number on your card. Sit down if the number on your card is the answer to:*
  - *72 subtract 42* (30)
  - *20 less than 49* (29)
  - *67 minus 24* (43)
  - *the difference between 59 and 32* (27)
  - *30 less than 91* (61)
  - *79 minus 41* (38)
  - *88 take away 14* (74)
  - *the difference between 87 and 24* (63)
  - *99 take away 21* (78)
  - *the difference between 74 and 22* (52)
  - *88 subtract 32* (56)

The winners are the children still standing with 45 on their cards.

(continued)

Who's left standing?

(continued)

Game 15: Add and subtract numbers mentally, including two 2-digit numbers

- Provide each child with a number card from '2-digit number cards'. (**Note:** Ensure you use the 12 number cards provided on the CD-ROM.)
- Say: *Everyone stand up. Look at the number on your card. Sit down if the number on your card is the answer to:*
  - *76 minus 31* (45)
  - *41 plus 11* (52)
  - *17 add 12* (29)
  - *62 subtract 32* (30)
  - *79 take away 41* (38)
  - *11 more than 16* (27)
  - *the difference between 78 and 35* (43)
  - *87 minus 26* (61)
  - *the sum of 42 and 32* (74)
  - *25 add 53* (78)
  - *87 subtract 24* (63)

The winners are the children still standing with 56 on their cards.

Game 16: Add numbers mentally, including adding three 1-digit numbers

- Provide each child with a 1–20 number card.
- Say: *Everyone stand up. Look at the number on your card. Sit down if the number on your card is the answer to:*
  - *2 plus 3 plus 1* (6)
  - *8 add 5 add 3* (16)
  - *5 add 4 add 3* (12)
  - *3 plus 4 plus 2* (9)
  - *the total of 8, 7 and 5* (20)
  - *9 plus 3 plus 7* (19)
  - *6 add 3 add 4* (13)
  - *1 plus 1 plus 2* (4)
  - *the sum of 6, 5 and 4* (15)
  - *4 add 3 add 3* (10)
  - *3 plus 2 plus 2* (7)
  - *the sum of 6, 4 and 4* (14)
  - *1 add 1 add 1* (3)
  - *9 add 7 add 2* (18)
  - *2 plus 1 plus 2* (5)
  - *the total of 2, 5 and 4* (11)
  - *1 add 0 add 0* (1)
  - *6 add 4 add 7* (17)
  - *3 plus 2 plus 3* (8)

The winners are the children still standing with 2 on their cards.

Stand up

Objectives

- Recall and use addition and subtraction facts to 20 fluently, and derive and use related facts up to 100
- Add and subtract numbers mentally, including a 2-digit number and ones, a 2-digit number and tens, two 2-digit numbers, and adding three 1-digit numbers

Teacher resources

- none

Pupil resources

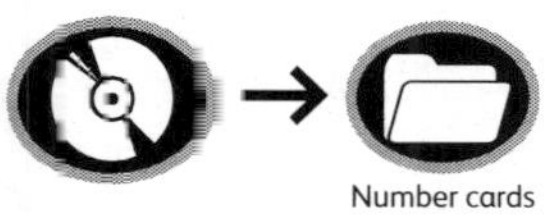

- '1–12 number cards' (one card per child, but only use the 1–9 number cards) or
- '1–20 number cards' (one card per child) or
- '2-digit number cards' (one card per child)

What to do

Game 1: Recall and use addition facts to 20

- Provide each child with a 1–9 number card.
- Say: *Look at the number on your card. Add 6 to the number on your card. If the total is 9, stand up.*
- Ask: *Who can tell me what number is on Sarah's and Peter's cards?* (3)
- Ask the children standing to show their cards.
- The children standing then sit down.
- Repeat for the following:
  - *Add 4 to the number on your card. If the total is 5, stand up.* (1)
  - *Add 3 to the number on your card. If the total is 7, stand up.* (4)
  - *Add 7 to the number on your card. If the sum is 12, stand up.* (5)
  - *Add 6 to the number on your card. If the total is 14, stand up.* (8)
  - *Add 8 to the number on your card. If the answer is 10, stand up.* (2)
  - *Add 5 to the number on your card. If the total is 11, stand up.* (6)
  - *Add 4 to the number on your card. If the answer is 13, stand up.* (9)
  - *Add 3 to the number on your card. If the sum is 10, stand up.* (7)

(continued)

Stand up

(continued)

Game 2: Recall and use subtraction facts to 20

- Provide each child with a 1–9 number card.
- Say: *Look at the number on your card. Stand up if your card shows the answer to 14 subtract 6.*
- Ask: *Who can tell me what number is on Amir's and Robert's cards?* (8)
- Ask the children standing to show their cards.
- The children standing then sit down.
- Repeat for the following:
  - *Stand up if your card shows the answer to 13 subtract 10.* (3)
  - *Stand up if your card shows the answer to 15 minus 9.* (6)
  - *Stand up if your card shows the answer to 8 subtract 7.* (1)
  - *Stand up if your card shows the answer to 13 take away 4.* (9)
  - *Stand up if your card shows the answer to 11 subtract 7.* (4)
  - *Stand up if your card shows the answer to 17 minus 10.* (7)
  - *Stand up if your card shows the answer to 10 subtract 8.* (2)
  - *Stand up if your card shows the answer to 12 take away 7.* (5)

Game 3: Recall and use addition and subtraction facts to 20

- Provide each child with a 1–9 number card.
- Say: *Look at the number on your card. Stand up if your card shows the answer to 11 subtract 8.*
- Ask: *Who can tell me what number is on Carl's and Sunita's cards?* (3)
- Ask the children standing to show their cards.
- The children standing then sit down.
- Repeat for the following:
  - *Add 6 to the number on your card. If the total is 8, stand up.* (2)
  - *Stand up if your card shows the answer to 17 subtract 9.* (8)
  - *Add 9 to the number on your card. If the answer is 16, stand up.* (7)
  - *Stand up if your card shows the answer to 14 take away 8.* (6)
  - *Add 14 to the number on your card. If the sum is 18, stand up.* (4)
  - *Stand up if your card shows the answer to 16 subtract 15.* (1)
  - *Stand up if your card shows the answer to 19 minus 10.* (9)
  - *Add 8 to the number on your card. If the answer is 13, stand up.* (5)

Stand up

(continued)

Game 4: Add numbers mentally, including a 2-digit number and ones

- Provide each child with a number card from '2-digit number cards'. (**Note:** Ensure you use the 12 number cards provided on the CD-ROM.)
- Say: *Look at the number on your card. Add 8 to the number on your card. If the total is 64, stand up.*
- Ask: *Who can tell me what number is on Harry's and Paul's cards?* (56)
- Ask the children standing to show their cards.
- The children standing then sit down.
- Repeat for the following:
  - *Add 6 to the number on your card. If the total is 67, stand up.* (61)
  - *Add 9 to the number on your card. If the total is 52, stand up.* (43)
  - *Add 7 to the number on your card. If the sum is 59, stand up.* (52)
  - *Add 5 to the number on your card. If the answer is 83, stand up.* (78)
  - *Add 3 to the number on your card. If the total is 30, stand up.* (27)
  - *Add 6 to the number on your card. If the total is 69, stand up.* (63)
  - *Add 4 to the number on your card. If the answer is 33, stand up.* (29)
  - *Add 8 to the number on your card. If the total is 82, stand up.* (74)
  - *Add 5 to the number on your card. If the total is 35, stand up.* (30)
  - *Add 7 to the number on your card. If the total is 45, stand up.* (38)
  - *Add 9 to the number on your card. If the answer is 54, stand up.* (45)

Game 5: Subtract numbers mentally, including a 2-digit number and ones

- Provide each child with a number card from '2-digit number cards'. (**Note:** Ensure you use the 12 number cards provided on the CD-ROM.)
- Say: *Look at the number on your card. Stand up if your card shows the answer to 50 subtract 5.*
- Ask: *Who can tell me what number is on Helen's and Oliver's cards?* (45)
- Ask the children standing to show their cards.
- The children standing then sit down.
- Repeat for the following:
  - *Stand up if your card shows the answer to 30 take away 3.* (27)
  - *Stand up if your card shows the answer to 67 minus 6.* (61)
  - *Stand up if your card shows the answer to 72 subtract 9.* (63)
  - *Stand up if your card shows the answer to 63 take away 7.* (56)
  - *Stand up if your card shows the answer to 47 subtract 4.* (43)
  - *Stand up if your card shows the answer to 86 minus 8.* (78)
  - *Stand up if your card shows the answer to 37 take away 7.* (30)
  - *Stand up if your card shows the answer to 56 minus 4.* (52)
  - *Stand up if your card shows the answer to 80 subtract 6.* (74)
  - *Stand up if your card shows the answer to 43 take away 5.* (38)
  - *Stand up if your card shows the answer to 32 minus 3.* (29)

(continued)

Stand up

(continued)

Game 6: Add and subtract numbers mentally, including a 2-digit number and ones

- Provide each child with a number card from '2-digit number cards'. (**Note:** Ensure you use the 12 number cards provided on the CD-ROM.)
- Say: *Look at the number on your card. Stand up if your card shows the answer to 59 subtract 3.*
- Ask: *Who can tell me what number is on Ali's and Greg's cards?* (56)
- Ask the children standing to show their cards.
- The children standing then sit down.
- Repeat for the following:
  - *Add 8 to the number on your card. If the total is 69, stand up.* (61)
  - *Stand up if your card shows the answer to 36 minus 7.* (29)
  - *Add 4 to the number on your card. If the total is 47, stand up.* (43)
  - *Stand up if the number on your card is 2 less than 32.* (30)
  - *Add 6 to the number on your card. If the answer is 58, stand up.* (52)
  - *Add 9 to the number on your card. If the total is 87, stand up.* (78)
  - *Add 7 to the number on your card. If the sum is 34, stand up.* (27)
  - *Stand up if your card shows the answer to 46 take away 8.* (38)
  - *Stand up if your card shows the answer to 79 subtract 5.* (74)
  - *Add 3 to the number on your card. If the total is 66, stand up.* (63)
  - *Stand up if your card shows the answer to 54 subtract 9.* (45)

Game 7: Add numbers mentally, including a 2-digit number and tens

- Provide each child with a number card from '2-digit number cards'. (**Note:** Ensure you use the 12 number cards provided on the CD-ROM.)
- Say: *Look at the number on your card. Add 30 to the number on your card. If the total is 91, stand up.*
- Ask: *Who can tell me what number is on Mile's and Tom's cards?* (61)
- Ask the children standing to show their cards.
- The children standing then sit down.
- Repeat for the following:
  - *Add 20 to the number on your card. If the sum is 72, stand up.* (52)
  - *Add 40 to the number on your card. If the total is 78, stand up.* (38)
  - *Add 10 to the number on your card. If the total is 84, stand up.* (74)
  - *Add 10 to the number on your card. If the sum is 37, stand up.* (27)
  - *Add 20 to the number on your card. If the total is 63, stand up.* (43)
  - *Add 30 to the number on your card. If the answer is 86, stand up.* (56)
  - *Add 10 to the number on your card. If the total is 40, stand up.* (30)
  - *Add 20 to the number on your card. If the answer is 65, stand up.* (45)
  - *Add 10 to the number on your card. If the total is 73, stand up.* (63)
  - *Add 50 to the number on your card. If the answer is 79, stand up.* (29)
  - *Add 20 to the number on your card. If the total is 98, stand up.* (78)

Stand up

(continued)

Game 8: Subtract numbers mentally, including a 2-digit number and tens

- Provide each child with a number card from '2-digit number cards'. (**Note:** Ensure you use the 12 number cards provided on the CD-ROM.)
- Say: *Look at the number on your card. Stand up if your card shows the answer to 73 subtract 30.*
- Ask: *Who can tell me what number is on Martin's and Paolo's cards?* (43)
- Ask the children standing to show their cards.
- The children standing then sit down.
- Repeat for the following:
  - *Stand up if your card shows the answer to 85 subtract 40.* (45)
  - *Stand up if your card shows the answer to 86 take away 30.* (56)
  - *Stand up if your card shows the answer to 81 minus 20.* (61)
  - *Stand up if your card shows the answer to 73 subtract 10.* (63)
  - *Stand up if your card shows the answer to 78 take away 40.* (38)
  - *Stand up if your card shows the answer to 89 minus 60.* (29)
  - *Stand up if your card shows the answer to 77 take away 50.* (27)
  - *Stand up if your card shows the answer to 72 minus 20.* (52)
  - *Stand up if your card shows the answer to 84 subtract 10.* (74)
  - *Stand up if your card shows the answer to 98 minus 20.* (78)
  - *Stand up if your card shows the answer to 80 take away 50.* (30)

Game 9: Add and subtract numbers mentally, including a 2-digit number and tens

- Provide each child with a number card from '2-digit number cards'. (**Note:** Ensure you use the 12 number cards provided on the CD-ROM.)
- Say: *Look at the number on your card. Stand up if your card shows the answer to 67 take away 40.*
- Ask: *Who can tell me what number is on Leroy's and Sally's cards?* (27)
- Ask the children standing to show their cards.
- The children standing then sit down.
- Repeat for the following:
  - *Add 50 to the number on your card. If the answer is 79, stand up.* (29)
  - *Add 10 to the number on your card. If the total is 84, stand up.* (74)
  - *Stand up if your card shows the answer to 92 minus 40.* (52)
  - *Add 40 to the number on your card. If the total is 70, stand up.* (30)
  - *Stand up if your card shows the answer to 73 subtract 30.* (43)
  - *Add 30 to the number on your card. If the total is 68, stand up.* (38)
  - *Stand up if your card shows the answer to 98 minus 20.* (78)
  - *Add 30 to the number on your card. If the total is 86, stand up.* (56)
  - *Add 40 to the number on your card. If the answer is 85, stand up.* (45)
  - *Stand up if your card shows the answer to 81 minus 20.* (61)
  - *Stand up if your card shows the answer to 93 subtract 30.* (63)

(continued)

Stand up

(continued)

Game 10: Add numbers mentally, including two 2-digit numbers

- Provide each child with a number card from '2-digit number cards'. (**Note:** Ensure you use the 12 number cards provided on the CD-ROM.)
- Say: *Look at the number on your card. Add 23 to the number on your card. If the answer is 68, stand up.*
- Ask: *Who can tell me what number is on Tina's and Zara's cards?* (45)
- Ask the children standing to show their cards.
- The children standing then sit down.
- Repeat for the following:
  - *Add 25 to the number on your card. If the total is 99, stand up.* (74)
  - *Add 24 to the number on your card. If the total is 87, stand up.* (63)
  - *Add 41 to the number on your card. If the answer is 70, stand up.* (29)
  - *Add 11 to the number on your card. If the total is 89, stand up.* (78)
  - *Add 52 to the number on your card. If the sum is 79, stand up.* (27)
  - *Add 36 to the number on your card. If the total is 97, stand up.* (61)
  - *Add 34 to the number on your card. If the sum is 86, stand up.* (52)
  - *Add 41 to the number on your card. If the total is 79, stand up.* (38)
  - *Add 25 to the number on your card. If the total is 68, stand up.* (43)
  - *Add 32 to the number on your card. If the answer is 88, stand up.* (56)
  - *Add 30 to the number on your card. If the total is 60, stand up.* (30)

Game 11: Subtract numbers mentally, including two 2-digit numbers

- Provide each child with a number card from '2-digit number cards'. (**Note:** Ensure you use the 12 number cards provided on the CD-ROM.)
- Say: *Look at the number on your card. Stand up if your card shows the answer to 79 minus 41.*
- Ask: *Who can tell me what number is on Eric's and John's cards?* (38)
- Ask the children standing to show their cards.
- The children standing then sit down.
- Repeat for the following:
  - *Stand up if your card shows the answer to 87 subtract 24.* (63)
  - *Stand up if your card shows the answer to 68 take away 41.* (27)
  - *Stand up if your card shows the answer to 75 subtract 32.* (43)
  - *Stand up if your card shows the answer to 89 minus 11.* (78)
  - *Stand up if your card shows the answer to 84 take away 54.* (30)
  - *Stand up if your card shows the answer to 67 subtract 22.* (45)
  - *Stand up if your card shows the answer to 78 minus 26.* (52)
  - *Stand up if your card shows the answer to 96 subtract 22.* (74)
  - *Stand up if your card shows the answer to 69 take away 13.* (56)
  - *Stand up if your card shows the answer to 74 minus 13.* (61)
  - *Stand up if your card shows the answer to 59 take away 30.* (29)

Stand up

(continued)

Game 12: Add and subtract numbers mentally, including two 2-digit numbers

- Provide each child with a number card from '2-digit number cards'. (**Note:** Ensure you use the 12 number cards provided on the CD-ROM.)
- Say: *Look at the number on your card. Stand up if your card shows the answer to 89 subtract 15.*
- Ask: *Who can tell me what number is on Fiona's and Kevin's cards?* (74)
- Ask the children standing to show their cards.
- The children standing then sit down.
- Repeat for the following:
  - *Add 34 to the number on your card. If the total is 95, stand up.* (61)
  - *Add 17 to the number on your card. If the sum is 69, stand up.* (52)
  - *Stand up if your card shows the answer to 88 take away 32.* (56)
  - *Stand up if your card shows the answer to 78 subtract 35.* (43)
  - *Add 26 to the number on your card. If the total is 56, stand up.* (30)
  - *Stand up if your card shows the answer to 79 minus 50.* (29)
  - *Add 34 to the number on your card. If the answer is 79, stand up.* (45)
  - *Add 21 to the number on your card. If the answer is 99, stand up.* (78)
  - *Stand up if your card shows the answer to 78 take away 51.* (27)
  - *Add 41 to the number on your card. If the total is 79, stand up.* (38)
  - *Stand up if your card shows the answer to 87 subtract 24.* (63)

Game 13: Add numbers mentally, including adding three 1-digit numbers

- Provide each child with a 1–12 number card.
- Say: *Look at the number on your card. Stand up if your card has the answer to 4 add 3 add 2.*
- Ask: *Who can tell me what number is on Leo's and Penny's cards?* (9)
- Ask the children standing to show their cards.
- The children standing then sit down.
- Repeat for the following:
  - *Stand up if your card has the answer to 3 plus 1 plus 1.* (5)
  - *Stand up if your card has the answer to 4 add 3 add 1.* (8)
  - *Stand up if this number is the sum of 7 plus 1 plus 2.* (10)
  - *Stand up if this number is the sum of 2 add 1 add 1.* (4)
  - *Stand up if your card has the answer to 4 plus 2 plus 5.* (11)
  - *Stand up if this number is the sum of 1 add 1 add 1.* (3)
  - *Stand up if your card has the answer to 2 add 3 add 1.* (6)
  - *Stand up if your card has the answer to 1 add 0 add 0.* (1)
  - *Stand up if your card has the answer to 4 plus 2 plus 1.* (7)
  - *Stand up if this number is the sum of 4 add 5 add 3.* (12)
  - *Stand up if your card has the answer to 1 plus 1 plus 0.* (2)

Whole-class, paired or individual activities

Using the Maths Facts in the *Facts and Games* book

Objectives

- Recall and use addition and subtraction facts to 20 fluently
- Add and subtract numbers mentally, including a 2-digit number and ones

Teacher resources

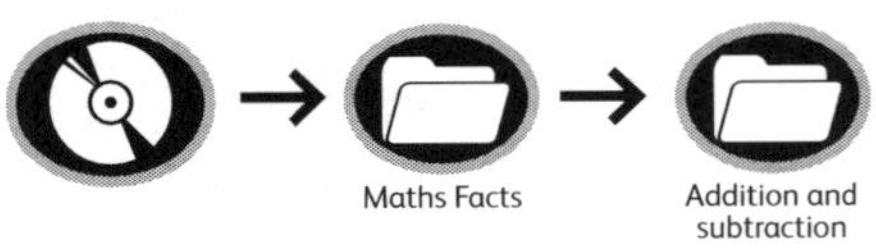

Pupil resources

- *Fluency in Number Facts: Facts and Games: Years 1 & 2* book pages 4–15 (per child or pair)

Introduction

The Maths Facts on pages 4–15 of the *Fluency in Number Facts: Facts and Games: Years 1 & 2* book cover the key addition and subtraction number facts that children need to be able to recall instantly by the end of Key Stage 1.

These pages aim to develop children's fluency by:

- securing a thorough conceptual understanding of the addition and subtraction number facts
- identifying patterns and the relationship between addition and subtraction
- developing strategic approaches to recalling and deriving the answers to addition and subtraction number facts.

To assist in achieving these aims, the addition and subtraction number facts contained in the *Facts and Games: Years 1 & 2* book are presented in the following ways:

- Addition and subtraction numbers facts to 20 (pages 4 – 6)
- Addition and subtraction trios to 20 (pages 7–13)
- Addition number facts to 5, 10 and 20 table (page 14)
- Addition of 1-digit and 2-digit numbers to 20 table (page 15)

The following pages include a brief description of each of these presentations, along with suggestions of how to focus on these Maths Facts either with the whole class, or with children working in pairs or individually.

Whole-class, paired or individual activities

Using the Maths Facts in the *Facts and Games* book

(continued)

Addition and subtraction numbers facts to 20
(pages 4–6)

The facts are organised into 'number fact families', for example, Number facts for 6, which are presented in two columns – an addition column and a subtraction column. This presentation shows the number pattern in each addition and subtraction 'family' as well as the relationship between the addition and the subtraction number facts.

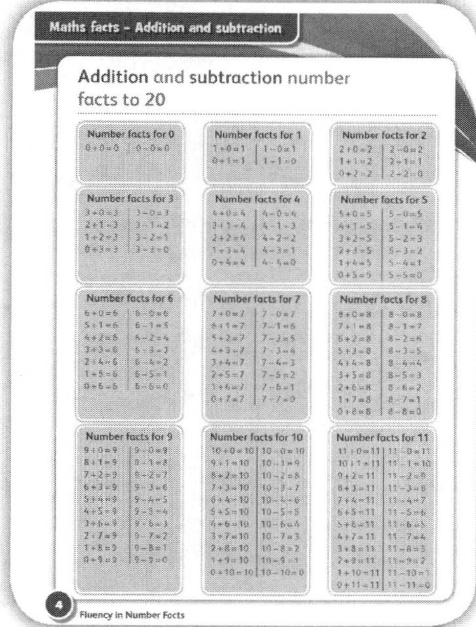
Maths facts – Addition and subtraction

Addition and subtraction number facts to 20

Number facts for 0
0 + 0 = 0 | 0 − 0 = 0

Number facts for 1
1 + 0 = 1 | 1 − 0 = 1
0 + 1 = 1 | 1 − 1 = 0

Number facts for 2
2 + 0 = 2 | 2 − 0 = 2
1 + 1 = 2 | 2 − 1 = 1
0 + 2 = 2 | 2 − 2 = 0

Number facts for 3
3 + 0 = 3 | 3 − 0 = 3
2 + 1 = 3 | 3 − 1 = 2
1 + 2 = 3 | 3 − 2 = 1
0 + 3 = 3 | 3 − 3 = 0

Number facts for 4
4 + 0 = 4 | 4 − 0 = 4
3 + 1 = 4 | 4 − 1 = 3
2 + 2 = 4 | 4 − 2 = 2
1 + 3 = 4 | 4 − 3 = 1
0 + 4 = 4 | 4 − 4 = 0

Number facts for 5
5 + 0 = 5 | 5 − 0 = 5
4 + 1 = 5 | 5 − 1 = 4
3 + 2 = 5 | 5 − 2 = 3
2 + 3 = 5 | 5 − 3 = 2
1 + 4 = 5 | 5 − 4 = 1
0 + 5 = 5 | 5 − 5 = 0

Number facts for 6
6 + 0 = 6 | 6 − 0 = 6
5 + 1 = 6 | 6 − 1 = 5
4 + 2 = 6 | 6 − 2 = 4
3 + 3 = 6 | 6 − 3 = 3
2 + 4 = 6 | 6 − 4 = 2
1 + 5 = 6 | 6 − 5 = 1
0 + 6 = 6 | 6 − 6 = 0

Number facts for 7
7 + 0 = 7 | 7 − 0 = 7
6 + 1 = 7 | 7 − 1 = 6
5 + 2 = 7 | 7 − 2 = 5
4 + 3 = 7 | 7 − 3 = 4
3 + 4 = 7 | 7 − 4 = 3
2 + 5 = 7 | 7 − 5 = 2
1 + 6 = 7 | 7 − 6 = 1
0 + 7 = 7 | 7 − 7 = 0

Number facts for 8
8 + 0 = 8 | 8 − 0 = 8
7 + 1 = 8 | 8 − 1 = 7
6 + 2 = 8 | 8 − 2 = 6
5 + 3 = 8 | 8 − 3 = 5
4 + 4 = 8 | 8 − 4 = 4
3 + 5 = 8 | 8 − 5 = 3
2 + 6 = 8 | 8 − 6 = 2
1 + 7 = 8 | 8 − 7 = 1
0 + 8 = 8 | 8 − 8 = 0

Number facts for 9
9 + 0 = 9 | 9 − 0 = 9
8 + 1 = 9 | 9 − 1 = 8
7 + 2 = 9 | 9 − 2 = 7
6 + 3 = 9 | 9 − 3 = 6
5 + 4 = 9 | 9 − 4 = 5
4 + 5 = 9 | 9 − 5 = 4
3 + 6 = 9 | 9 − 6 = 3
2 + 7 = 9 | 9 − 7 = 2
1 + 8 = 9 | 9 − 8 = 1
0 + 9 = 9 | 9 − 9 = 0

Number facts for 10
10 + 0 = 10 | 10 − 0 = 10
9 + 1 = 10 | 10 − 1 = 9
8 + 2 = 10 | 10 − 2 = 8
7 + 3 = 10 | 10 − 3 = 7
6 + 4 = 10 | 10 − 4 = 6
5 + 5 = 10 | 10 − 5 = 5
4 + 6 = 10 | 10 − 6 = 4
3 + 7 = 10 | 10 − 7 = 3
2 + 8 = 10 | 10 − 8 = 2
1 + 9 = 10 | 10 − 9 = 1
0 + 10 = 10 | 10 − 10 = 0

Number facts for 11
11 + 0 = 11 | 11 − 0 = 11
10 + 1 = 11 | 11 − 1 = 10
9 + 2 = 11 | 11 − 2 = 9
8 + 3 = 11 | 11 − 3 = 8
7 + 4 = 11 | 11 − 4 = 7
6 + 5 = 11 | 11 − 5 = 6
5 + 6 = 11 | 11 − 6 = 5
4 + 7 = 11 | 11 − 7 = 4
3 + 8 = 11 | 11 − 8 = 3
2 + 9 = 11 | 11 − 9 = 2
1 + 10 = 11 | 11 − 10 = 1
0 + 11 = 11 | 11 − 11 = 0

4 Fluency in Number Facts

How to use the Maths Facts

Whole class

- Focus on just one 'number fact family' at a time, for example, 'Number facts for 6'. (The eventual aim is to have the class focus on several 'number fact families' simultaneously.)
- Display the appropriate PDF file (CD-ROM: Maths Facts / Addition and Subtraction) and provide each child or pair with a copy of the *Facts and Games: Years 1 & 2* book and direct their attention to the relevant 'number fact family' on pages 4–6.
- Begin by asking the children to identify different patterns in both lists of calculations and discuss these with the class.
- Can the children see any relationships between the two columns of calculations?
- Ask individual children to chant the facts, for example:
  – *Michael, please read out all the addition number facts for 6.*
  – *Julia, please tell us all the subtraction number facts for 6.*
- Ask specific groups of children to chant the facts, for example:
  – *6 add 0 is 6* (boys); *5 add 1 is 6* (girls); *4 add 2 is 6* (boys); *3 add 3 is 6* (girls)…
  – *6 add 0 is 6* (Group A); *5 add 1 is 6* (Group B); *4 add 2 is 6* (Group C); *3 add 3 is 6* (Group A)…
- Tell the children to spend just two or three minutes looking at the addition and subtraction facts with the aim of focussing their attention on learning these facts off by heart.
- Conclude by hiding the PDF file, asking the children to close their copy of the *Facts and Games: Years 1 & 2* book and ask the class questions similar to the following:
  – *What is 4 add 2?*
  – *How many more do you need to add to 3 to make 6?*
  – *4 and what other number total 6?*
  – *What is 6 subtract / minus / take away 1?*
  – *What is the difference between 6 and 5?*
  – *What is 2 less than 6?*

(continued)

Whole-class, paired or individual activities

Using the Maths Facts in the *Facts and Games* book

(continued)

Pairs

- Begin by asking the children to focus on just one 'number fact family', for example, 'Number facts for 6'. (The eventual aim is to have the children focus on several 'number fact families' simultaneously.)
- Provide each pair with a copy of the *Facts and Games: Years 1 & 2* book and direct their attention to the relevant 'number fact family' on pages 4–6. Alternatively, ask the children to choose a 'family' that they know they need to develop greater fluency of.
- Children spend just two or three minutes individually looking at the addition and subtraction facts with the aim of learning these facts off by heart.
- Children then take it in turns to take charge of the book and ask each other questions similar to those on page 71.

Individual

- Begin by asking the child to focus on just one 'number fact family', for example, 'Number facts for 6'. (The eventual aim is to have the child focus on several 'number fact families' simultaneously.)
- Provide the child with a copy of the *Facts and Games: Years 1 & 2* book and direct their attention to the relevant 'number fact family' on pages 4–6. Alternatively, ask the child to choose a 'family' that they know they need to develop greater fluency of.
- It is recommended that the child spends just five or ten minutes each time, focussing their attention on learning the addition and subtraction facts off by heart.
- To provide some personal challenge, suggest the child covers the addition number facts with their hand and recites the facts to themselves. They then repeat this for the related subtraction number facts.

Whole-class, paired or individual activities

Using the Maths Facts in the *Facts and Games* book

(continued)

Addition and subtraction trios to 20 (pages 7–13)

'Trios' show the relationship between the three numbers that make up an addition fact and the related subtraction fact. They also show that addition of two numbers can be done in any order (commutative) and how this law does *not* apply to subtraction.

How to use the Maths Facts

Whole class

- Focus on just one set of addition and subtraction 'trios' at a time, for example, Addition and subtraction trios for 6'.
- Display the appropriate PDF file (CD-ROM: Maths Facts / Addition and Subtraction) and provide each child or pair with a copy of the *Facts and Games: Years 1 & 2* book and direct their attention to the relevant trios on pages 7–13.
- Begin by asking the children to identify different patterns between the four calculations in the first trio.
- Ensure the children realise that each trio consists of only three numbers, i.e. 0, 6 and 6, and that these three numbers produce four calculations: two addition calculations (6 + 0 = 6 and 0 + 6 = 6), and two subtraction calculations (6 – 0 = 6 and 6 – 6 = 0).
- Referring to the two addition calculations, discuss with the children how addition of two numbers can be done in any order (commutative law).
- Then, referring to the two subtraction calculations, discuss with the children how the commutative law does *not* apply to subtraction.
- Move on to discussing the inverse relationship between addition and subtraction.
- Repeat the above for the remaining trios in the set.
- Next tell the children to spend just two or three minutes looking at the set of addition and subtraction trios with the aim of focussing their attention on learning the facts off by heart.
- Conclude by hiding the PDF file, asking the children to close their copy of the *Facts and Games: Years 1 & 2* book and ask the class questions similar to the following:
  - *Tell me an addition calculation you can make using only the numbers 2, 4 and 6.*
  - *Can you tell me another addition calculation that only uses the same three numbers?*
  - *Tell me a subtraction calculation that only uses the numbers 2, 4 and 6.*
  - *Is there another subtraction calculation that only uses these numbers?*

(*continued*)

Whole-class, paired or individual activities

Using the Maths Facts in the *Facts and Games* book

(continued)

Pairs

- Provide each pair with a copy of the *Facts and Games: Years 1 & 2* book and direct their attention to the relevant set of addition and subtraction trios on pages 7–13. Alternatively, ask the children to choose a set of trios that they know they need to develop greater fluency of.
- Children take turns to choose one of the trios and place their hand/fingers over the list of four calculations.
- Referring to the three numbers on the triangle, the other child has to say the two addition and two subtraction number facts.
- Once they have done this, the child covering the facts removes their hand/finger to reveal the four calculations.

Individual

- Provide each child with a copy of the *Facts and Games: Years 1 & 2* book and direct their attention to the relevant set of addition and subtraction trios on pages 7–13. Alternatively, ask the child to choose a set of trios that they know they need to develop greater fluency of.
- It is recommended that the child spends just five or ten minutes each time, focussing their attention on one set of addition and subtraction trios with the aim of learning the facts off by heart.
- To provide some personal challenge, as for the paired activity above, suggest the child places their hand/fingers over the list of four calculations and recites the facts to themselves.

Whole-class, paired or individual activities

Using the Maths Facts in the *Facts and Games* book

(continued)

Addition number facts to 5, 10 and 20 table (page 14)

Addition of 1-digit and 2-digit numbers to 20 table (page 15)

The table on page 14 shows all of the addition number facts to 20 involving the numbers 0 to 10. The answers in red are all the number facts to 5, the answers in blue are all the number facts from 6 to 10, and the answers in green are all the number facts from 11 to 20. The table therefore, shows children the progressive nature of the number facts from 5 to 10 and then to 20.

The table on page 15 shows all of the addition number facts to 20 involving the 1 to 9 digits and the 'teen' numbers.

The tables also show that addition of two numbers can be done in any order (commutative) and that addition is the opposite (inverse) of subtraction.

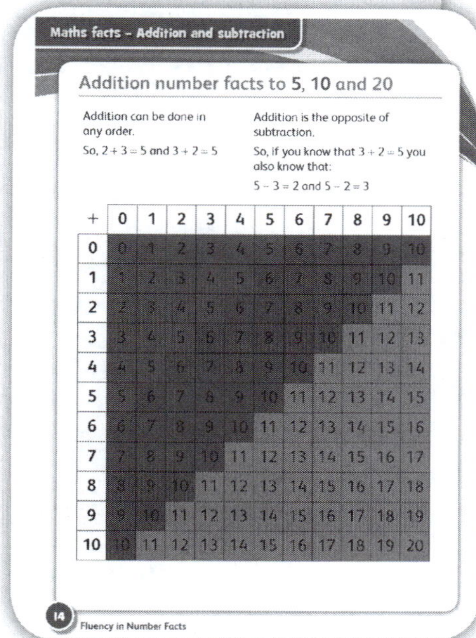

Maths facts – Addition and subtraction

Addition number facts to 5, 10 and 20

Addition can be done in any order.

So, 2 + 3 = 5 and 3 + 2 = 5

Addition is the opposite of subtraction.

So, if you know that 3 + 2 = 5 you also know that:

5 – 3 = 2 and 5 – 2 = 3

+	0	1	2	3	4	5	6	7	8	9	10
0	0	1	2	3	4	5	6	7	8	9	10
1	1	2	3	4	5	6	7	8	9	10	11
2	2	3	4	5	6	7	8	9	10	11	12
3	3	4	5	6	7	8	9	10	11	12	13
4	4	5	6	7	8	9	10	11	12	13	14
5	5	6	7	8	9	10	11	12	13	14	15
6	6	7	8	9	10	11	12	13	14	15	16
7	7	8	9	10	11	12	13	14	15	16	17
8	8	9	10	11	12	13	14	15	16	17	18
9	9	10	11	12	13	14	15	16	17	18	19
10	10	11	12	13	14	15	16	17	18	19	20

14 Fluency in Number Facts

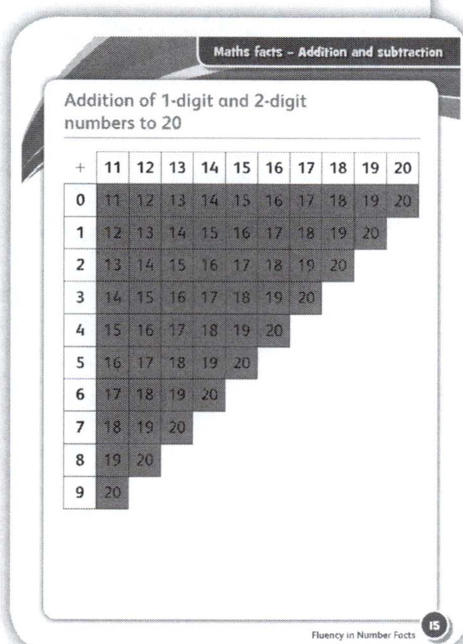

Maths facts – Addition and subtraction

Addition of 1-digit and 2-digit numbers to 20

+	11	12	13	14	15	16	17	18	19	20
0	11	12	13	14	15	16	17	18	19	20
1	12	13	14	15	16	17	18	19	20	
2	13	14	15	16	17	18	19	20		
3	14	15	16	17	18	19	20			
4	15	16	17	18	19	20				
5	16	17	18	19	20					
6	17	18	19	20						
7	18	19	20							
8	19	20								
9	20									

Fluency in Number Facts 15

How to use the Maths Facts

Whole class

- Display the appropriate PDF file (CD-ROM: Maths Facts / Addition and Subtraction) and provide each child or pair with a copy of the *Facts and Games: Years 1 & 2* book and direct their attention to the two tables on pages 14 and 15.
- Begin by discussing the 'Addition number facts to 5, 10 and 20 table' on page 14 with the children. Ask the children to identify different patterns in the table and discuss these with the class. Draw their attention to the patterns of numbers in each row, column and diagonal. In particular, highlight the row of numbers at the top of the table and the column of numbers down the left-hand side of the table.
- Next, move onto showing the children how to use the table. Put one finger on 2 in the column of numbers down the left-hand side of the table and another finger on 3 in the row of numbers at the top of the table, and then move both fingers across and down the table until they meet at the answer, i.e. 5.

(*continued*)

Whole-class, paired or individual activities

Using the Maths Facts in the *Facts and Games* book

(continued)

- Discuss with the children how 2 + 3 is the same as 3 + 2 (commutative).
- Repeat several times.
- Once the children are secure with reading the table for addition, show them how the table can also be used for subtraction. Put one finger on 2 in the column of numbers down the left-hand side of the table, and then move another finger across the row until you land on 5. Once your finger is on 5, move up the column until you land on 3 in the row of numbers at the top of the table.
- Discuss with the children that if they know that 2 + 3 = 5 then they also know that 5 – 3 = 2 and 5 – 2 = 3.
- Repeat several times.
- Next, ask the children to spend just four or five minutes becoming familiar with the table.
- Referring to the PDF file on display, conclude by asking the class questions similar to the following:
  - *Kevin, will you come out and show us how to get the answer to 7 add 5?*
  - *So, if we know that 7 add 5 is 12, what is the answer to 5 add 7? How can we check this on the table?*
  - *If we know that 7 plus 5 is 12, and 5 add 7 is 12, what is the answer to 12 subtract 7? How does the table help us check? What about 12 minus 5?*
- Repeat the above for the 'Addition of 1-digit and 2-digit numbers to 20' on page 15.

Pairs

- Provide each pair with a copy of the *Facts and Games: Years 1 & 2* book and direct their attention to one, or both, of the tables on pages 14 and 15.
- Children spend just two or three minutes individually looking at the table(s) with the aim of learning these facts off by heart.
- Children then take it in turns to ask each other questions similar to the following:
  - *Can you show me how to find the answer to 8 add 7?*
  - *What is 4 plus 7?*
  - *What is 9 subtract 5?*
  - *What is the difference between 13 and 7?*

Individual

- Provide each child with a copy of the *Facts and Games: Years 1 & 2* book and direct their attention to one, or both, of the tables on pages 14 and 15.
- It is recommended that the child spends just five or ten minutes each time, focussing their attention on learning the addition and subtraction facts off by heart.
- To provide some personal challenge, suggest the child covers the answers on the table leaving only the numbers in the top row and left-hand column visible. The child tests themselves on the addition number facts to 5, 10 and 20 (page 14) and/or the addition of 1-digit and 2-digit numbers to 20 (page 15).

Firework additions

Objective

- Recall addition facts to 20 fluently

Pupil resources

- *Fluency in Number Facts: Facts and Games: Years 1 & 2* book pages 38 and 39 (per pair); PDFs:

- two 0–9 dice (per pair)
- 12 counters: 6 for each player (per pair)

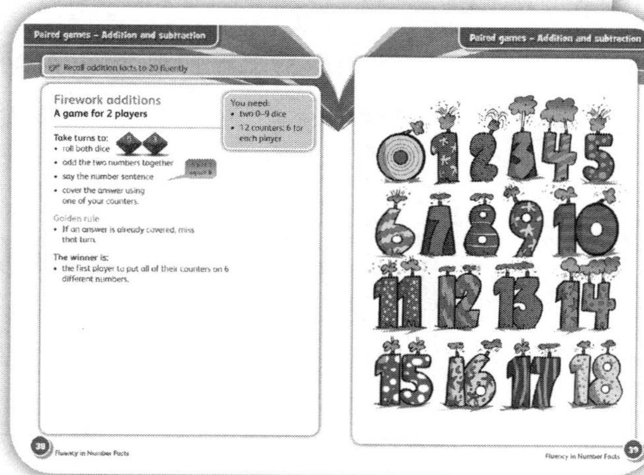

Variations

- Children play the game in groups of three. Each player has 4 counters. The winner is the first player to put all of their counters on 4 different numbers.

or Add three 1-digit numbers

- Rather than using two 0–9 dice, use three 1–6 dice and add the three numbers together.

Before you start:

- Decide who will win on even totals and who will win on odd totals.

What to do:

- Each player rolls one of the 0–9 dice.
- If the total of the two dice is even, the player who wins on the even totals covers that number with one of their counters. If the total of the two dice is odd, the player who wins on the odd totals covers that number with one of their counters.

The winner is:

- the first player to put all of their counters on 6 different numbers.

- Children play the game individually, using all 12 counters. In addition to the resources listed, provide each child with a small container.

What to do:

- roll both dice
- add the two numbers together
- say the number sentence
- cover the answer using one of your counters. If that number already has a counter on it, discard the counter into the container.

Golden rule:

- Each number can only take one counter.

You win the game if:

- you have put a counter on 8 numbers before using all your counters.

Shipwreck subtractions

Objective

- Recall subtraction facts to 20 fluently

Pupil resources

- *Fluency in Number Facts: Facts and Games: Years 1 & 2* book pages 40 and 41 (per pair); PDFs:

→ Paired games and activities → Paired games from the *Facts and Games: Years 1 & 2* book

- 14 counters: 7 of one colour, 7 of another colour (per pair)
- pencil and paperclip (for the spinner) (per pair)
- 0–9 dice (per pair)

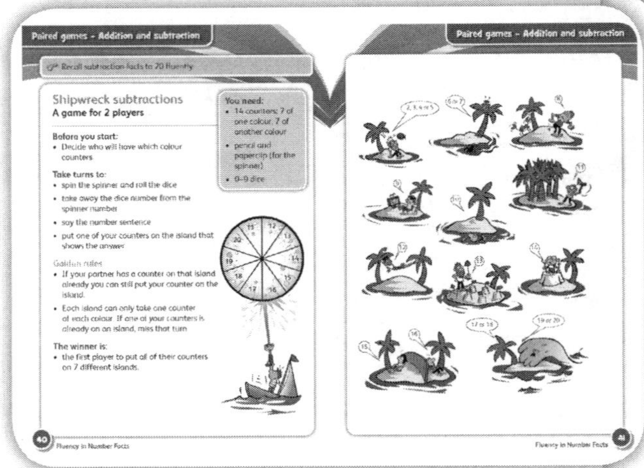

Paired games – Addition and subtraction

Recall subtraction facts to 20 fluently

Shipwreck subtractions
A game for 2 players

You need:
- 14 counters: 7 of one colour, 7 of another colour
- pencil and paperclip (for the spinner)
- 0–9 dice

Before you start:
- Decide who will have which colour counters.

Take turns to:
- spin the spinner and roll the dice
- take away the dice number from the spinner number
- say the number sentence
- put one of your counters on the island that shows the answer

Golden rules:
- If your partner has a counter on that island already you can still put your counter on the island.
- Each island can only take one counter of each colour. If one of your counters is already on an island, miss that turn.

The winner is:
- the first player to put all of their counters on 7 different islands.

40 Fluency in Number Facts

Paired games – Addition and subtraction

Fluency in Number Facts 41

Variations

- Children play the game in groups of three. You need 18 counters: 6 each of three different colours. The winner is the first player to put all of their counters on 6 different islands.

Golden rule:

- Each island can only take one counter. The first player to put a counter on an island 'owns' that island.
- If an island is already 'owned', miss that turn.

The winner is:

- the first player to 'own' 4 islands.

- Children play the game individually, using all 14 counters. In addition to the resources listed, provide each child with a small container.

What to do:

- spin the spinner and roll the dice
- take away the dice number from the spinner number
- say the number sentence
- put one of your counters on the island that shows the answer. If that island already has a counter on it, discard a counter into the container.

Golden rule:

- Each island can only take one counter.

You win the game if:

- you have put a counter on 8 islands before using all your counters.

Fruity facts

Objective

- Recall addition and subtraction facts to 20 fluently

Pupil resources

- *Fluency in Number Facts: Facts and Games: Years 1 & 2* book pages 42 and 43 (per pair); PDFs:

Paired games and activities → Paired games from the *Facts and Games: Years 1 & 2* book

- 16 counters: 8 of one colour, 8 of another colour (per pair)
- two 0–9 dice (per pair)

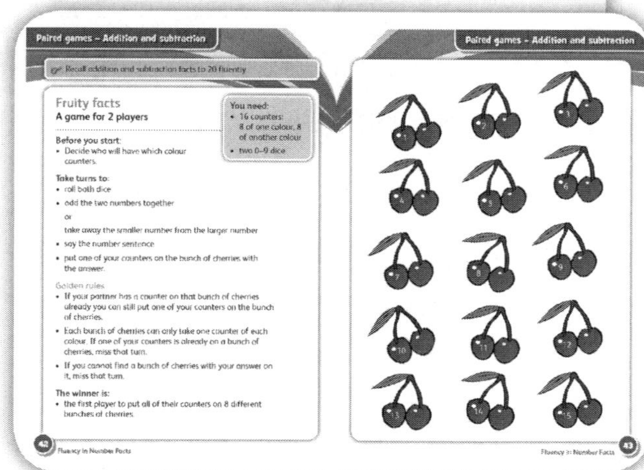
Paired games – Addition and subtraction

Recall addition and subtraction facts to 20 fluently

Fruity facts

A game for 2 players

You need:
- 16 counters: 8 of one colour, 8 of another colour
- two 0–9 dice

Before you start:
- Decide who will have which colour counters.

Take turns to:
- roll both dice
- add the two numbers together

  or

  take away the smaller number from the larger number
- say the number sentence
- put one of your counters on the bunch of cherries with the answer.

Golden rules
- If your partner has a counter on that bunch of cherries already you can still put one of your counters on the bunch of cherries.
- Each bunch of cherries can only take one counter of each colour. If one of your counters is already on a bunch of cherries, miss that turn.
- If you cannot find a bunch of cherries with your answer on it, miss that turn.

The winner is:
- the first player to put all of their counters on 8 different bunches of cherries.

42 Fluency in Number Facts

Paired games – Addition and subtraction

Fluency in Number Facts 43

Variations

- Children play the game in groups of three. You need 24 counters: 8 each of three different colours.

or Add three 1-digit numbers

- Rather than using two 0–9 dice, use three 1–6 dice and add the three numbers together.

- Children play the game individually, using all 16 counters. In addition to the resources listed, provide each child with a small container.

What to do:

- add the two numbers together or take away the smaller number from the larger number
- say the number sentence
- put one of your counters on the bunch of cherries with the answer. If that bunch of cherries already has a counter on it, discard a counter into the container.

Golden rule:

- Each bunch of cherries can only take one counter.

You win the game if:

- you have put a counter on 12 bunches of cherries before using all your counters.

Alien invasion

Objective

- Add three 1-digit numbers

Pupil resources

- *Fluency in Number Facts: Facts and Games: Years 1 & 2* book pages 44 and 45 (per pair); PDFs:

→ Paired games and activities → Paired games from the *Facts and Games: Years 1 & 2* book

- 20 counters (per pair)
- three 1–6 dice (per pair)

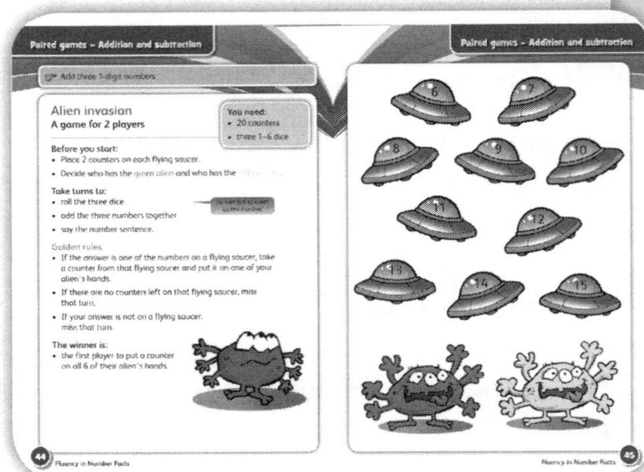

Variations

- Children play the game in groups of three. You need 30 counters. Use the blue alien at the bottom of the instructions page (page 44) for the third player.

You need:

- 10 counters
- three 1–6 dice

Before you start:

- Decide who has the green alien and who has the yellow alien.
- Place a counter on 5 of your alien's hands.

Take turns to:

- roll the three dice
- add the three numbers together
- say the number sentence.

Golden rules:

- If the answer is one of the numbers on a flying saucer, take one of your counters off your alien's hands and place it on that flying saucer.
- If there is already a counter on that flying saucer, miss that turn.
- If your answer is not on a flying saucer, miss that turn.

The winner is:

- the first player to put all of their alien's counters on a flying saucer.

- Children play the game individually, using only 10 counters and placing only one counter on each flying saucer. Use either the green or the yellow alien – not both.

Golden rules:

- If the answer is one of the numbers on a flying saucer, take a counter from that flying saucer and put it on one of your alien's hands.
- If there are no counters left on that flying saucer, miss that turn.
- If your answer is not on a flying saucer, remove a counter from your alien and discard it.

You win the game if:

- your alien can collect 5 counters.

Boating bonanza

Addition
Subtraction

Objective

- Add and subtract a 2-digit number and ones

Pupil resources

- *Fluency in Number Facts: Facts and Games: Years 1 & 2* book pages 46 and 47 (per pair); PDFs:

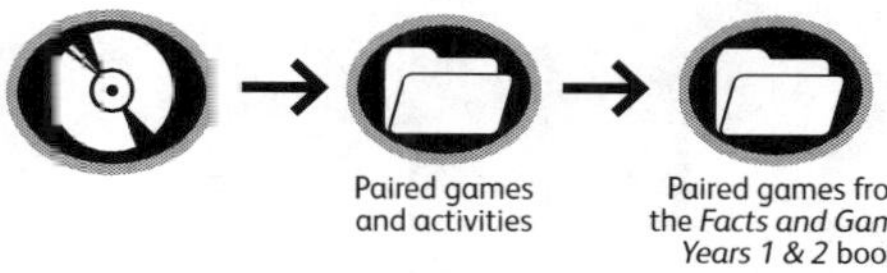

- button (per pair)
- two 0–9 dice: 1 for each player (per pair)
- 10 counters: 5 for each player (per pair)

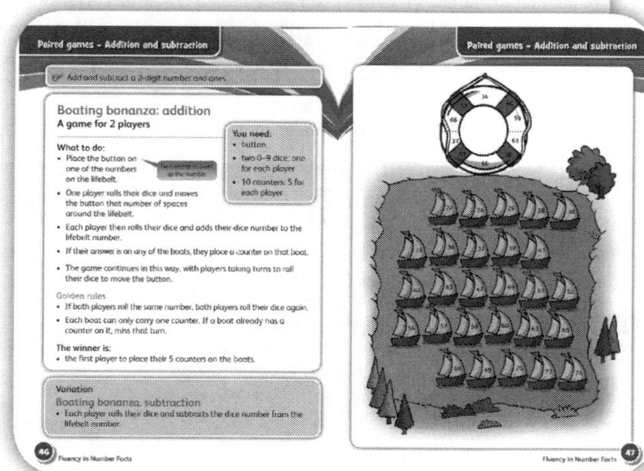

Paired games - Addition and subtraction

Add and subtract a 2-digit number and ones

Boating bonanza: addition
A game for 2 players

You need:
- button
- two 0–9 dice: one for each player
- 10 counters: 5 for each player

What to do:
- Place the button on one of the numbers on the lifebelt.
- One player rolls their dice and moves the button that number of spaces around the lifebelt.
- Each player then rolls their dice and adds their dice number to the lifebelt number.
- If their answer is on any of the boats, they place a counter on that boat.
- The game continues in this way, with players taking turns to roll their dice to move the button.

Golden rules
- If both players roll the same number, both players roll their dice again.
- Each boat can only carry one counter. If a boat already has a counter on it, miss that turn.

The winner is:
- the first player to place their 5 counters on the boats.

Variation
Boating bonanza: subtraction
- Each player rolls their dice and subtracts the dice number from the lifebelt number.

46 Fluency in Number Facts

Paired games - Addition and subtraction

47 Fluency in Number Facts

Variations

- Children play the game in groups of three. You need three 0–9 dice: 1 for each player, and 15 counters: 5 for each player.

- Children play the game individually, using all 10 counters and only one 0–9 dice. In addition to the resources listed, provide each child with a small container.

What to do:
- Place the button on one of the numbers on the lifebelt.
- Roll the dice and move the button that number of spaces around the lifebelt.
- Roll the dice again and add the dice number to the lifebelt number.
- If the answer is on any of the boats, place a counter on that boat. If the answer is not on any of the boats, discard the counter into the container.

Golden rule:
- Each boat can only carry one counter. If a boat already has a counter on it, discard the counter into the container.

You win the game if:
- you put 5 counters on the boats before using all your counters.

- Children play the game described in the second variation above; however the child subtracts the dice number from the lifebelt number.

Paired games and activities

Jack-in-a-box

Addition
Subtraction
Addition or subtraction

Objective

- Add and subtract a 2-digit number and tens

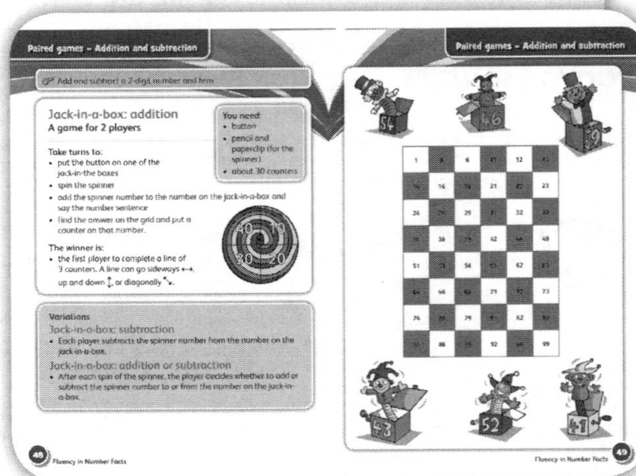
Paired games – Addition and subtraction
Add and subtract a 2-digit number and tens
Jack-in-a-box: addition
A game for 2 players
You need:
- button
- pencil and paperclip (for the spinner)
- about 30 counters

Take turns to:
- put the button on one of the jack-in-the boxes
- spin the spinner
- add the spinner number to the number on the jack-in-a-box and say the number sentence
- find the answer on the grid and put a counter on that number.

The winner is:
- the first player to complete a line of 3 counters. A line can go sideways ↔, up and down ↕, or diagonally.

Variations
Jack-in-a-box: subtraction
- Each player subtracts the spinner number from the number on the jack-in-a-box.

Jack-in-a-box: addition or subtraction
- After each spin of the spinner, the player decides whether to add or subtract the spinner number to or from the number on the jack-in-a-box.

48 Fluency in Number Facts
Fluency in Number Facts 49

Pupil resources

- *Fluency in Number Facts: Facts and Games: Years 1 & 2* book pages 48 and 49 (per pair); PDFs:

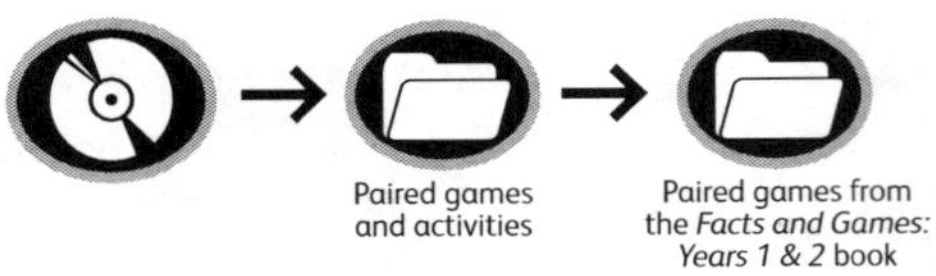

- button (per pair)
- pencil and paperclip (for the spinner) (per pair)
- about 30 counters (per pair)

Variations

- Children play the game in groups of three.

or

- The winner is the first player to complete a square of 4 counters
- Children play the game individually using only 9 counters.

You win the game if:

- you can complete line of 3 counters. A line can go sideways, up and down or diagonally.

The caterpillar's boots

Addition
Subtraction

Objective

- Add and subtract two 2-digit numbers

Pupil resources

- *Fluency in Number Facts: Facts and Games: Years 1 & 2* book pages 50 and 51 (per pair); PDFs:

Paired games and activities → Paired games from the *Facts and Games: Years 1 & 2* book

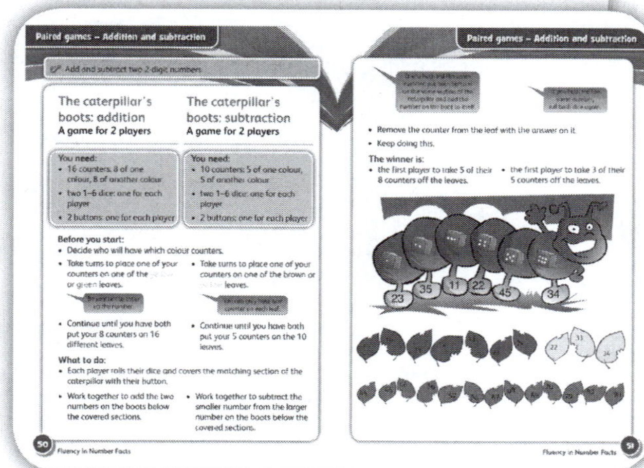

Paired games – Addition and subtraction

Add and subtract two 2-digit numbers

The caterpillar's boots: addition
A game for 2 players

You need:
- 16 counters: 8 of one colour, 8 of another colour
- two 1–6 dice: one for each player
- 2 buttons: one for each player

The caterpillar's boots: subtraction
A game for 2 players

You need:
- 10 counters: 5 of one colour, 5 of another colour
- two 1–6 dice: one for each player
- 2 buttons: one for each player

Before you start:
- Decide who will have which colour counters.
- Take turns to place one of your counters on one of the yellow or green leaves. / Take turns to place one of your counters on one of the brown or yellow leaves.
- Continue until you have both put your 8 counters on 16 different leaves. / Continue until you have both put your 5 counters on the 10 leaves.

What to do:
- Each player rolls their dice and covers the matching section of the caterpillar with their button.
- Work together to add the two numbers on the boots below the covered sections. / Work together to subtract the smaller number from the larger number on the boots below the covered sections.

50 Fluency in Number Facts

Paired games – Addition and subtraction

- Remove the counter from the leaf with the answer on it.
- Keep doing this.

The winner is:
- the first player to take 5 of their 8 counters off the leaves. / the first player to take 3 of their 5 counters off the leaves.

Fluency in Number Facts 51

- For *The caterpillar's boots (Addition):* 16 counters: 8 of one colour, 8 of another colour (per pair)
- For *The caterpillar's boots (Subtraction):* 10 counters: 5 of one colour, 5 of another colour (per pair)
- two 1–6 dice: one for each player (per pair)
- two buttons: one for each player (per pair)

Note:

- As this game is aimed at consolidating children's understanding of adding and subtracting mentally two 2-digit numbers, it is recommended that it be played with more able children.
- Some children may have difficulty in understanding the rules of this game so it is also recommended that you spend time playing the game with them before they play it together.

Odd or even fingers

Objective

- Recall addition facts to 20 fluently

Pupil resources

- 10 counters (per pair)

What to do

- Players decide who is going to be 'even' and who is going to be 'odd'.
- Both players say 'Ready, steady, go!' and simultaneously hold up between 1 and 10 fingers.
- If the total number of fingers is odd, the 'odd' player takes a counter. If the total number of fingers is even, the 'even' player takes a counter.
- The winner is the player with more counters after 10 rounds.

Paired games and activities

Adding the dice

Objective

- Recall and use addition facts to 20 fluently

Pupil resources

Whole-class games and activities → Hands-on game boards

- 'Hands-on: Numbers 1–12' (per pair)
- two 1–6 dice (per pair)
- 20 counters: 10 of one colour, 10 of another colour (per pair)

What to do

- Before you start decide who will have which colour counters.
- Take turns to:
  - roll both dice, for example, 6 and 3
  - add the two numbers together, i.e. 9
  - cover the answer, i.e. 9, using one of your counters.
- If the number is already covered, miss that turn.
- The winner is the player with more counters on the game board once all the numbers, except for number 1, have a counter on them.

Variation

- Use the 'Hands-on: Numbers 1–20 game board' (per pair), two 0–9 dice and 24 counters: 12 of one colour, 12 of another colour (per pair)
- The winner is the player with more counters on the game board once all the numbers, except for numbers 19 and 20, have a counter on them.

Making 10

Objective

- Recall and use addition facts for 10 fluently

Pupil resources

→ Whole-class games and activities → Hands-on game boards

- 'Hands-on: Numbers 1–10' (per pair)
- 0–9 dice (per pair)
- 24 counters: 12 of one colour, 12 of another colour (per pair)

What to do

- Before you start decide who will have which colour counters.
- Take turns to:
  - roll the dice, for example, 6
  - work out what number needs to be added to the dice number to make 10, i.e. 4
  - cover the answer, i.e. 4, using one of your counters.
- If the number is already covered, miss that turn.
- The winner is the player with more counters on the game board once all the numbers have a counter on them.

Making 20

Objective

- Recall and use addition facts for 20 fluently

Pupil resources

→ Whole-class games and activities → Hands-on game boards

- 'Hands-on: Numbers 1–20' (per pair)
- 1–20 dice (per pair)
- 30 counters: 15 of one colour, 15 of another colour (per pair)

What to do

- Before you start decide who will have which colour counters.
- Take turns to:
  - roll the dice, for example, 13
  - work out what number needs to be added to the dice number to make 20, i.e. 7
  - cover the answer, i.e. 7, using one of your counters.
- If the number is already covered, miss that turn.
- The winner is the player with more counters on the game board once all the numbers, except for number 20, have a counter on them.

Individual activities

Addition and subtraction Flip Facts cards

Objective

- Recall and use addition and subtraction facts to 20 fluently

Resources:

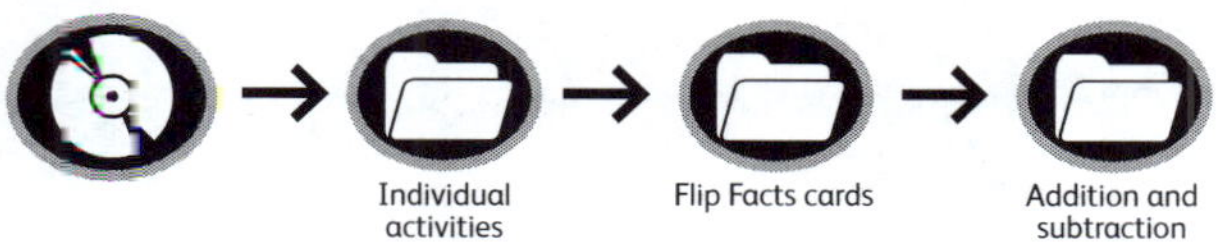

- 'Addition and subtraction Flip Facts cards'
- scissors
- glue
- hole punch
- small piece of string or paper fastener

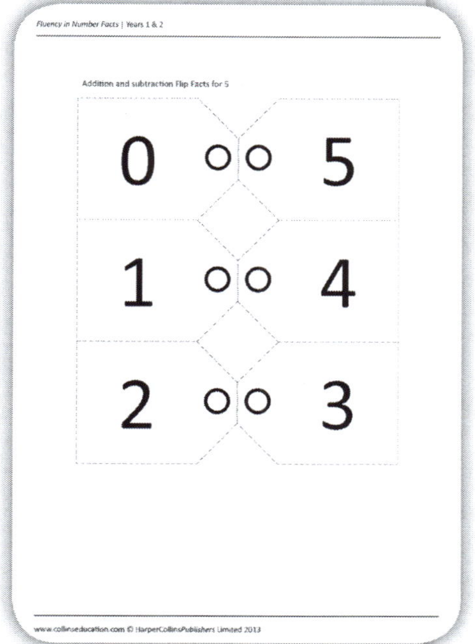
Fluency in Number Facts | Years 1 & 2

Addition and subtraction Flip Facts for 5

0 5

1 4

2 3

www.collinseducation.com © HarperCollinsPublishers Limited 2013

What to do

- Cut out the cards along the dashed lines.
- Fold each card along the dotted lines to form two-sided cards.
- Glue together the back of each card.
- Punch a hole in the centre of each card.
- Arrange the cards in order with the smallest number on top.
- Fasten the set of cards together with string or a paper fastener.

To practise the addition facts for 10

- Use the 'Addition and subtraction Flip Facts cards for 10'.
- Start with the 0 card on top.
- Ask yourself: *0, how many more to make 10?* (10) Turn over the card to check. *1, how many more to make 10?* (9) Turn over the card to check. 2, how many more to make 10? (8) Turn over the card to check.
- Continue until you reach the card showing 5 and once again ask: *5, how many more to make 10?* (5).
- Now turn the pack of cards around asking: *5, how many more to make 10?* (5). Turn over the card to check. *4, how many more to make 10?* (6) and so on.
- Repeat several times, quickening the pace as you go.

To practise the subtraction facts for 10

- Use the 'Addition and subtraction Flip Facts cards for 10'.
- Start with the 0 card on top.
- Ask yourself: *10 take away 0 is?* (10). Turn over the card to check. *10 take away 1 is?* (9). Turn over the card to check. *10 take away 2 is?* (8). Turn over the card to check.
- Continue until you reach the card showing 5 and once again ask: *10 take away 5 is?* (5).
- Now turn the pack of cards around, asking: *10 take away 5 is?* (5). Turn over the card to check. *10 take away 6 is?* (4) and so on.
- Repeat several times, quickening the pace as you go.
- Children spend just five or ten minutes each time, focussing their attention on learning the addition and subtraction facts off by heart.

Variation

- Use other sets of Flip Facts cards to practise the addition and subtraction facts for 1–9, 11–20.

Hold it up

Objective

- Recall and use multiplication and division facts for the 2, 5 and 10 multiplication tables

Teacher resources

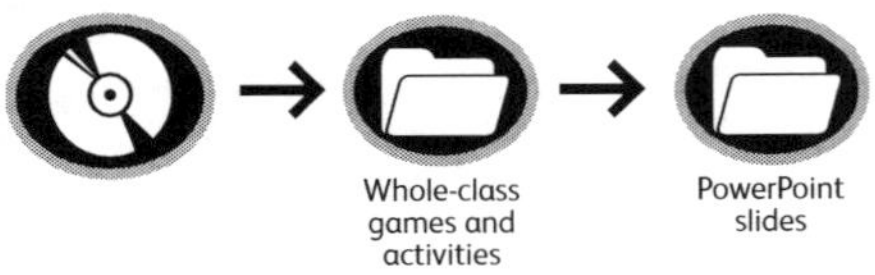

- 'Hold it up'

Pupil resources

- set of 0–9 number cards or small individual whiteboard and pen (per child)

What to do

- Using either the 'Hold it up: Numbers 1–10' slide or 'Hold it up: Numbers 1–12' slide, write '× 2', '× 5' or '× 10' in the box at the top of the slide.
- Point to one of the coloured 1–10 or 1–12 numbers on the slide.
- Children work out the answer and hold up the appropriate number card(s).
- Repeat several times.

Variations

- Use the 'Hold it up: 2 times table' slide to practise the division facts for the 2 multiplication table.
- Use the 'Hold it up: 5 times table' slide to practise the division facts for the 5 multiplication table.
- Use the 'Hold it up: 10 times table' slide to practise the division facts for the 10 multiplication table.

Around the clock

Objective

- Recall and use multiplication and division facts for the 2, 5 and 10 multiplication tables

Teacher resources

Whole-class games and activities → PowerPoint slides

- 'Around the clock'

Pupil resources

Number cards

- set of 'Multiples of 2 number cards', set of 'Multiples of 5 number cards', or set of 'Multiples of 10 number cards', or small individual whiteboard and pen (per child)

What to do

- Decide which multiplication facts you want the children to practise and consolidate.
- Using the 'Around the clock' slide, write '× 2', '× 5' or '× 10' on the circle in the centre of the clock.
- Provide each child with the corresponding multiples of 2, 5 or 10 number cards or an individual whiteboard and pen.
- Point to one of the 1–12 numbers on the clock face.
- Children work out the answer and hold up the appropriate multiples card or write the answer on their whiteboard.
- Repeat several times.

Variations

- Provide pairs of children with a set of multiples cards, and ask them to work together.
- Don't write '× 2', '× 5' or '× 10' on the circle in the centre of the clock and don't provide the children with the multiples of 2, 5 or 10 number cards. Point to one of the 1–12 numbers on the clock face, say: *times 2, times 5* or *times 10*. Children work out the answer and put up their hand or write the answer on their whiteboard.

Gladiators

Objective

- Recall and use multiplication and division facts for the 2, 5 and 10 multiplication tables

Teacher resources

→ Whole-class games and activities → PowerPoint slides

- Gladiators

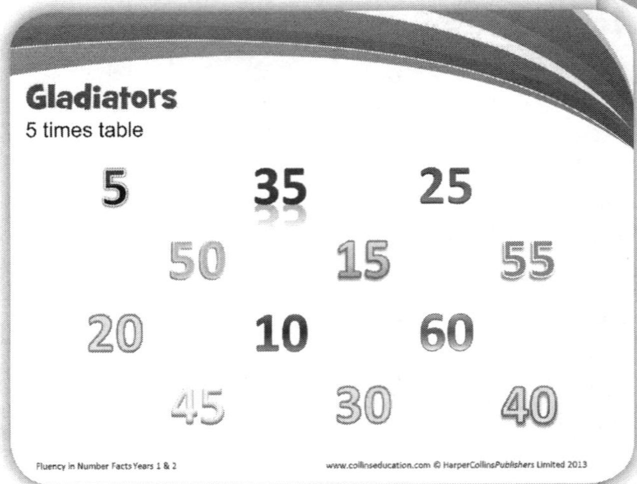

Pupil resources

- 2 × rulers or 'swords'

What to do

- Decide which multiplication table you want the children to practise and consolidate and display the appropriate Gladiators times table slide.
- Ask two children to stand either side of the numbers.
- Ask a multiplication fact for the corresponding multiplication table, for example: *3 times 5 is…*
- The first child to point to the correct answer stays in. The other child sits down.
- Quickly choose another child to come and take the place of the child that just sat down.
- Continue as above.
- Which child can stay in the longest?

Variations

- The children sitting down ask the two children standing by the numbers a question where the answer is on the slide.
- To quicken the game, have two children standing either side of the numbers, one behind the other. When a child loses and has to sit down, there is an immediate replacement.
- Use the other 'Gladiators: times tables' slides and the 'Gladiators: Division facts' slide.

Hands-on

Objective

- Recall and use multiplication and division facts for the 2, 5 and 10 multiplication tables

Teacher resources

- none

Pupil resources

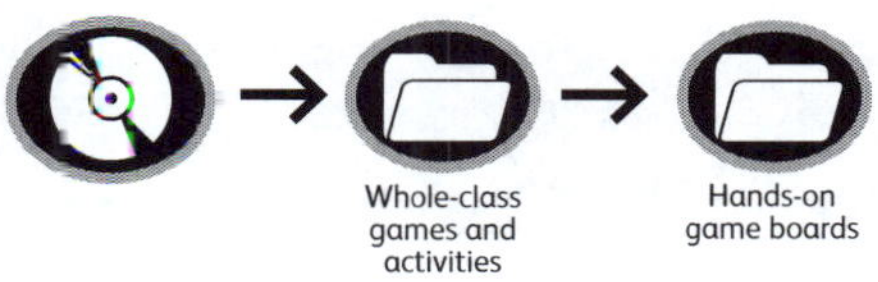

- 'Hands-on: Multiples of 2' game board (per pair) or
- 'Hands-on: Multiples of 5' game board (per pair) or
- 'Hands-on: Multiples of 10' game board (per pair) or
- 'Hands-on: Numbers 1–12' game board (per pair)

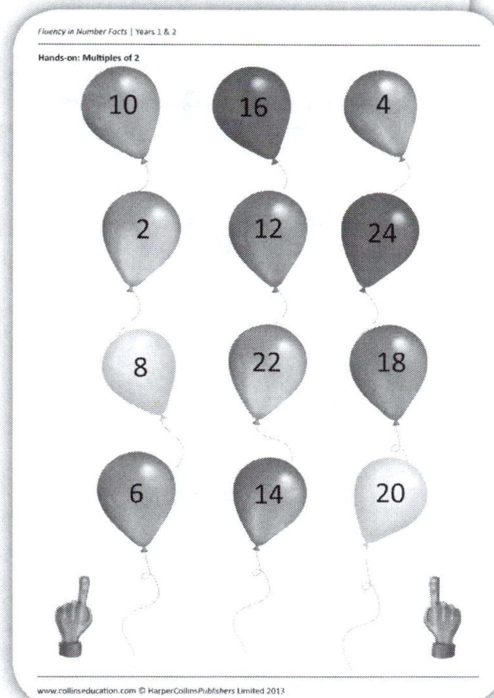
Fluency in Number Facts | Years 1 & 2

Hands-on: Multiples of 2

10 16 4
2 12 24
8 22 18
6 14 20

www.collinseducation.com © HarperCollinsPublishers Limited 2013

What to do

- Decide whether you want the children to practise and consolidate the multiplication or division facts for the 2, 5 or 10 multiplication table.
- Arrange the children into pairs and provide each pair with a copy of the appropriate 'Hands-on' game board.
- Tell the children to put the game board between them and for each child to put their index finger on a hand at the bottom of the game board.
- Ask an appropriate multiplication or division fact for the multiplication table the children are practising, for example: *6 times 5* (if practising the multiplication facts for the 5 multiplication table) or *12 divided by 2* (if practising the division facts for the 2 multiplication table).
- The first child to point to the correct answer wins.
- Children keep count of how many games they win.
- Play for as long as is appropriate.
- The winner in each pair is the child who wins more rounds.

Variation

- Provide each pair with a pile of counters. As a child wins a game they take a counter. The winner in each pair is the child who wins more counters.

Bingo

Objective

- Recall and use multiplication and division facts for the 2, 5 and 10 multiplication tables

Teacher resources

→ Whole-class games and activities → PowerPoint slides

- 'Bingo'

Pupil resources

- pencil and paper or small individual whiteboard and pen (per child)

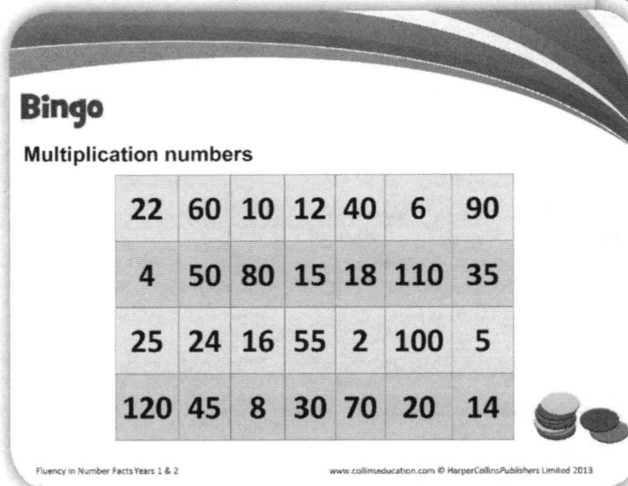

What to do

- Display the 'Bingo: Multiplication numbers' slide.
- Ask each child to write down any five numbers from the slide.
- Ask questions involving the multiplication facts for the 2, 5 and 10 multiplication tables.
- Children look to see if any of their five numbers numbers is the answer to the question.
- If a child has the answer, they cross out that number.
- The winner is the first child to cross out all five of their numbers and call out *Bingo!*

(**Note:** Be sure to keep a record of the answers for checking purposes.)

Variations

- Ask the children to write down more or fewer than five numbers from the slide.
- Use the 'Bingo: Multiplication and division numbers' slide. Ask the children questions involving the multiplication and division facts for the 2, 5 and 10 multiplication tables.

Four in a row

Objective

- Recall and use multiplication facts for the 2, 5 and 10 multiplication tables

Teacher resources

→ Whole-class games and activities → PowerPoint slides

- 'Four in a row'
- 1–12 dice

Pupil resources

- none

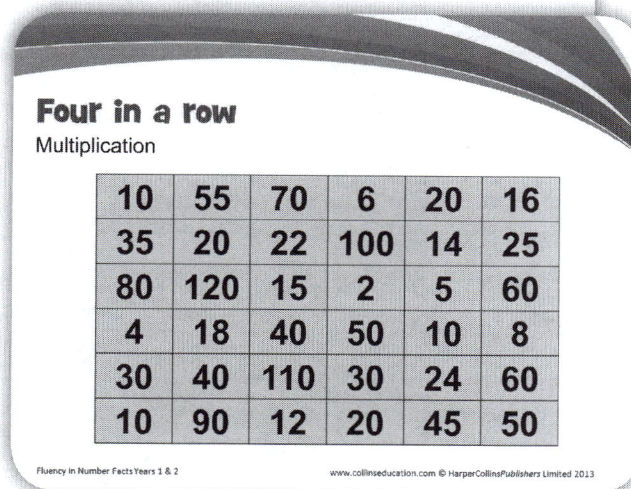

10	55	70	6	20	16
35	20	22	100	14	25
80	120	15	2	5	60
4	18	40	50	10	8
30	40	110	30	24	60
10	90	12	20	45	50

What to do

- Divide the class into two teams – a red team and a blue team.
- Display the 'Four in a row: Multiplication' slide.
- Explain that the object of the game is for a team to highlight a row of four numbers either side to side, up and down or diagonally.
- To highlight a number, a team must successfully answer a 2, 5 or 10 times table question.
- Invite a child from the red team to roll the dice and say the number, for example: 4.
- Look at the numbers on the slide, and choosing an answer that appears on the slide, decide whether to multiply the dice number by 2, 5 or 10 to form a question that gives an answer that appears on the slide. Ask the children the question, for example: *4 times 10*.
- Select a child from the red team to call out the answer.
- If correct, this number is highlighted in red on the slide. If incorrect, ask a child from the blue team to give the answer. If correct, this number is highlighted in blue.
- Next, invite a child from the blue team to roll the dice.
- Repeat above, at a quick pace, until one team has highlighted a row of four numbers.

Variation

- The team that rolls the dice decides whether to multiply the dice number by 2, 5 or 10.

Tell me the facts

Objective

- Recall and use multiplication and division facts for the 2, 5 and 10 multiplication tables

Teacher resources

→ Whole-class games and activities → PowerPoint slides

- 'Tell me the facts'

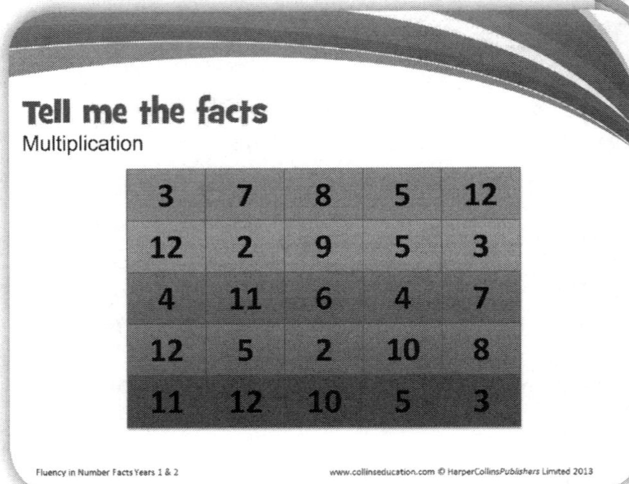

Pupil resources

- none

What to do

- Display the 'Tell me the facts: Multiplication' slide.
- Ask a child to highlight two numbers next to each other either side to side, up and down, or diagonally and say a known multiplication number fact about these two numbers, i.e. *I know that 4 times 2 equals 8.*
- Repeat asking other children to come and highlight two other numbers, saying a known multiplication fact about the two numbers.

Variations

- Ask questions such as:
  - *Point to two numbers next to each other that when multiplied together make 35.*
- Use the 'Tell me the facts: Division' slide, asking questions such as:
  - *Point to two numbers next to each other that when the larger number is divided by the smaller number gives an answer of 6.*

Who's left standing?

Objective

- Recall and use multiplication and division facts for the 2, 5 and 10 multiplication tables

Teacher resources

- none

Pupil resources

Number cards

- 'Multiples of 2 number cards'(one card per child) or
- 'Multiples of 5 number cards' (one card per child) or
- 'Multiples of 10 number cards' (one card per child) or
- '1–12 number cards' (one card per child)

What to do

Game 1: Recall and use multiplication facts for the 2 multiplication table

- Provide each child with a card from 'Multiples of 2 number cards'.
- Say: *Everyone stand up. Look at the number on your card. Sit down if the number on your card is the answer to:*
  - *4 times 2* (8)
  - *7 multiplied by 2* (14)
  - *12 times 2* (24)
  - *8 sets of 2* (16)
  - *2 times 2* (4)
  - *9 lots of 2* (18)
  - *1 times 2* (2)
  - *3 groups of 2* (6)
  - *11 multiplied by 2* (22)
  - *10 times 2* (20)
  - *5 times 2* (10)

The winners are the children still standing with 12 on their cards.

Game 2: Recall and use multiplication facts for the 5 multiplication table

- Provide each child with a card from 'Multiples of 5 number cards'.
- Say: *Everyone stand up. Look at the number on your card. Sit down if the number on your card is the answer to:*
  - *3 lots of 5* (15)
  - *9 multiplied by 5* (45)
  - *6 groups of 5* (30)
  - *11 multiplied by 5* (55)
  - *1 times 5* (5)
  - *5 times 5* (25)
  - *2 multiplied by 5* (10)
  - *10 times 5* (50)
  - *7 sets of 5* (35)
  - *12 times 5* (60)
  - *4 times 5* (20)

The winners are the children still standing with 40 on their cards.

(*continued*)

Who's left standing?

(continued)

Game 3: Recall and use multiplication facts for the 10 multiplication table

- Provide each child with a card from 'Multiples of 10 number cards'.
- Say: *Everyone stand up. Look at the number on your card. Sit down if the number on your card is the answer to:*
  - *3 times 10* (30)
  - *8 lots of 10* (80)
  - *9 multiplied by 10* (90)
  - *2 groups of 10* (20)
  - *11 multiplied by 10* (110)
  - *6 times 10* (60)
  - *1 multiplied by 10* (10)
  - *5 sets of 10* (50)
  - *12 times 10* (120)
  - *7 times 10* (70)
  - *4 times 10* (40)

The winners are the children still standing with 100 on their cards.

Game 4: Recall and use division facts for the 2 multiplication table

- Provide each child with a card from '1–12 number cards'.
- Say: *Everyone stand up. Look at the number on your card. Sit down if the number on your card is the answer to:*
  - *14 shared between 2* (7)
  - *16 divided by 2* (8)
  - *6 shared between 2* (3)
  - *24 divided by 2* (12)
  - *18 shared between 2* (9)
  - *8 divided by 2* (4)
  - *20 divided by 2* (10)
  - *10 divided by 2* (5)
  - *4 shared between 2* (2)
  - *22 divided by 2* (11)
  - *2 divided by 2* (1)

The winners are the children still standing with 6 on their cards.

Game 5: Recall and use division facts for the 5 multiplication table

- Provide each child with a card from '1–12 number cards'.
- Say: *Everyone stand up. Look at the number on your card. Sit down if the number on your card is the answer to:*
  - *10 shared between 5* (2)
  - *20 divided by 5* (4)
  - *55 divided by 5* (11)
  - *50 divided by 5* (10)
  - *30 divided by 5* (6)
  - *15 shared between 5* (3)
  - *40 divided by 5* (8)
  - *25 shared between 5* (5)
  - *5 divided by 5* (1)
  - *35 shared between 5* (7)
  - *60 divided by 5* (12)

The winners are the children still standing with 9 on their cards.

Who's left standing?

(continued)

Game 6: Recall and use division facts for the 10 multiplication table

- Provide each child with a card from '1–12 number cards'.
- Say: *Everyone stand up. Look at the number on your card. Sit down if the number on your card is the answer to:*
  - *80 divided by 10* (8)
  - *30 shared between 10* (3)
  - *50 shared between 10* (5)
  - *90 shared between 10* (9)
  - *120 divided by 10* (12)
  - *110 divided by 10* (11)
  - *20 shared between 10* (2)
  - *100 divided by 10* (10)
  - *60 divided by 10* (6)
  - *40 divided by 10* (4)
  - *10 divided by 10* (1)

The winners are the children still standing with 7 on their cards.

Game 7: Recall and use division facts for the 2, 5 and 10 multiplication tables

- Provide each child with a card from '1–12 number cards'.
- Say: *Everyone stand up. Look at the number on your card. Sit down if the number on your card is the answer to:*
  - *20 divided by 5* (4)
  - *100 divided by 10* (10)
  - *12 divided by 2* (6)
  - *20 shared between 10* (2)
  - *5 divided by 5* (1)
  - *70 shared between 10* (7)
  - *40 divided by 5* (8)
  - *6 shared between 2* (3)
  - *60 divided by 5* (12)
  - *90 shared between 10* (9)
  - *22 divided by 2* (11)

The winners are the children still standing with 5 on their cards.

Forming groups

Objectives

- Recognise odd and even numbers
- Recall and use multiplication and division facts for the 2, 5 and 10 multiplication tables

Teacher resources

- none

Pupil resources

Number cards

- '2-digit number cards' (one card per child) or
- 'Multiples of 2 number cards' (one card per child) or
- 'Multiples of 5 number cards' (one card per child) or
- 'Multiples of 10 number cards' (one card per child)

What to do

Game 1: Recognise odd and even numbers (multiples of 2)

- Provide each child with a card from '2-digit number cards'.
- Point and say: *Everyone stand up. Look at the number on your card. When I say 'Go!' I want everyone with an even number to move to this side of the room, and everyone with an odd number to move to this side of the room. Ready? Go!*
- Once the two groups have formed, ask the members of each group in turn to call out their number. Say: *Everyone hold up your number card. The even group, starting with Rebecca, call out your numbers. Now the odd group, starting with Leroy, tell us your numbers.*

Variations

- Rather than using the criteria of odd or even numbers to sort the cards, ask the children to sort the cards using the criteria: a multiple of 2 / not a multiple of 2.
- Provide each child with a card from 'Multiples of 2 number cards' or from '2-digit number cards'.

Forming groups

(continued)

Game 2: Recognise multiples of 5

- Provide each child with a card from either '2-digit number cards' or 'Multiples of 5 number cards'.
- Point and say: *Everyone stand up. Look at the number on your card. When I say 'Go!' I want everyone who has a card with a number on it that is an answer to the five times table (a multiple of 5) to move to this side of the room, and everyone who has a card with a number on it that is not an answer to the five times table (not a multiple of 5) to move to this side of the room. Ready? Go!*
- Once the two groups have formed, ask the members of each group in turn to call out their number. Say: *Everyone hold up your number card. The group with the answers to the five times table (multiples of 5), starting with Susie, call out your numbers. Now the group with the numbers that are not the answers to the five times table (not multiples of 5), starting with Arshin, tell us your numbers.*

Game 3: Recognise multiples of 10

- Provide each child with a card from either '2-digit number cards' or 'Multiples of 10 number cards'.
- Point and say: *Everyone stand up. Look at the number on your card. When I say 'Go!' I want everyone who has a card with a number on it that is an answer to the ten times table (a multiple of 10) to move to this side of the room, and everyone who has a card with a number on it that is not an answer to the ten times table (not a multiple of 10) to move to this side of the room. Ready? Go!*
- Once the two groups have formed, ask the members of each group in turn to call out their number. Say: *Everyone hold up your number card. The group with the answers to the ten times table (multiples of 10), starting with Emily, call out your numbers. Now the group with the numbers that are not the answers to the ten times table (not multiples of 10), starting with Kasim, tell us your numbers.*

Stand up

Objective

- Recall and use multiplication and division facts for the 2, 5 and 10 multiplication tables

Teacher resources

- none

Pupil resources

Number cards

- '1–12 number cards' (one card per child)

What to do

- Decide which multiplication or division facts for the 2, 5 and 10 multiplication tables you want the children to practise and consolidate.
- Provide each child with a card from '1–12 number cards'.

To practise the multiplication facts for the 2 multiplication table:

- Say: *Look at the number on your card. Multiply the number on your card by 2. Stand up if the answer is 12.*
- Ask: *Who can tell me what number is on Michael's and William's cards?* (6)
- Ask the children standing to show their cards.
- The children standing then sit down.
- Repeat saying: *Multiply the number on your card by 2. Stand up if the answer is:*

  10 (5)   *22* (11)   *4* (2)   *20* (10)   *14* (7)   *8* (4)
  24 (12)   *6* (3)   *18* (9)   *2* (1)   *16* (8)

To practise the division facts for the 2 multiplication table:

- Say: *Divide 16 by 2. Look at the number on your card. If you have the answer on your card, stand up.*
- Ask: *Who can tell me what number is on Fiona's and Sharik's cards?* (8)
- Ask the children standing to show their cards.
- The children standing then sit down.
- Repeat for the following:

  12 (6)   *4* (2)   *22* (11)   *10* (5)   *20* (10)   *14* (7)
  2 (1)   *8* (4)   *24* (12)   *6* (3)   *18* (9)

Variations

To practise the multiplication facts for the 5 multiplication table:

- Say: *Look at the number on your card. Multiply the number on your card by 5. Stand up if the answer is:*

40 (8)	*25* (5)	*60* (12)	*35* (7)	*10* (2)	*55* (11)
20 (4)	*45* (9)	*5* (1)	*15* (3)	*30* (6)	*50* (10)

To practise the division facts for the 5 multiplication table:

- Say: *Divide 35 by 5. Look at the number on your card. If you have the answer on your card, stand up.* (7). Repeat for the following:

25 (5)	*5* (1)	*50* (10)	*60* (12)	*30* (6)	*10* (2)
40 (8)	*45* (9)	*15* (3)	*55* (11)	*20* (4)	

To practise the multiplication facts for the 10 multiplication table:

- Say: *Look at the number on your card. Multiply the number on your card by 10. Stand up if the answer is:*

30 (3)	*50* (5)	*70* (7)	*60* (6)	*40* (4)	*80* (8)
120 (12)	*90* (9)	*110* (11)	*20* (2)	*100* (10)	*10* (1)

To practise the division facts for the 10 multiplication table:

- Say: *Divide 60 by 10. Look at the number on your card. If you have the answer on your card, stand up.* (6). Repeat for the following:

40 (4)	*10* (1)	*120* (12)	*90* (9)	*30* (3)	*80* (8)
70 (7)	*100* (10)	*20* (2)	*110* (11)	*50* (5)	

Whole-class, paired or individual activities

Using the Maths Facts in the *Facts and Games* book

Objective

- Recall and use multiplication and division facts for the 2, 5 and 10 multiplication tables

Teacher resources

→ Maths Facts → Multiplication and division

Pupil resources

- *Fluency in Number Facts: Facts and Games: Years 1 & 2* book pages 16–23 (per child or pair)

Introduction

The Maths Facts on pages 4 –15 of the *Fluency in Number Facts: Facts and Games: Years 1 & 2* book cover the key multiplication and division number facts that children need to be able to recall instantly by the end of Key Stage 1.

These pages aim to develop children's fluency by:

- securing a thorough conceptual understanding of the multiplication and division number facts
- identifying patterns and the relationship between multiplication and division
- developing strategic approaches to recalling and deriving the answers to multiplication and division number facts.

To assist in achieving these aims, the multiplication and division number facts contained in the *Facts and Games: Years 1 & 2* book are presented in the following ways:

- 2, 5 and 10 times tables facts (page 16)
- Division facts relating to the 2, 5 and 10 times tables facts (page 17)
- Multiples of 2, 5 and 10 (page 18)
- 2, 5 and 10 multiplication facts table (pages 19 and 20)
- Trios for the 2, 5 and 10 times tables and the related division facts (pages 21–23)

The following pages include a brief description of each of these presentations, along with suggestions of how to focus on these Maths Facts either with the whole class, or with children working in pairs or individually.

Whole-class, paired or individual activities

Using the Maths Facts in the *Facts and Games* book

(continued)

2, 5 and 10 times tables facts (page 16)

This page shows, in three columns, the 2, 5 and 10 times tables facts up to the 12th multiple, i.e. 12 × 2, 12 × 5 and 12 × 10.

The 2 times table is in red, the 5 times table in blue, and the 10 times table in green. This corresponds with the colours used on pages 17–23. The use of colour will become increasingly important throughout Lower Key Stage 2 as children learn the multiplication and division facts for the 3, 4 and 8 multiplication tables and then the 6, 7, 9, 11 and 12 multiplication tables.

The 2, 5 and 10 times tables facts also shows the four 'keys facts', i.e. 1 ×, 2 ×, 5 × and 10 ×. These 'key facts', once secure, can be used to help derive the answers to unknown related facts.

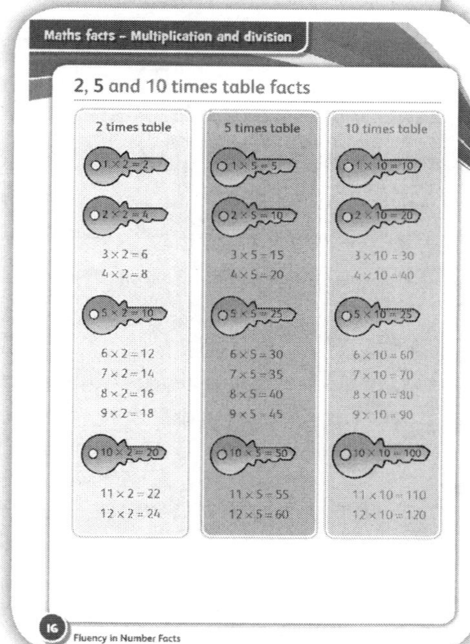
Maths facts – Multiplication and division

2, 5 and 10 times table facts

2 times table	5 times table	10 times table
1 × 2 = 2	1 × 5 = 5	1 × 10 = 10
2 × 2 = 4	2 × 5 = 10	2 × 10 = 20
3 × 2 = 6	3 × 5 = 15	3 × 10 = 30
4 × 2 = 8	4 × 5 = 20	4 × 10 = 40
5 × 2 = 10	5 × 5 = 25	5 × 10 = 50
6 × 2 = 12	6 × 5 = 30	6 × 10 = 60
7 × 2 = 14	7 × 5 = 35	7 × 10 = 70
8 × 2 = 16	8 × 5 = 40	8 × 10 = 80
9 × 2 = 18	9 × 5 = 45	9 × 10 = 90
10 × 2 = 20	10 × 5 = 50	10 × 10 = 100
11 × 2 = 22	11 × 5 = 55	11 × 10 = 110
12 × 2 = 24	12 × 5 = 60	12 × 10 = 120

16 Fluency in Number Facts

How to use the Maths Facts

Whole class

- Focus on the multiplication facts for the 2 or 5 or 10 multiplication table. However, the eventual aim is to have the class focussing on two or three tables at a time. It is also recommended that you begin by simultaneously working on both the multiplication and division facts for the same multiplication table so that children gain a deeper understanding of the relationship between multiplication and division.
- Display the appropriate PDF file (CD-ROM / Maths Facts / Multiplication and division) and provide each child or pair with a copy of the *Facts and Games: Years 1 & 2* book and direct their attention to the relevant multiplication facts on page 16.
- Begin by asking the children to identify different patterns in the list of calculations and discuss these with the class. What do they notice about the first, the second and in particular the third number in each calculation? Can the children see any relationships between these numbers?

(continued)

Whole-class, paired or individual activities

Using the Maths Facts in the *Facts and Games* book

(continued)

- Next, draw children's attention to the four 'key facts', i.e. 1 ×, 2 ×, 5 ×, 10 ×. Discuss with the children how it is important that they learn and remember these 'key facts' first as, once secure, they can use them to help derive the answers to unknown related facts.
- Ask individual children to chant the facts, for example: *Faith, please read out the 2 times table facts.* After the child has said approximately half of the facts, say: *Declan, please continue the 2 times table facts.*
- Ask specific groups of children to chant the facts, for example:
  - *1 times 2 is 2* (boys); *2 times 2 is 4* (girls); *3 times 2 is 6* (boys); *4 times 2 is 8* (girls)...
  - *1 times 2 is 2* (Group A); *2 times 2 is 4* (Group B); *3 times 2 is 6* (Group C); *4 times 2 is 8* (Group A)...
- Ask the whole class to chant the facts.
- Tell the children to spend just two or three minutes looking at the multiplication facts with the aim of focussing their attention on learning these facts off by heart.
- Conclude by hiding the PDF file and asking the children to close their copy of the *Facts and Games: Years 1 & 2* book and ask the class questions similar to the following:
  - *What is 5 times 2?*
  - *What is 7 multiplied by 2?*
  - *What is 8 lots of 2?*
  - *What is 10 groups of 2?*
- After several sessions once you have repeated the above several times for the 2, 5 and 10 multiplication tables, draw children's attention to the use of colour, i.e. the 2 times table is in red, the 5 times table in blue, and the 10 times table in green.

Pairs

- Begin by asking the children to focus on the multiplication facts for the 2 or 5 or 10 multiplication table. However, the eventual aim is to have the children focus on two or three multiplication tables simultaneously.
- Provide each pair with a copy of the *Facts and Games: Years 1 & 2* book and direct their attention to the relevant multiplication facts on page 16. Alternatively, ask the children to choose the multiplication tables that they know they need to develop greater fluency of.
- Children spend just two or three minutes individually looking at the multiplication facts with the aim of learning these facts off by heart.
- Children then take turns to take charge of the book and ask each other questions similar to those above.

Whole-class, paired or individual activities

Using the Maths Facts in the *Facts and Games* book

(continued)

Individual

- Begin by asking the child to focus on the multiplication facts for the 2 or 5 or 10 multiplication table. However, the eventual aim is to have the child focus on two or three multiplication tables simultaneously.
- Provide the child with a copy of the *Facts and Games: Years 1 & 2* book and direct their attention to the relevant multiplication facts on page 16. Alternatively, ask the child to choose the multiplication tables that they know they need to develop greater fluency of.
- It is recommended that the child spends just five or ten minutes each time, focussing their attention on learning the multiplication facts off by heart.
- To provide some personal challenge, suggest the child covers the multiplication facts and recites the facts to themselves.

(*continued*)

Whole-class, paired or individual activities

Using the Maths Facts in the *Facts and Games* book

(continued)

Division facts relating to the 2, 5 and 10 times tables facts (page 17)

This page shows, in three columns, the division facts relating to the 2, 5 and 10 times tables facts up to the 12th multiple, i.e. 24 ÷ 2, 60 ÷ 5 and 120 ÷ 10.

The division facts for the 2 times table is in red, the division facts for the 5 times table in blue, and the division facts for the 10 times table in green. This corresponds with the colours used on pages 16, 18–23. The use of colour will become increasingly important throughout Lower Key Stage 2 as children learn the multiplication and division facts for the 3, 4 and 8 multiplication tables and then the 6, 7, 9, 11 and 12 multiplication tables.

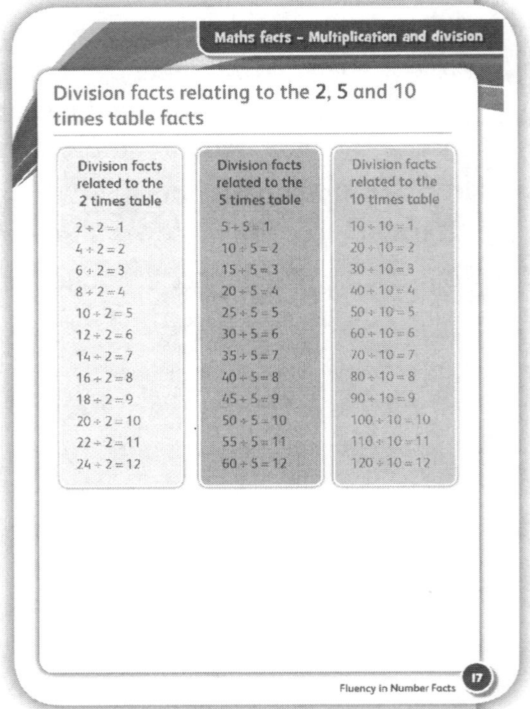
Maths facts – Multiplication and division

Division facts relating to the 2, 5 and 10 times table facts

Division facts related to the 2 times table	Division facts related to the 5 times table	Division facts related to the 10 times table
2 ÷ 2 = 1	5 ÷ 5 = 1	10 ÷ 10 = 1
4 ÷ 2 = 2	10 ÷ 5 = 2	20 ÷ 10 = 2
6 ÷ 2 = 3	15 ÷ 5 = 3	30 ÷ 10 = 3
8 ÷ 2 = 4	20 ÷ 5 = 4	40 ÷ 10 = 4
10 ÷ 2 = 5	25 ÷ 5 = 5	50 ÷ 10 = 5
12 ÷ 2 = 6	30 ÷ 5 = 6	60 ÷ 10 = 6
14 ÷ 2 = 7	35 ÷ 5 = 7	70 ÷ 10 = 7
16 ÷ 2 = 8	40 ÷ 5 = 8	80 ÷ 10 = 8
18 ÷ 2 = 9	45 ÷ 5 = 9	90 ÷ 10 = 9
20 ÷ 2 = 10	50 ÷ 5 = 10	100 ÷ 10 = 10
22 ÷ 2 = 11	55 ÷ 5 = 11	110 ÷ 10 = 11
24 ÷ 2 = 12	60 ÷ 5 = 12	120 ÷ 10 = 12

Fluency in Number Facts 17

How to use the Maths Facts

Whole class

- Focus on the division facts for the 2 or 5 or 10 multiplication table. However, the eventual aim is to have the class focussing on the division facts for two or three multiplication tables at a time. It is also recommended that you begin by simultaneously working on both the multiplication and division facts for the same multiplication table so that children gain a deeper understanding of the relationship between multiplication and division.
- Display the appropriate PDF file (CD-ROM / Maths Facts / Multiplication and division) and provide each child or pair with a copy of the *Facts and Games: Years 1 & 2* book and direct their attention to the relevant division facts on page 17.
- Begin by asking the children to identify different patterns in the list of calculations and discuss these with the class. What do they notice about the first, the second and the third number in each calculation? Can the children see any relationships between these numbers?
- Next, draw children's attention to the corresponding multiplication facts on the appropriate PDF file (CD-ROM / Maths Facts / Multiplication and division) and page 16 of the *Facts and Games: Years 1 & 2* book. In particular, ensure they are made aware of how the same colour has been used to link the related multiplication and division facts.
- Discuss with the children the inverse relationship between multiplication and division and how they can use a known multiplication fact to help them derive the answer to an unknown division fact (and vice versa), for example, 8 × 2 = 16 and 16 ÷ 2 = 8.
- Ask individual children to chant the facts, for example: *Leroy, will you read out the division facts for the 2 times table?* After the child has said approximately half of the facts, say: *Yolanda, please continue to say the facts.*

Whole-class, paired or individual activities

Using the Maths Facts in the *Facts and Games* book

(continued)

- Ask specific groups of children to chant the facts, for example:
  - *2 divided by 2 is 1* (boys); *4 divided by 2 is 2* (girls); *6 divided by 2 is 3* (boys); *8 divided by 2 is 4* (girls)…
  - *2 divided by 2 is 1* (Group A); *4 divided by 2 is 2* (Group B); *6 divided by 2 is 3* (Group C); *8 divided by 2 is 4* (Group A)…
- Ask the whole class to chant the facts.
- Ask the children to spend just two or three minutes looking at the division facts with the aim of focussing their attention on learning these facts off by heart.
- Conclude by hiding the PDF file and asking the children to close their copy of the *Facts and Games: Years 1 & 2* book, and ask the class questions similar to the following:
  - *What is 12 divided by 2?*
  - *What is 20 shared between 2?*
  - *How many twos are there in 16?*
  - *Share 24 between 2. How many is this each?*

Pairs

- Begin by asking the children to focus on the division facts for the 2 or 5 or 10 multiplication table. However, the eventual aim is to have the children focus on two or three multiplication tables simultaneously.
- Provide each pair with a copy of the *Facts and Games: Years 1 & 2* book and direct their attention to the relevant division facts on page 17. Alternatively, ask the children to choose the division facts that they know they need to develop greater fluency of.
- Children spend just two or three minutes individually looking at the division facts with the aim of learning these facts off by heart.
- Children then take turns to take charge of the book and ask each other questions similar to those above.

Individual

- Begin by asking the child to focus on the division facts for the 2 or 5 or 10 multiplication table. However, the eventual aim is to have the child focus on two or three multiplication tables simultaneously.
- Provide the child with a copy of the *Facts and Games: Years 1 & 2* book and direct their attention to the relevant division facts on page 17. Alternatively, ask the child to choose the division facts that they know they need to develop greater fluency of.
- It is recommended that the child spends just five or ten minutes each time, focussing their attention on learning the division facts off by heart.
- To provide some personal challenge, suggest the child covers the division facts and recites the facts to themselves.

(continued)

Whole-class, paired or individual activities

Using the Maths Facts in the *Facts and Games* book

(continued)

Multiples of 2, 5 and 10 (page 18)

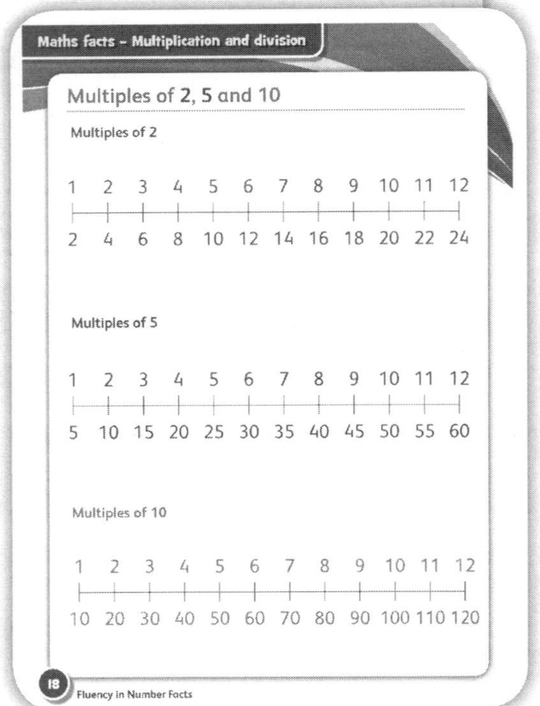

Maths facts – Multiplication and division

Multiples of 2, 5 and 10

Multiples of 2

1	2	3	4	5	6	7	8	9	10	11	12
2	4	6	8	10	12	14	16	18	20	22	24

Multiples of 5

1	2	3	4	5	6	7	8	9	10	11	12
5	10	15	20	25	30	35	40	45	50	55	60

Multiples of 10

1	2	3	4	5	6	7	8	9	10	11	12
10	20	30	40	50	60	70	80	90	100	110	120

18 Fluency in Number Facts

This page shows the multiplication and related division facts for 2, 5 and 10 up to the 12th multiple, i.e. 24 (× 2), 60 (× 5) and 120 (× 10).

The multiples of 2 are in red, the multiples of 5 in blue, and the multiples of 10 in green. This corresponds with the colours used on pages 16, 17 and 19–23. The use of colour will become increasingly important throughout Lower Key Stage 2 as children learn the multiplication and division facts for the 3, 4 and 8 multiplication tables and then the 6, 7, 9, 11 and 12 multiplication tables.

These number lines are a simple way of showing the relationship between the increasing steps and the corresponding products. They also highlight the link between multiplication and division.

How to use the Maths Facts

Whole class

- Focus on the multiplication and division facts for the 2 or 5 or 10 multiplication table. However, the eventual aim is to have the class focussing on two or three tables at a time.
- Display the appropriate PDF file (CD-ROM / Maths Facts / Multiplication and division) and provide each child or pair with a copy of the *Facts and Games: Years 1 & 2* book and direct their attention to the relevant multiples of 2, 5 and 10 number line on page 18.
- Begin by discussing with the children how the line is simply a number line but instead of having one set of numbers along the line, there are two sets of numbers – one set above the line (the numbers 1 to 12) and another set below the line (the corresponding multiples).
- Ask the children to identify any patterns or relationships between the numbers on the number line.
- Then, pointing in turn to each of the numbers 1 to 12 above the number line, and then the corresponding multiples below the line, say the multiplication facts to the children, for example:
  - *1 times 2 is 2*
  - *2 times 2 is 4*
  - *3 times 2 is 6*
  - *4 times 2 is 8…*
- Once the class are secure in using the number line to identify the multiplication facts, ask individual children to repeat the above, chanting the multiplication facts.

Whole-class, paired or individual activities

Using the Maths Facts in the *Facts and Games* book

(continued)

- Next, pointing in turn to each of the multiples below the number line, and then the corresponding number 1–12 above the line, say the division facts to the children, for example:
  - *2 divided by 2 is 1*
  - *4 divided by 2 is 2*
  - *6 divided by 2 is 3*
  - *8 divided by 2 is 4…*
- Once the class are secure in using the number line to identify the division facts, ask individual children to repeat the above, chanting the division facts.
- Ask the children to spend just two or three minutes looking at the number line with the aim of focussing their attention on learning the multiplication and division facts for the multiplication table off by heart.
- Conclude by hiding the PDF file and asking the children to close their copy of the *Facts and Games: Years 1 & 2* book. Ask the class questions similar to the following:
  - *What is 2 times / multiplied by / lots of / groups of 8?*
  - *What is 18 divided by / shared between 2?*
  - *How many twos are there in 18?*
  - *Share 22 between 2, how many is this each?*

Pairs

- Begin by asking the children to focus on the multiplication and division facts for the 2 or 5 or 10 multiplication table. However, the eventual aim is to have the children focus on two or three multiplication tables simultaneously.
- Provide each pair with a copy of the *Facts and Games: Years 1 & 2* book and direct their attention to the relevant multiples of 2, 5 or 10 number line on page 18. Alternatively, ask the children to choose the multiplication and division facts that they know they need to develop greater fluency of.
- Children spend just two or three minutes individually using the number line to assist them in learning the multiplication and division facts off by heart.
- Children then take turns to take charge of the book and ask each other questions similar to those above.

(*continued*)

Whole-class, paired or individual activities

Using the Maths Facts in the *Facts and Games* book

(continued)

Individual

- Begin by asking the child to focus on the multiplication and division facts for the 2 or 5 or 10 multiplication table. However, the eventual aim is to have the child focus on two or three multiplication tables simultaneously.
- Provide the child with a copy of the *Facts and Games: Years 1 & 2* book and direct their attention to the relevant multiples of 2, 5 or 10 number line on page 18. Alternatively, ask the child to choose the multiplication and division facts that they know they need to develop greater fluency of.
- It is recommended that the child spends just five or ten minutes each time, focussing their attention on learning the multiplication and division facts off by heart.
- To provide some personal challenge, suggest the child covers the numbers (multiples) below the number line and recites the multiplication facts to themselves and/or cover the numbers 1–12 above the number line and recite the division facts to themselves.

Whole-class, paired or individual activities

Using the Maths Facts in the *Facts and Games* book

(continued)

2, 5 and 10 multiplication facts table (pages 19 and 20)

The table on page 19 shows the calculations (without the answers) that make up the 2, 5 and 10 multiplication facts up to the 12th multiple. The table on page 20 shows the answers (multiples) corresponding to the 2, 5 and 10 multiplication calculations. These tables can be used to show that multiplication of two numbers can be done in any order (commutative). The table on page 20 can also be used to show the relationship between multiplication and division.

The multiplication calculations and corresponding multiples of 2 are in red, the calculations and multiples of 5 in blue, and the calculations and multiples of 10 in green. This corresponds with the colours used on pages 16–18 and 21–23. The use of colour will become increasingly important throughout Lower Key Stage 2 as children learn the multiplication and division facts for the 3, 4 and 8 multiplication tables and then the 6, 7, 9, 11 and 12 multiplication tables.

Maths facts – Multiplication and division

2, 5 and 10 multiplication facts

×	2	5	10
1	1 × 2	1 × 5	1 × 10
2	2 × 2	2 × 5	2 × 10
3	3 × 2	3 × 5	3 × 10
4	4 × 2	4 × 5	4 × 10
5	5 × 2	5 × 5	5 × 10
6	6 × 2	6 × 5	6 × 10
7	7 × 2	7 × 5	7 × 10
8	8 × 2	8 × 5	8 × 10
9	9 × 2	9 × 5	9 × 10
10	10 × 2	10 × 5	10 × 10
11	11 × 2	11 × 5	11 × 10
12	12 × 2	12 × 5	12 × 10

Fluency in Number Facts 19

Maths facts – Multiplication and division

×	2	5	10
1	2	5	10
2	4	10	20
3	6	15	30
4	8	20	40
5	10	25	50
6	12	30	60
7	14	35	70
8	16	40	80
9	18	45	90
10	20	50	100
11	22	55	110
12	24	60	120

20 Fluency in Number Facts

How to use the Maths Facts

Whole class

- Display the appropriate PDF file (CD-ROM / Maths Facts / Multiplication and division) and and provide each child or pair with a copy of the *Facts and Games: Years 1 & 2* book and direct their attention to the two tables on pages 19 and 20.
- Begin by discussing the 2, 5 and 10 multiplication facts table on page 19 with the children. Ask the children to identify different patterns in the table and discuss these with the class. Draw their attention to the row of three numbers at the top of the table and the column of 12 numbers down the left-hand side of the table.
- Next, move on to showing the children how to use the table. Put one finger on 6 in the column of numbers down the left-hand side of the table and another finger on 2 in the row of numbers at the top of the table, and then move both fingers across and down the table until they meet at the calculation, i.e. 6 × 2.
- Next, display page 20 to the children, which shows the answers (multiples) to the calculations on page 19.
- As with page 19, demonstrate to the children how to find the answer to 6 × 2.
- Repeat the above several times for other calculations, moving between pages 19 and 20 as you go.

(continued)

Whole-class, paired or individual activities

Using the Maths Facts in the *Facts and Games* book

(continued)

- Once the children are secure with using the tables and identifying a calculation and finding the corresponding answer (multiple), use the tables to demonstrate to the children how, for example, 2 × 6 is the same as 6 × 2 (commutative).
- Repeat several times.
- Next, tell the children to spend just four or five minutes becoming familiar with the tables.
- Referring to the table on page 19, conclude by asking the class questions similar to the following:
  - *What is 9 times 2?*
  - *What is 3 multiplied by 2?*
  - *What is 6 lots of 2?*
  - *What is 12 groups of 2?*
- After each question, display the table on page 20 to check the answer.
- The multiplication table on page 20 can also be used to show the relationship between multiplication and division. Once the children are confident in using the table to recall the answers to the multiplication facts, demonstrate how to use the table to help them recall the answers to division facts and their inverse relationship to multiplication.

Pairs

- Begin by asking the children to focus on the multiplication facts for the 2 or 5 or 10 multiplication table. However, the eventual aim is to have the children focus on two or three multiplication tables simultaneously.
- Provide each pair with a copy of the *Facts and Games: Years 1 & 2* book and direct their attention to one of the columns on the 2, 5 and 10 multiplication facts table on page 19. Alternatively, ask the children to choose the multiplication facts that they know they need to develop greater fluency of.
- Children stand the book up so that one child is looking at page 19, while the other child is looking at page 20.

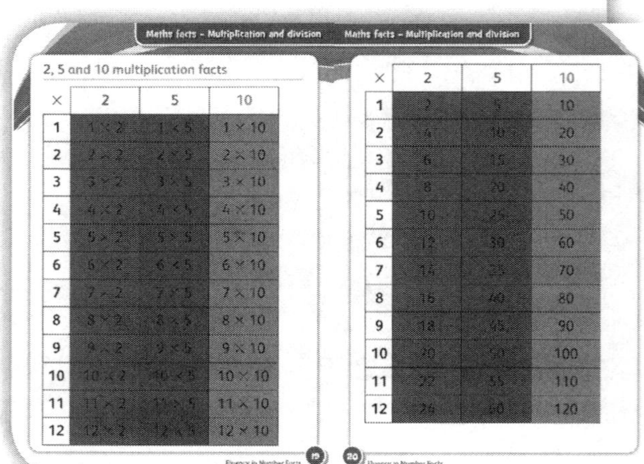

- The child looking at page 20 identifies a multiplication calculation using the row of numbers at the top of the table and the column of numbers down the left-hand side of the table and says the calculation to their partner, for example: *8 times 2*.
- The child looking at page 19 finds that calculation on the table, works out the answer and says it to their partner.
- The child looking at page 20 then says whether this answer is correct or not.
- After about five minutes, children swap roles and repeat.
- To use the tables to practise and consolidate division facts, children refer to the multiplication table on page 20. They cover the numbers in the left-hand column (or top row) and take turns to ask each other division questions. They check the answer each time by removing the cover on the left-hand column (or top row).

Whole-class, paired or individual activities

Using the Maths Facts in the *Facts and Games* book

(continued)

Individual

- Begin by asking the child to focus on the multiplication facts for the 2 or 5 or 10 multiplication table. However, the eventual aim is to have the child focus on two or three multiplication tables simultaneously.
- Provide the child with a copy of the *Facts and Games: Years 1 & 2* book and direct their attention to one of the columns on the 2, 5 and 10 multiplication facts table on page 19. Alternatively, ask the child to choose the multiplication facts that they know they need to develop greater fluency of.
- Beginning on page 19, the child points to one of the calculations and recalls the answer.
- They then turn over to page 20 to check whether this answer is correct or not.
- It is recommended that the child spends just five or ten minutes each time, focussing their attention on learning the multiplication facts off by heart.
- To use the table to practise and consolidate division facts, the child uses the multiplication table on page 20. They cover the numbers in the left-hand column (or top row) and ask themselves a division question. They check the answer each time by removing the cover on the left-hand column (or top row).

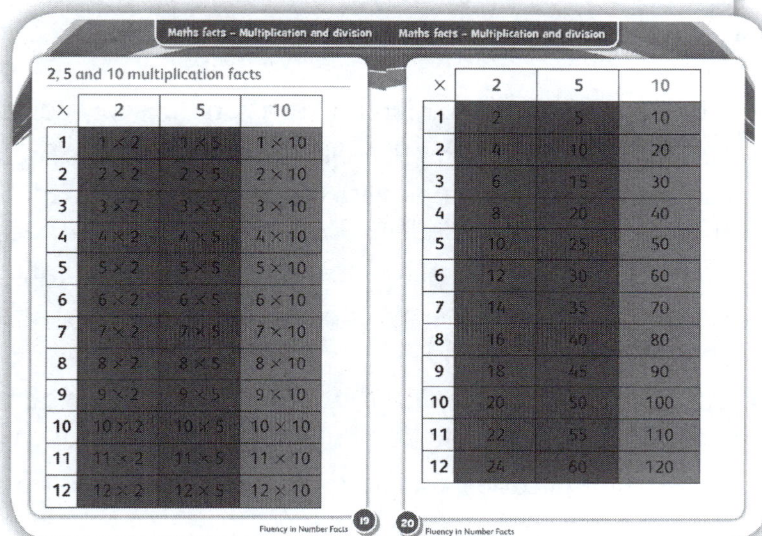
Maths facts – Multiplication and division

2, 5 and 10 multiplication facts

×	2	5	10
1	1 × 2	1 × 5	1 × 10
2	2 × 2	2 × 5	2 × 10
3	3 × 2	3 × 5	3 × 10
4	4 × 2	4 × 5	4 × 10
5	5 × 2	5 × 5	5 × 10
6	6 × 2	6 × 5	6 × 10
7	7 × 2	7 × 5	7 × 10
8	8 × 2	8 × 5	8 × 10
9	9 × 2	9 × 5	9 × 10
10	10 × 2	10 × 5	10 × 10
11	11 × 2	11 × 5	11 × 10
12	12 × 2	12 × 5	12 × 10

Fluency in Number Facts 19

Maths facts – Multiplication and division

×	2	5	10
1	2	5	10
2	4	10	20
3	6	15	30
4	8	20	40
5	10	25	50
6	12	30	60
7	14	35	70
8	16	40	80
9	18	45	90
10	20	50	100
11	22	55	110
12	24	60	120

20 Fluency in Number Facts

(*continued*)

Whole-class, paired or individual activities

Using the Maths Facts in the *Facts and Games* book

(continued)

Trios for the 2, 5 and 10 times tables and the related division facts (pages 21–23)

'Trios' show the relationship between the three numbers that make up a multiplication fact and the related division fact. They can be used to show that multiplication of two numbers can be done in any order (commutative) and how this law does not apply to division.

The 'trios' for 2 are in red, the 'trios' for 5 in blue, and the 'trios' for 10 in green. This corresponds with the colours used on pages 16–20. The use of colour will become increasingly important throughout Lower Key Stage 2 as children learn the multiplication and division facts for the 3, 4 and 8 multiplication tables and then the 6, 7, 9, 11 and 12 multiplication tables.

How to use the Maths Facts

Whole class

- Focus on the multiplication and division facts for the 2 or 5 or 10 multiplication table.
- Display the appropriate PDF file (CD-ROM / Maths Facts / Multiplication and division) and provide each child or pair with a copy of the *Facts and Games: Years 1 & 2* book and direct their attention to the relevant times tables and related division facts on pages 21–23.
- There are 12 sets of 'trios' for each multiplication table, so begin by referring to each set of 'trios' in turn, asking the children to identify different patterns between the four calculations in the 'trio'.
- Ensure the children realise that each 'trio' consists of only three numbers, for example, 5, 2 and 10, and that these three numbers produce four calculations:
  - two multiplication calculations: $5 \times 2 = 10$ and $2 \times 5 = 10$
  - two division calculations: $10 \div 2 = 5$ and $10 \div 5 = 2$.

Whole-class, paired or individual activities

Using the Maths Facts in the *Facts and Games* book

(continued)

- Referring to the two multiplication calculations, discuss with the children how multiplication of two numbers can be done in any order (commutative law).
- Then, referring to the two division calculations, discuss with the children how the commutative law does not apply to division.
- Move on to discussing the inverse relationship between multiplication and division.
- Next, ask the children to spend just two or three minutes looking at the set of four multiplication and division facts for each 'trio' with the aim of focussing their attention on learning the facts off by heart.
- Conclude by hiding the PDF file and asking the children to close their copy of the *Facts and Games: Years 1 & 2* book. Ask the class questions similar to the following:
  - *Tell me a multiplication calculation you can make using only the numbers 2, 5 and 10.*
  - *Can you tell me another multiplication calculation that only uses the same three numbers?*
  - *Tell me a division calculation that uses only the numbers 2, 5 and 10.*
  - *Is there another division calculation that uses only these numbers?*
- Repeat the above for the remaining 11 sets of 'trios' as and when appropriate.

Pairs

- Provide each pair with a copy of the *Facts and Games: Years 1 & 2* book and direct their attention to the relevant times tables and related division facts on pages 21–23. Alternatively, ask the children to choose the multiplication table that they know they need to develop greater fluency of.
- Children take turns to choose one of the trios and place their hand/fingers over the list of four calculations.
- Referring to the three numbers on the triangle, the other child says the two multiplication and two division number facts.
- Once they have done this, the child covering the facts removes their hand/finger to reveal the four calculations.

Individual

- Provide the child with a copy of the *Facts and Games: Years 1 & 2* book and direct their attention to the relevant times tables and related division facts on pages 21–23. Alternatively, ask the child to choose the multiplication table that they know they need to develop greater fluency of.
- It is recommended that the child spends just five or ten minutes each time, focussing their attent on on learning the multiplication and division facts off by heart.
- To provide some personal challenge, as for the paired activity above, suggest the child places their hand/fingers over the list of four calculations and recites the facts to themselves.

Toy train

Objective

- Recall multiplication facts for the 2 multiplication table

Pupil resources

- *Fluency in Number Facts: Facts and Games: Years 1 & 2* book pages 52 and 53 (per pair); PDFs:

Paired games and activities

Paired games from the *Facts and Games: Years 1 & 2* book

- button (per pair)
- 1–6 dice (per pair)
- 10 counters: 5 for each player (per pair)

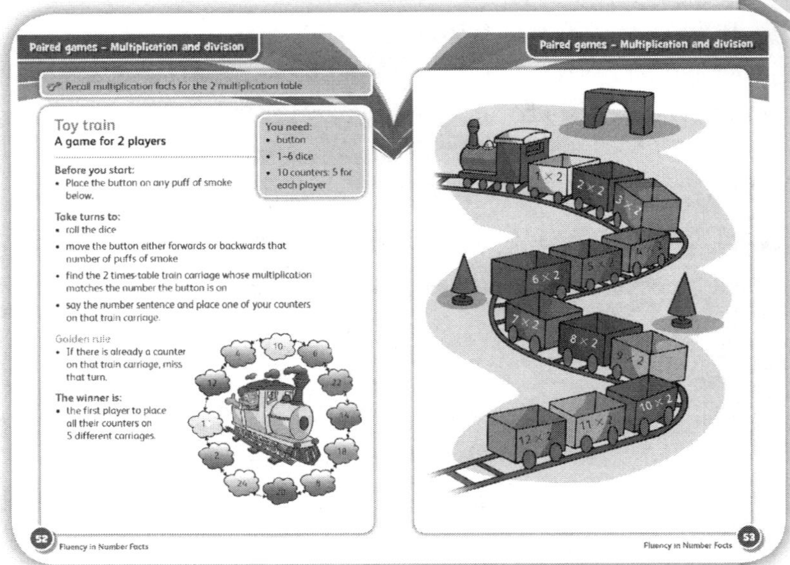

Paired games – Multiplication and division

Recall multiplication facts for the 2 multiplication table

Toy train
A game for 2 players

You need:
- button
- 1–6 dice
- 10 counters: 5 for each player

Before you start:
- Place the button on any puff of smoke below.

Take turns to:
- roll the dice
- move the button either forwards or backwards that number of puffs of smoke
- find the 2 times-table train carriage whose multiplication matches the number the button is on
- say the number sentence and place one of your counters on that train carriage.

Golden rule
- If there is already a counter on that train carriage, miss that turn.

The winner is:
- the first player to place all their counters on 5 different carriages.

52 Fluency in Number Facts

Paired games – Multiplication and division

Fluency in Number Facts 53

Variations

- Children play the game in groups of three. You need 12 counters: 4 for each player. The winner is the first player to put all of their counters on four different carriages.
- Use 12 counters instead of ten counters (per pair).

Before you start:

- Place a counter on each of the carriages, ensuring not to cover the calculation.
- Place the button on any puff of smoke.

Take turns to:

- roll the dice
- move the button either forwards or backwards that number of puffs of smoke
- find the 2 times table train carriage that matches the number the button is on
- say the number sentence and take the counter.

Golden rule:

- If there is no counter on that train carriage, miss that turn.

The winner is:

- the first player to collect five counters.

Paired games and activities

Clowning around

Objective

- Recall multiplication facts for the 5 multiplication table

Pupil resources

- *Fluency in Number Facts: Facts and Games: Years 1 & 2* book pages 54 and 55 (per pair); PDFs:

→ Paired games and activities → Paired games from the *Facts and Games: Years 1 & 2* book

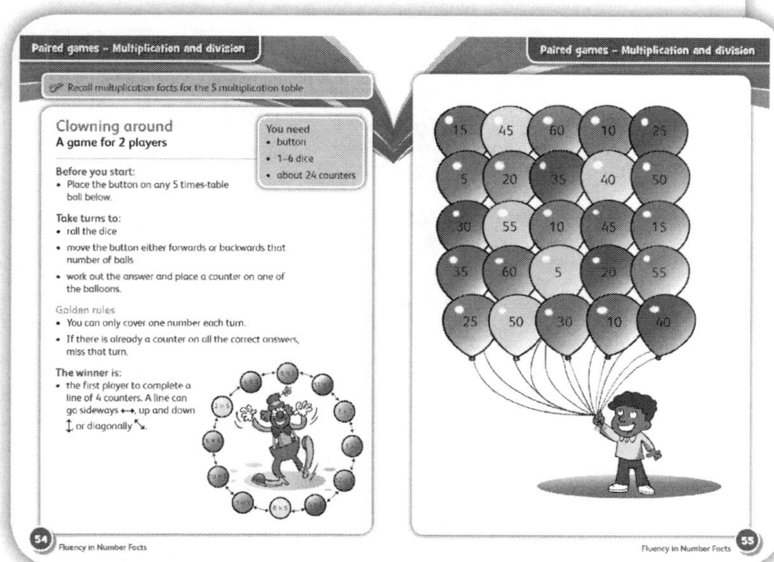
Paired games – Multiplication and division

Recall multiplication facts for the 5 multiplication table

Clowning around
A game for 2 players

You need
- button
- 1–6 dice
- about 24 counters

Before you start:
- Place the button on any 5 times-table ball below.

Take turns to:
- roll the dice
- move the button either forwards or backwards that number of balls
- work out the answer and place a counter on one of the balloons.

Golden rules
- You can only cover one number each turn.
- If there is already a counter on all the correct answers, miss that turn.

The winner is:
- the first player to complete a line of 4 counters. A line can go sideways ↔, up and down ↕ or diagonally ⤡.

54 Fluency in Number Facts

Paired games – Multiplication and division

15 45 60 10 25
5 20 35 40 50
30 55 10 45 15
35 60 5 20 55
25 50 30 10 40

Fluency in Number Facts 55

- button (per pair)
- 1–6 dice (per pair)
- about 24 counters (per pair)

Variations

- Children play the game in groups of three.

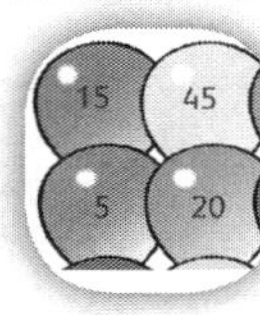

or

- Use a 1–12 dice instead of the spinner, multiplying the dice number by 5.

or

- The winner is the first player to complete a square of four counters.

- Children play the game individually with 12 instead of 24 counters.

You win the game if:

- you can complete a line of four counters. A line can go sideways, up and down or diagonally.

Sandcastles

Objectives

- Recall multiplication facts for the 10 multiplication table

Pupil resources

- *Fluency in Number Facts: Facts and Games: Years 1 & 2* book pages 56 and 57 (per pair); PDFs:

- button (per pair)
- 1–6 dice (per pair)
- 10 counters: 5 for each player (per pair)

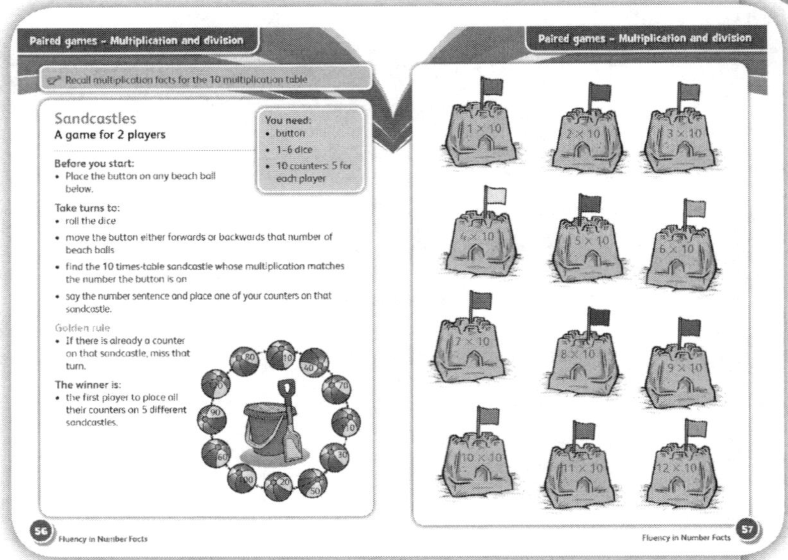
Paired games – Multiplication and division

Recall multiplication facts for the 10 multiplication table

Sandcastles
A game for 2 players

You need:
- button
- 1–6 dice
- 10 counters: 5 for each player

Before you start:
- Place the button on any beach ball below.

Take turns to:
- roll the dice
- move the button either forwards or backwards that number of beach balls
- find the 10 times-table sandcastle whose multiplication matches the number the button is on
- say the number sentence and place one of your counters on that sandcastle.

Golden rule
- If there is already a counter on that sandcastle, miss that turn.

The winner is:
- the first player to place all their counters on 5 different sandcastles.

56 Fluency in Number Facts

Paired games – Multiplication and division

Fluency in Number Facts 57

Variations

- Children play the game in groups of three. You need 12 counters: 4 for each player. The winner is the first player to put all of their counters on four different sandcastles.
- Use 12 counters instead of ten counters (per pair).

Before you start:

- Place a counter on each of the sandcastles ensuring not to cover the calculation.
- Place the button on any beach ball.

Take turns to:

- roll the dice
- move the button either forwards or backwards that number of beach balls
- find the 10 times table sandcastle that matches the number the button is on
- say the number sentence and take the counter.

Golden rule:

- If there is no counter on that sandcastle, miss that turn.

The winner is:

- the first player to collect five counters.

Starburst

Objective

- Recall multiplication facts for the 2, 5 and 10 multiplication tables

Pupil resources

- Fluency in Number Facts: *Facts and Games: Years 1 & 2* book pages 58 and 59 (per pair); PDFs:

- 1–12 dice (per pair)
- about 30 counters (per pair)

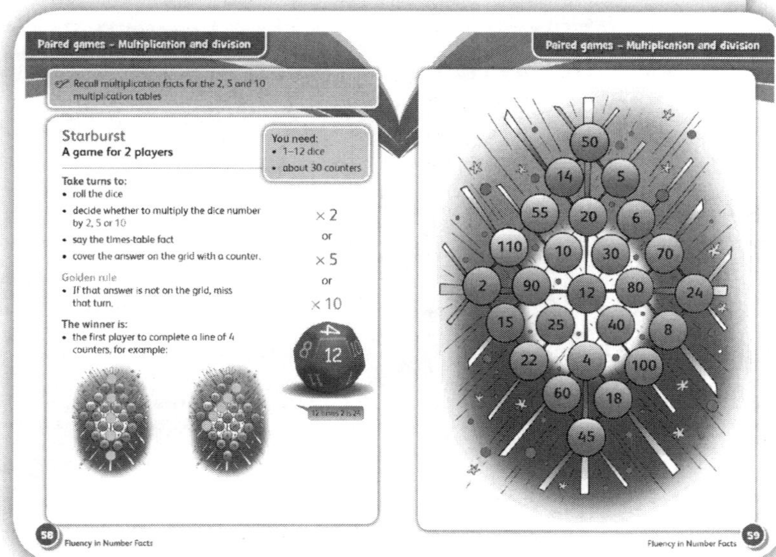

Paired games – Multiplication and division

Recall multiplication facts for the 2, 5 and 10 multiplication tables

Starburst
A game for 2 players

You need:
- 1–12 dice
- about 30 counters

Take turns to:
- roll the dice
- decide whether to multiply the dice number by 2, 5 or 10
- say the times-table fact
- cover the answer on the grid with a counter.

×2 or ×5 or ×10

Golden rule
- If that answer is not on the grid, miss that turn.

The winner is:
- the first player to complete a line of 4 counters, for example:

58 Fluency in Number Facts

Paired games – Multiplication and division

Fluency in Number Facts 59

Variations

- Children play the game in groups of three.
- The winner is the first player to complete a diamond of four counters.
- Children play the game individually using 12 counters.

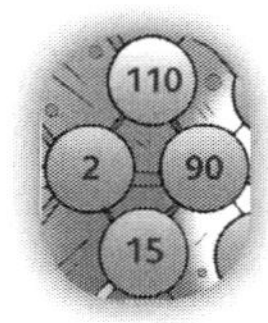

You win the game if:

- you can complete a line of 4 counters.

Paired games and activities

Round the racetrack

Objective

- Recall division facts for the 2, 5 and 10 multiplication tables

Pupil resources

- *Fluency in Number Facts: Facts and Games: Years 1 & 2* book pages 60 and 61 (per pair); PDFs:

→ Paired games and activities → Paired games from the *Facts and Games: Years 1 & 2* book

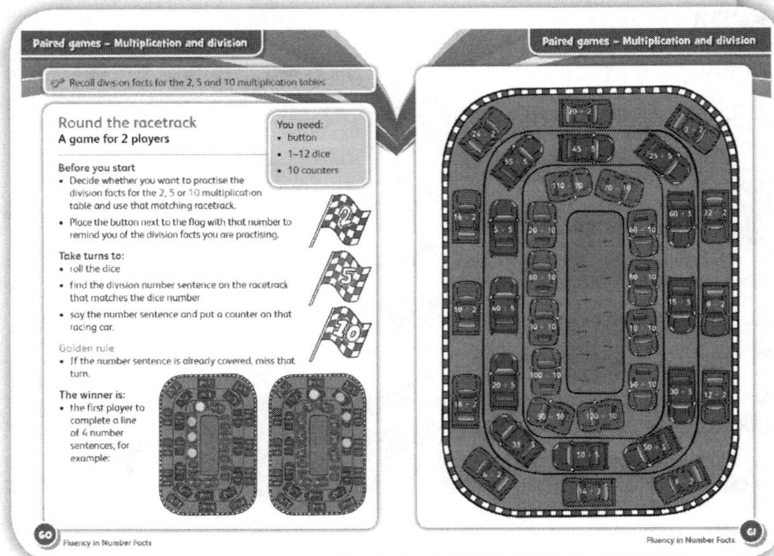
Paired games – Multiplication and division
Recall division facts for the 2, 5 and 10 multiplication tables

Round the racetrack
A game for 2 players

You need:
- button
- 1–12 dice
- 10 counters

Before you start
- Decide whether you want to practise the division facts for the 2, 5 or 10 multiplication table and use that matching racetrack.
- Place the button next to the flag with that number to remind you of the division facts you are practising.

Take turns to:
- roll the dice
- find the division number sentence on the racetrack that matches the dice number
- say the number sentence and put a counter on that racing car.

Golden rule
- If the number sentence is already covered, miss that turn.

The winner is:
- the first player to complete a line of 4 number sentences, for example:

60 Fluency in Number Facts

Paired games – Multiplication and division

Fluency in Number Facts 61

- button (per pair)
- 1–12 dice (per pair)
- 10 counters (per pair)

Variations

- Children play the game in groups of three.

You need

- 2 × 1–12 dice: 1 for each player (per pair)
- 20 counters (per pair)

Before you start:

- Decide whether you want to use the 2, 5 or 10 racetrack. Each player must use a different racetrack.

What to do:

- Both players roll their dice.
- Each player finds the division number sentence on their racetrack that matches the dice number.
- Each player says the number sentence and puts a counter on that racing car.

Golden rule:

- If the number sentence is already covered, miss that turn.

The winner is:

- the first player to complete a line of four number sentences on their racetrack.

- Children play the game individually using eight counters instead of 10.

You win the game if:

- you can complete a line of four counters.

Paired games and activities

Duck division

Objective

- Recall division facts for the 2, 5 and 10 multiplication tables

Pupil resources

- *Fluency in Number Facts: Facts and Games: Years 1 & 2 book* pages 62 and 63 (per pair); PDFs:

- 1–12 dice (per pair)
- 12 counters (per pair)

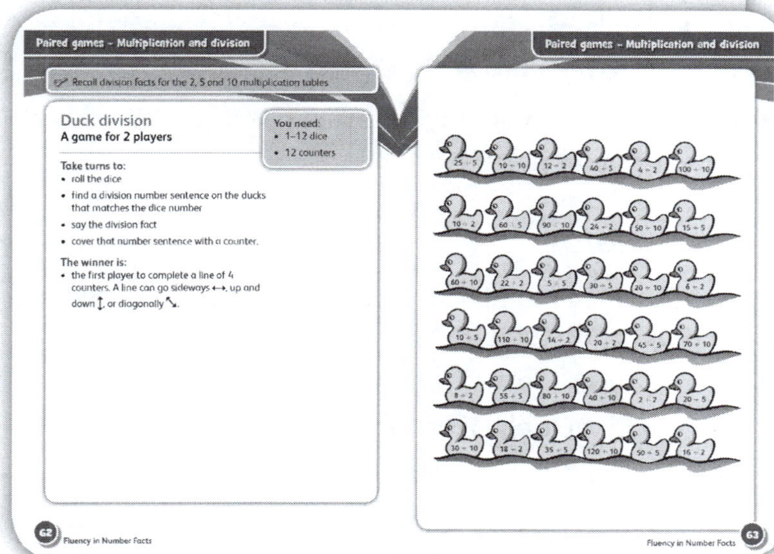

Paired games – Multiplication and division

Recall division facts for the 2, 5 and 10 multiplication tables

Duck division
A game for 2 players

You need:
- 1–12 dice
- 12 counters

Take turns to:
- roll the dice
- find a division number sentence on the ducks that matches the dice number
- say the division fact
- cover that number sentence with a counter.

The winner is:
- the first player to complete a line of 4 counters. A line can go sideways ⟷, up and down ↕, or diagonally ⤡.

62 Fluency in Number Facts

Paired games – Multiplication and division

25 ÷ 5	10 ÷ 10	12 ÷ 2	40 ÷ 5	4 ÷ 2	100 ÷ 10
10 ÷ 2	60 ÷ 5	90 ÷ 10	24 ÷ 2	50 ÷ 10	15 ÷ 5
60 ÷ 10	22 ÷ 2	5 ÷ 5	30 ÷ 5	20 ÷ 10	6 ÷ 2
10 ÷ 5	110 ÷ 10	14 ÷ 2	20 ÷ 2	45 ÷ 5	70 ÷ 10
8 ÷ 2	55 ÷ 5	80 ÷ 10	40 ÷ 10	2 ÷ 2	20 ÷ 5
30 ÷ 10	18 ÷ 2	35 ÷ 5	120 ÷ 10	50 ÷ 5	16 ÷ 2

Fluency in Number Facts 63

Variations

- Children play the game in groups of three.

or

- The winner is the first player to complete a square of four counters.

- Children play the game individually using 12 counters.

You win the game if:

- you can complete a line of four counters. A line can go sideways, up and down or diagonally.

Times-table practice

Objective

- Recall multiplication facts for the 2, 5 and 10 multiplication tables

Pupil resources

- 1–12 dice (per pair)
- 20 counters: 10 counters for each player (per pair)
- container (per pair)

What to do

- Decide which multiplication table you want the children to practise, for example, 5 multiplication table.
- Children take turns to roll the dice.
- Each child multiplies the dice number by 5.
- The first child to call out the correct answer places one of their counters into the container.
- The winner is the first player to place all their counters into the container.

Win the counters

Objective

- Recall multiplication facts for the 2, 5 and 10 multiplication tables

Pupil resources

→ Whole-class games and activites → Hands-on game boards

- 'Hands-on: Multiples of 2' game board or
- 'Hands-on: Multiples of 5' game board or
- 'Hands-on: Multiples of 10' game board (per pair)
- 1–12 dice (per pair)
- 20 counters (per pair)

What to do

- Decide which multiplication table you want the children to practise, for example, 5 multiplication table, and provide them with the appropriate game board, i.e. 'Hands on: Multiples of 5' game board.
- Each player puts their index finger on one of the hands at the bottom of the game board.
- One child rolls the dice, for example, 6.
- Both children multiply the dice number by the multiplication table they are practising, for example, 5 multiplication table.
- The first player to point to the correct answer on the game board, i.e. 30, wins a counter.
- The winner is the player with more counters once all 20 counters have been won.

Cover the multiples

Objective

- Recall multiplication facts for the 2, 5 and 10 multiplication tables

Pupil resources

→ Whole-class games and activites → Hands-on game boards

- 'Hands-on: Multiples of 2' game board or
- 'Hands-on: Multiples of 5' game board or
- 'Hands-on: Multiples of 10' game board (per pair)
- 1–12 dice (per pair)
- 20 counters: 10 of one colour, 10 of another colour (per pair)

What to do

- Decide which multiplication table you want the children to practise, for example, 2 multiplication table, and provide them with the appropriate game board, i.e. 'Hands-on: Multiples of 2' game board.
- Children decide who will have which colour counters.
- Children take turns to:
  - roll the dice, for example, 8
  - multiply the dice number by the multiplication table they are practising, for example, 2 multiplication table, and say the answer, i.e. 16.
- If the answer is correct, they place one of their counters on that number on the game board.
- If the number is already covered, they miss that turn.
- The winner is the player with more counters on the game board once all the numbers have a counter on them.

Stack them up

Objective

- Recall multiplication facts for the 2, 5 and 10 multiplication tables

Pupil resources

- ‘Hands-on: Multiples of 2’ game board or
- ‘Hands-on: Multiples of 5’ game board or
- ‘Hands-on: Multiples of 10’ game board (per pair)
- 1–12 dice (per pair)
- 20 counters: 10 of one colour, 10 of another colour (per pair)

What to do

- Decide which multiplication table you want the children to practise, for example, 10 multiplication table, and provide them with the appropriate game board, i.e. ‘Hands-on: Multiples of 10’ game board.
- Children decide who will have which colour counters.
- Children take turns to:
  - roll the dice, for example, 6
  - multiply the dice number by the multiplication table they are practising, for example, 10 multiplication table, and say the answer, i.e. 60.
- If their answer is correct, they place one of their counters on that number (but making sure not to cover the number) on the game board.
- If the number already has a counter on it, either with one of their own counters, or one the other player’s counters, they place their counter on top of the pile.
- The player whose colour counter is on top ‘owns’ the pile.
- Children keep going, taking turns, until each player has put their ten counters on the game board.
- Each player then carefully removes all the piles where the top counter is their colour.
- Each player then counts how many counters they have altogether (of both colours).
- The winner is the player with more counters.

Individual activities

Multiplication and division Flip Facts cards

Objective

- Recall and use multiplication and division facts for the 2, 5 and 10 multiplication tables

Resources

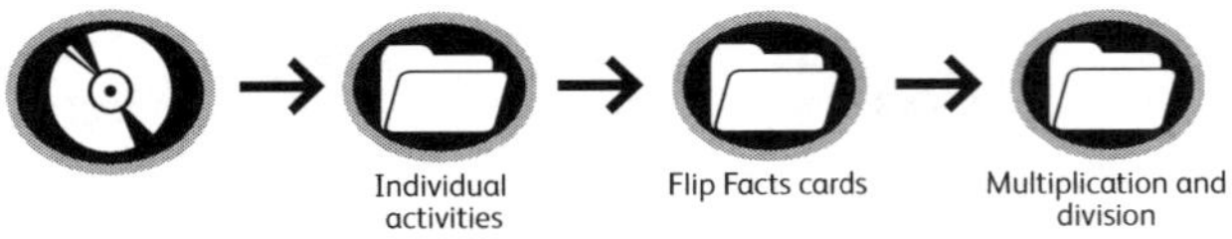

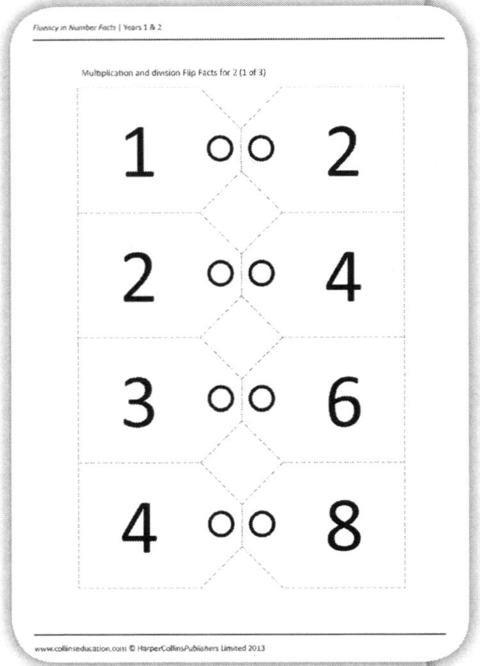

- 'Multiplication and division Flip Facts cards'
- scissors
- glue
- hole punch
- small piece of string or paper fastener

What to do

- Cut out the cards along the dashed lines.
- Fold each card along the dotted lines to form two-sided cards.
- Glue together the back of each card.
- Punch a hole in the centre of each card.
- Arrange the cards in order with the smallest number on top.
- Fasten the set of cards together with string or a paper fastener.

To practise the multiplication facts for the 2 multiplication table

- Use the Multiplication and division Flip Facts cards for 2
- Start with the 1 card on top.
- Ask yourself: *1 multiplied by 2 is?* (2) Turn over the card to check. *2 multiplied by 2 is?* (4) Turn over the card to check. *3 multiplied by 2 is?* (6) Turn over the card to check.
- Continue until you reach the card showing 12 and ask: *12 multiplied by 2 is* (24).
- Repeat several times, quickening the pace as you go.

Individual activities

To practise the division facts for the 2 multiplication table

- Use the 'Multiplication and division Flip Facts cards for 2'.
- Start with the 24 card on top.
- Ask yourself: *24 divided by 2 is…?* (12) Turn over the card to check. *22 divided by 2 is…?* (11) Turn over the card to check. *20 divided by 2 is…?* (10) Turn over the card to check.
- Continue until you reach the card showing 2 and ask: *2 divided by 2 is…?* (1)
- Repeat several times, quickening the pace as you go.

- Children spend just five or ten minutes each time, focussing their attention on learning the multiplication and division facts off by heart.

Variations

- Use the 'Multiplication and division Flip Facts cards for 5' to practise the multiplication and division facts for the 5 multiplication table.
- Use the 'Multiplication and division Flip Facts cards for 10' to practise the multiplication and division facts for the 10 multiplication table.

Number and place value | Addition and subtraction facts | Multiplication and division facts

Sit down, stand up

Objectives

- Compare and order numbers from 0 up to 100
- Recognise the place value of each digit in a 2-digit number (tens, ones)
- Recall and use addition and subtraction facts to 20 fluently, and derive and use related facts up to 100
- Add and subtract numbers mentally, including a 2-digit number and ones, a 2-digit number and tens, two 2-digit numbers, adding three 1-digit numbers
- Recall and use multiplication and division facts for the 2, 5 and 10 multiplication tables

Teacher resources

→ Whole-class games and activities → PowerPoint slides

- 'Sit down, stand up'

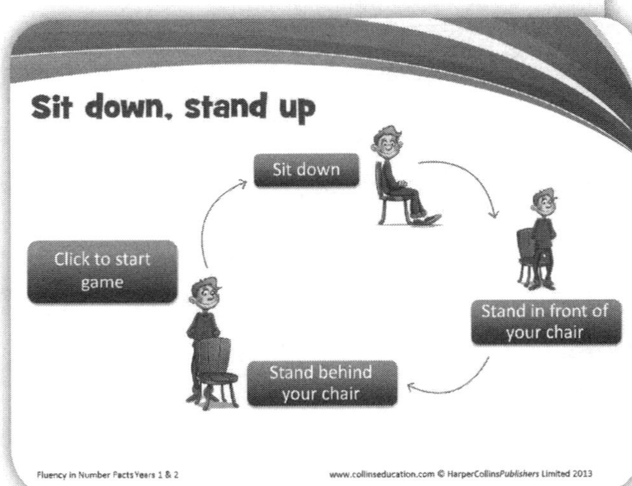

Pupil resources

- none

What to do

- Explain to the children that this a game of honesty.
- Display the first 'Sit down, stand up' slide:
  - sit down
  - stand in front of your chair
  - stand behind your chair
- All the children start the game by sitting.
- Ask the class an appropriate question, for example: *What is 5 times 7*?
- Ask a child for the answer, i.e. 35.
- All the children that worked out the correct answer stand up in front of their chair.
- Continue asking questions.
- Each time a child works out the correct answer to a question, they move to a different position following the order on the slide.
- If a child works out an incorrect answer to a question they stay in their current position.
- Continue asking questions until there are some children sitting down, some children standing in front of their chair and other children standing behind their chair.
- Finally, in rapid succession display slides 2 to 7 (which form a continual loop), eventually stopping on one of the slides.
- All the children in the position displayed on the slide are the winners.

Number and place value

Addition and subtraction facts

Multiplication and division facts

Target boards

Objectives

- Compare and order numbers from 0 up to 100
- Recognise the place value of each digit in a 2-digit number (tens, ones)
- Recall addition and subtraction facts to 20 fluently
- Add and subtract numbers mentally, including a 2-digit number and ones, a 2-digit number and tens, two 2-digit numbers, adding three 1-digit numbers
- Recall and use multiplication and division facts for the 2, 5 and 10 multiplication tables

Teacher resources

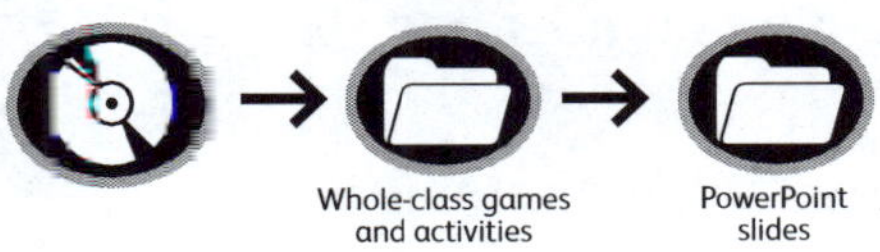

- 'Target boards'

Pupil resources

- none

What to do

- Display the first 'Target boards' slide.
- Ask questions similar to the following:
  - *Which numbers are even/odd?*
  - *Which numbers are less than / more than 8?*
  - *How many more green stars are there than blue stars?*
  - *Which two numbers make 12? Can you find another pair of numbers that make 12?*
  - *Which two numbers have a difference of 3? Can you find another pair of numbers that have a difference of 3?*
  - *Which number is 1 more than / 1 less than 6?*
  - *Which number on the slide is the next number in this pattern: 2, 4, 6, 8, 10…?*
- Ask children to point and say different calculations and expressions using the numbers and symbols on the board, for example: 18 > 2, 5 + 2 = 7.

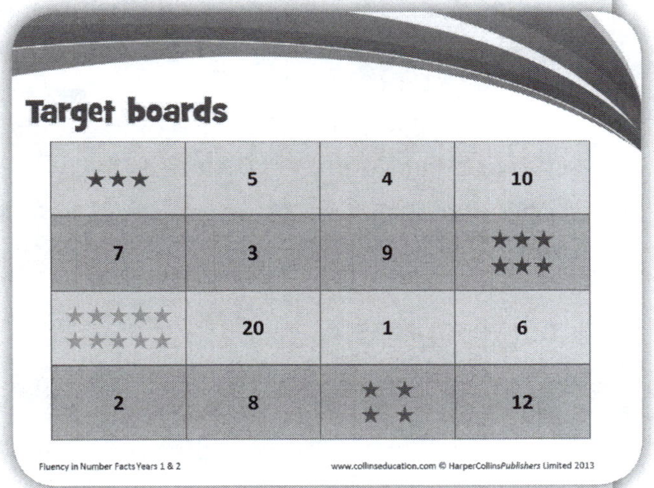

Target boards

★★★	5	4	10
7	3	9	★★★ ★★★
★★★★★ ★★★★★	20	1	6
2	8	★★ ★★	12

Fluency in Number Facts Years 1 & 2 www.collinseducation.com © HarperCollinsPublishers Limited 2013

Variations

- Use the second 'Target boards' slide.
- Change the content in either of the target boards.
- Present the children with a target board where some of the boxes are empty. Ask the children to suggest the content for the missing boxes on the target board.

Number and place value

Addition and subtraction facts

Multiplication and division facts

Hand me your cards

Objectives

- Count in steps of 1, 2, 3, 5 and 10 from any number, forward or backward (Game 1)
- Recognise the place value of each digit in a 2-digit number (tens, ones) (Game 2)
- Given a number, identify one more, one less, ten more and ten less (Game 3)
- Compare and order numbers from 0 up to 100 (Game 4)
- Recall addition and subtraction facts to 20 fluently (Game 5)
- Recall addition and subtraction facts to 20 fluently; add numbers mentally, including adding three 1-digit numbers (Game 6)
- Add numbers mentally, including a 2-digit number and ones; a 2-digit number and tens; two 2-digit numbers (Game 7)
- Subtract numbers mentally, including a 2-digit number and ones; a 2-digit number and tens; two 2-digit numbers (Game 8)
- Recall and use multiplication and division facts for the 2, 5 and 10 multiplication tables (Game 9)

Teacher resources

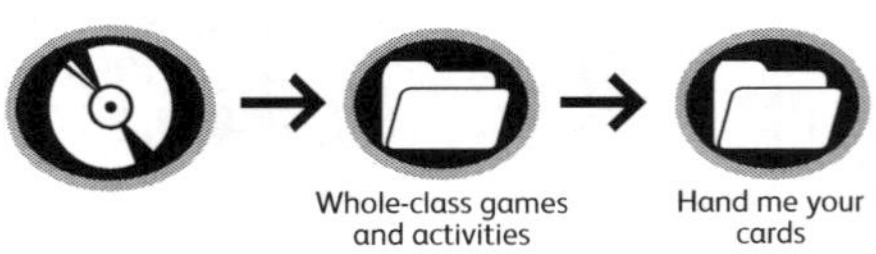

- 'Hand me your cards' (Teacher's call card)

Pupil resources

- 'Hand me your cards' (the white and grey answer cards, ideally printed onto card)

What to do

- Choose the appropriate game for the objective(s) you want the children to practise and consolidate (see above).
- Arrange the class into four teams.
- Separately shuffle and distribute the white and grey answer cards. Each team must have nine answer cards – either all white cards or all grey answer cards. Depending on the number of children in the class, some children may have more than one card. Cards with the Challenge 1 icon denote the answer to an easier question. Cards with the Challenge 3 icon denote the answer to a more difficult question.

- Read out the 'What to say' questions from the Teacher's call card (but not the answers!). Read the questions from the top to the bottom of each column, asking all the questions in the left-hand column first, then all the questions in the right-hand column. Note that there are two answer cards for each number, to ensure there is competition to 'be the first' to call out the answer.
- The first child who has the correct answer on their card, and who calls out this answer, hands their card to the teacher. Team members may assist each other, but only the child that is holding the card can call out the answer.
- Once a child has handed in his/her card(s), they may still assist their team members with the remaining cards. As before, however, he/she is not allowed to call out the answer to the teacher – only the child that is holding the card can call it out.
- Continue asking the questions from the Teacher's call card.
- The winner is the first team with all their answer cards handed in.
- Continue to play the game to see which teams come second and third.

Variations

- Arrange the class into different number of teams:
  - two teams, giving each team 18 cards
  - three teams, giving each team 12 cards (**Note:** One team will have six white answer cards and six grey answer cards.)
  - six teams, giving each team six cards.
- Read the questions from the bottom to the top of each column, asking the questions in the left-hand column first, then the questions in the right-hand column. Or ask the questions in the right-hand column first.
- Put the answer cards in the middle of the table so the group can help each other from the start.

Number and place value

Addition and subtraction facts

Multiplication and division facts

Loop cards

Objectives

- Count in steps of 1, 2, 3, 5 and 10 from any number, forward or backward (Game 1)
- Recognise the place value of each digit in a 2-digit number (tens, ones) (Game 2)
- Given a number, identify one more, one less, ten more and ten less (Game 3)
- Compare and order numbers from 0 up to 100 (Game 4)
- Recall addition and subtraction facts to 20 fluently; add and subtract numbers mentally, including adding three 1-digit numbers (Game 5)
- Add numbers mentally, including a 2-digit number and ones; a 2-digit number and tens; two 2-digit numbers (Game 6)
- Subtract numbers mentally, including a 2-digit number and ones; a 2-digit number and tens; two 2-digit numbers (Game 7)
- Add and subtract numbers mentally, including a 2-digit number and ones; a 2-digit number and tens; two 2-digit numbers (Game 8)
- Recall and use multiplication and division facts for the 2, 5 and 10 multiplication tables (Game 9)

Teacher resources

- none

→ Whole-class games and activities → Loop cards

Pupil resources

- 'Loop cards' (ideally printed onto card)

What to do

- Choose the appropriate game for the objective(s) you want the children to practise and consolidate (see above).
- Shuffle the cards and hand them out to the children. Every card must be used, so if necessary give some children more than one card. Cards with the Challenge 1 icon denote the answer to an easier question. Cards with the Challenge 3 icon denote the answer to a more difficult question.
- Decide who will start the game (the game can begin with any card).
- The first player reads aloud the text on the right-hand side of the card, for example: *Who has 13 plus 7?*
- The rest of the children work out the answer, and the child who has the correct answer on the left-hand side of their card reads it out, for example: *I have 20.* If the answer is correct, that player then reads the text on the right-hand side of their card, for example: *Who has 9 subtract 5?*
- The game continues in this way.
- The game ends when the child who started the game reads out the answer on the left-hand side of their card.

Variation

- To encourage a brisk pace and increase fluency, use a timer and display the 'time to beat'.

Number and place value

Addition and subtraction facts

Multiplication and division facts

Around the room

Objectives

- Count in steps of 2, 3 and 5 from 0, and count in tens from any number, forward or backward
- Compare and order numbers from 0 up to 100
- Recognise the place value of each digit in a 2-digit number (tens, ones)
- Recall and use addition and subtraction facts to 20 fluently, and derive and use related facts up to 100
- Add and subtract numbers mentally, including a 2-digit number and ones, a 2-digit number and tens, two 2-digit numbers, adding three 1-digit numbers
- Recall and use multiplication and division facts for the 2, 5 and 10 multiplication tables

Teacher resources

- none

Pupil resources

- none

What to do

- Children either sit in a circle or at their tables as long as there is a logical 'path' from one child/table to the next.
- Ask one child to go and stand behind the child who is sitting next to them.
- Ask an appropriate question to these two children, for example: *What is 14 add 3? What is the next number in this pattern: 3, 6, 9, 12…?*
- If the child who is standing calls out the correct answer first, they move and stand behind the next child.
- If the child that is sitting calls out the correct answer first, they stand up and go behind the next child. The child that was just standing sits in the place of the child they were just standing behind.
- The game continues in this way around the room.
- When you have gone around the class say: *All change!* and children can go back to their original positions.

Number and place value

Addition and subtraction facts

Multiplication and division facts

One name left

Objectives

- Count in steps of 2, 3 and 5 from 0, and count in tens from any number, forward or backward
- Compare and order numbers from 0 up to 100
- Recognise the place value of each digit in a 2-digit number (tens, ones)
- Recall and use addition and subtraction facts to 20 fluently, and derive and use related facts up to 100
- Add and subtract numbers mentally, including a 2-digit number and ones, a 2-digit number and tens, two 2-digit numbers, adding three 1-digit numbers
- Recall and use multiplication and division facts for the 2, 5 and 10 multiplication tables

Teacher resources

- small box or container

Pupil resources

- small slip of paper or card (per child)
- pencil (per child)

What to do

- Ask the children to write their name on the small slip of paper or card and fold it in half.
- Collect the slips and put them into the box or container.
- Choose two names from the box.
- Ask these two children to stand.
- Ask an appropriate question to these two children, for example: *What is 20 subtract 5? What is the next number in this pattern: 50, 45, 40, 35, 30…?*
- For the child who answers correctly first, put their slip of paper into a separate 'still in' pile. For the child who answers incorrectly, or is beaten on speed by the other child, put their card in an 'out' pile.
- Continuing choosing two names from the box and asking a question.
- When all the names have been chosen from the box, put the children's names that are in the 'still in' pile back into the box.
- Continue the game as before, choosing two names, asking a question and putting the names into 'still in' and 'out' piles.
- Continue the game until only two children, then finally one child is left.

Whole-class games and activities

Number and place value

Addition and subtraction facts

Multiplication and division facts

Whispers

Objectives

- Given a number, identify one more, one less, ten more and ten less
- Recall and use addition and subtraction facts to 20 fluently, and derive and use related facts up to 100
- Add and subtract numbers mentally, including a 2-digit number and ones, a 2-digit number and tens, two 2-digit numbers, adding three 1-digit numbers
- Recall and use multiplication and division facts for the 2, 5 and 10 multiplication tables

Teacher resources

- small slip of paper or card with an appropriate question written on it, for example: 2 + 5 =, 8 – 3 =, 10 × 4 =, 45 ÷ 5 = …

Pupil resources

- none

What to do

- Arrange the class into two or three teams. Ideally, there should be the same number of children in each team.
- Each team stands or sits in a line.
- Secretly show the first child in each team the slip of paper or card showing an appropriate question written on it, for example 2 + 5 = .
- When the first child in each team has seen the slip of paper say *Go!*
- The first child then works out the answer to the question and thinks of a different question that has the same answer, for example: 10 – 3. They then whisper this calculation to the second child in the line.
- The second child works out the answer, thinks of a different question with the same answer and whispers this calculation to the third child in the line.
- The activity continues as described above.
- When the last child in each team has worked out the answer to the question they are given, they call out the answer. Does the last child's answer match the original question on the slip of paper? If so, this is a winning team.

Variation

- An easier version is to show the first child in each team a number, which teams then whisper to each other.

Number and place value

Addition and subtraction facts

Multiplication and division facts

Folding numbers

Objectives

- Count in steps of 2, 3 and 5 from 0, and count in tens from any number, forward or backward
- Compare and order numbers from 0 up to 100
- Recognise the place value of each digit in a 2-digit number (tens, ones)
- Given a number, identify one more, one less, ten more and ten less
- Recall addition and subtraction facts to 20 fluently
- Add and subtract numbers mentally, including a 2-digit number and ones, a 2-digit number and tens, two 2-digit numbers, adding three 1-digit numbers
- Recall and use multiplication and division facts for the 2, 5 and 10 multiplication tables

Teacher resources

- none

Pupil resources

- *The first time you do this activity:* coloured pencils, crayons, and/or felt-tips, sheet of A4 paper (per child and yourself)

Note to the teacher

This activity is not just about children answering mathematical questions. More importantly, it is about encouraging children to *ask* mathematical questions.

What to do – *The first time you do this activity*

- Provide each child, and yourself, with a sheet of A4 paper, and each group with some coloured pencils, crayons and/or felt-tips.
- Demonstrate and ask the children to:
  – place their sheet of paper in the landscape position on the table in front of them
  – write their name in large writing in the middle of the sheet of paper.
- Demonstrate and ask the children to:

Easier version:

  – fold their sheet of paper in half, side to side (it doesn't matter whether the writing is on the inside or the outside of the fold)
  – fold their sheet of paper a second time, top to bottom
  – fold their sheet of paper a third time, side to side.

More challenging version:

  – fold their sheet of paper a fourth time, top to bottom.

Folding numbers

(continued)

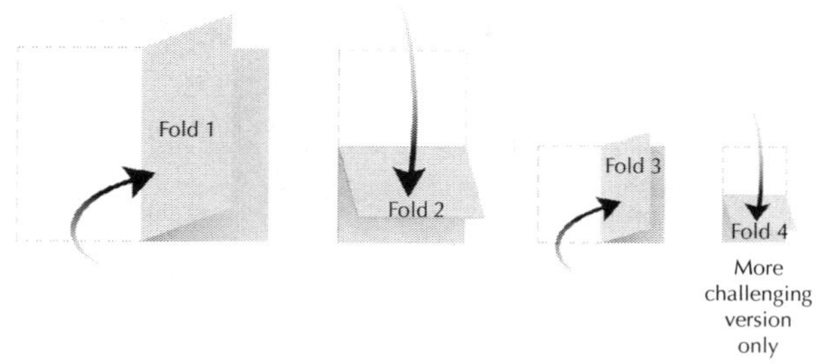

- Demonstrate and tell the children to open out their sheet of paper to the blank side (not the side that has their name written on it). For the easier version there should be eight small rectangles; for the more challenging version there should 16 small rectangles.

Easier version:

- Demonstrate and ask the children to use the coloured pencils, crayons, and/or felt-tips to write neatly, in large writing, each of the digits 1 to 8, in any order, one digit in each small rectangle, for example:

3	5	7	2
8	1	4	6

More challenging version:

- Demonstrate and ask the children to write, in large writing, each of the numbers 0 to 9, in any order, one number in each small rectangle. Then in the six remaining empty rectangles, to repeat any six of the numbers, for example:

9		6	2
5	1		
		3	8
4	7	0	

→

9	8	6	2
5	1	9	4
2	6	3	8
4	7	0	5

- Once all the children have done this, ask them to look carefully at the numbers on their sheet.
- Demonstrate to the children how the sheet of paper can be folded to show different 1-digit, 2-digit and, if appropriate, 3-digit numbers (*more challenging version only*).

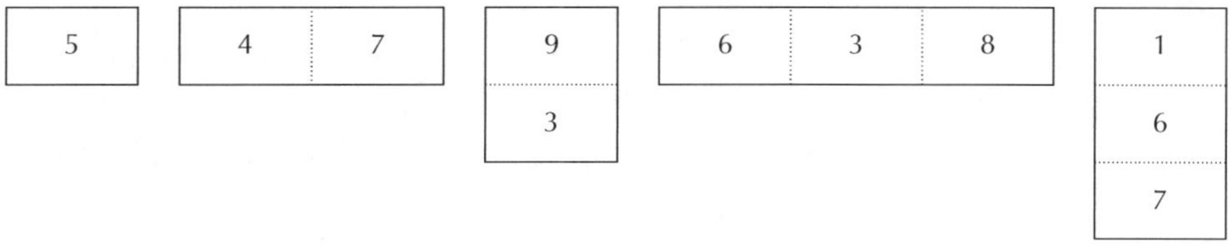

(continued)

Folding numbers

(continued)

- Next, ask the children to fold their sheet of paper to show you the number 6.
- Repeat several times asking questions similar to the following until the children are confident in folding their sheet of paper in different ways to display different 1-digit, 2-digit and, if appropriate, 3-digit numbers.
  - *Show me the number 1.*
  - *Show me the number between 2 and 4.*
  - *Show me a number less than 5.*
  - *Show me an even number greater than 10.*
  - *Show me an odd 2-digit number.*
  - *Show me a number between 20 and 60.*
  - *Show me an odd number greater than 100.*
  - *Show me an even 3-digit number.*
  - *Show me a number between 300 and 700.*
- Once children are confident in using their 'Folding numbers' sheet, demonstrate the following to the class, asking a confident child to come out to the front to be your partner:
  - Look at the child's 'Folding numbers' sheet and ask them a question similar to those above where the answer can be displayed on their 'Folding numbers' sheet.
  - Once the child has successfully done this, ask them to carefully look at *your* 'Folding numbers' sheet and to ask you a question where the answer can be displayed on your 'Folding numbers' sheet.
  - Repeat if necessary, being sure to demonstrate more open-ended types of questions to the class.
- Once children are familiar with this, arrange them into pairs.
- Tell the children to take turns in asking each other questions where the answer can be displayed on their partners 'Folding numbers' sheet. Remind the children that they need to think carefully about what questions to ask, as their partner must be able to show the answer on their 'Folding numbers' sheet.
- After a sufficient length of time, bring the class back together again and discuss with the children the range of questions that they asked. It is important to elicit from the children the difference between a 'poor' question, for example: *Can you show me the number 12?*, and a 'good' question, for example: *Can you show me a number between 10 and 15?*
- Keep the 'Folding numbers' sheets for when you revisit the activity.

Folding numbers

(continued)

What to do – *Revisiting the activity*

- Ask the children to look at their 'Folding numbers' sheet again.
- Arrange the children into pairs.
- Tell the children to take turns in asking each other questions where the answer can be displayed on their partners 'Folding numbers' sheet. Remind the children that they need to think carefully about what questions to ask, as their partner must be able to show the answer on their 'Folding numbers' sheet.
- After a sufficient length of time, bring the class back together again and briefly discuss the activity with the children.
- Keep the 'Folding numbers' sheets for the next time you revisit the activity.

Whole-class, group or individual activities

Number and place value

Addition and subtraction facts

Multiplication and division facts

Written activities

Objectives

- Compare and order numbers from 0 up to 100
- Given a number, identify one more, one less, ten more and ten less
- Recall addition and subtraction facts to 20 fluently
- Add and subtract numbers mentally, including a 2-digit number and ones, a 2-digit number and tens, two 2-digit numbers
- Recall and use multiplication and division facts for the 2, 5 and 10 multiplication tables

Teacher resources

→ Written activities

- scissors

Pupil resources

- Written activities sheet (per child)
- pencil (per child)

Introduction

Fluency in Number Facts: Facts and Games: Years 1 & 2 includes a set of Written activities, presented as templates. They are aimed at providing children with further practice and consolidation and also at offering teachers a means of assessing individual children's proficiency in number. They can be used with the whole class, specific groups or individual children.

Although designed to be reproduced onto sheets of A4 paper, many of the templates show the same type of activity presented three times with the following icons used to allow for differentiation: Challenge 1 (easy), Challenge 2 (average) and Challenge 3 (challenging). The intention is that once the teacher has filled in and copied the template that these are then cut into smaller pieces of paper for the children to complete. However, even for those templates that do not include these differentiation icons, these Written activities can also be adapted easily to meet a range of abilities. It is important therefore that these Written activities are viewed as generic worksheets that teachers fill in and adapt in order to meet the different needs and abilities of their children.

Whole-class, group or individual activities

It is envisaged that, whether it be one of the full A4 activities (for example, '16 calculations', '49 calculations' or '100 calculations') or one of the activities that are presented to the children on a smaller piece of paper (for example, 'Across and up', 'Calculation boxes' or 'Dice calculations'), each Written activity should take no longer than ten minutes for the children to complete. Alternatively, to encourage speed and recall, set the children to work, and as they finish the activity they raise their hand and you tell them how long it took them to complete it.

It is recommended that children do the same type of activity (perhaps even involving the same numbers) on two or three consecutive days. This way, the majority of children will see themselves making progress over the two or three days, thus providing greater encouragement and self-motivation.

What to do

- Choose an appropriate Written activity for the whole class, specific groups or individual children, taking careful consideration of the different needs and abilities of the children.
- Fill in the template on screen, then name this version and save it to use again later on. Alternatively, print one copy of the template and fill it in by hand. Detailed guidance regarding possible differentiated content (Challenge 1, Challenge 2, Challenge 3) to use for each of the templates is given below on pages 142–161.
- Once filled in, photocopy as many copies as is required for the number of children you want to complete the Written activity. If required, cut the sheets into two or three smaller strips of paper.
- Distribute the activities to the children, taking care to provide each child with the appropriate differentiated version of the activity. Also ensure that each child has a sharpened pencil!
- If it is the first time that children are doing one of the Written activities, spend time explaining how to do the activity. If appropriate, display the saved template on the interactive whiteboard (IWB) to help with the explanation.
- Allow the children approximately ten minutes to complete the activity or set the activity as a timed exercise.
- Once the children have finished, immediately mark the activity. You may want to mark the activity with the children's help, asking children to mark their own sheet or swapping and marking someone else's sheet.
- Be sure to discuss the results of the activity with the children, asking them which questions they found easy, which they found more difficult, and also referring to specific questions, asking them how they worked out the answer. This should provide some excellent data to help identify common errors or misconceptions that children may have. You can then either follow on with some brief impromptu teaching, assisting children to overcome the errors or misconceptions or, alternatively, keep this information in mind for some further teaching at a later date.
- And finally…remember to repeat the same type of activity (perhaps even involving the same numbers) on two or three consecutive days.

Whole-class, group or individual activities

Order the numbers

Number and place value

Notes for the teacher

- Children need to be familiar with the traditional 1–100 number square in order to complete this activity successfully.
- For each grid, write four or five numbers, making sure that you write the numbers in the correct positions as located on a 1–100 number square.

Notes for the children

- Ensure children understand that each of the grids is a different section of a 1–100 number square. Some of the numbers have been given, and they have to work out which numbers belong in the empty squares.

Example of differentiation content

Challenge 1

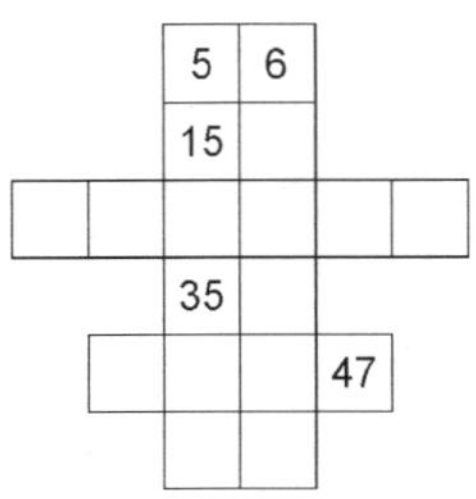

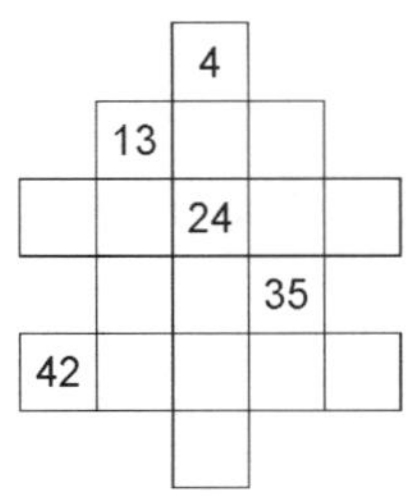

Variations

- If necessary, provide children with a 1–100 number square to consult.
- Provide the children with more numbers already on the grid.

Challenge 2

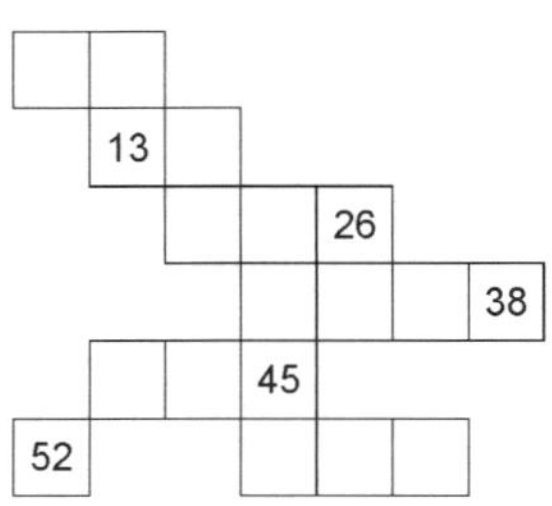

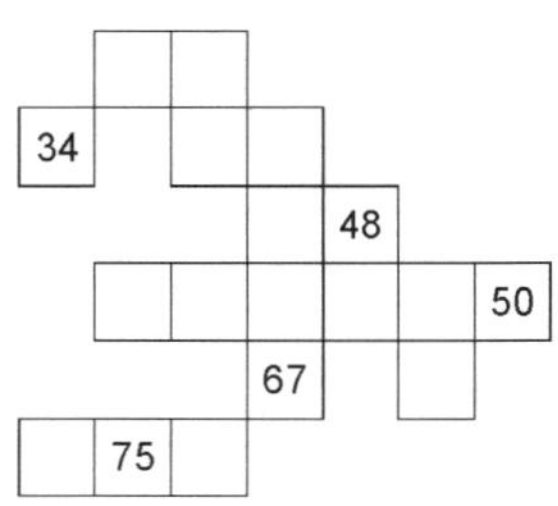

Challenge 3

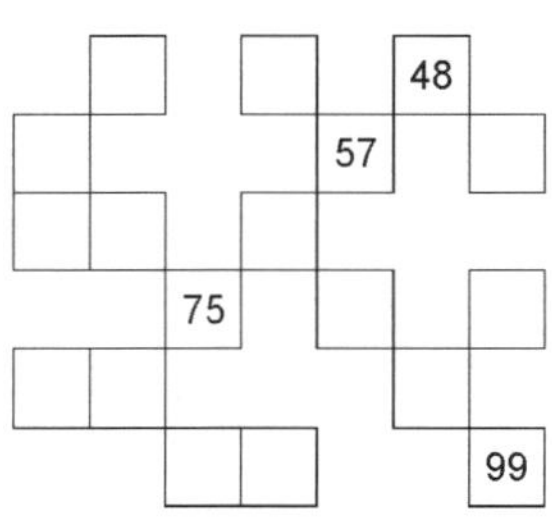

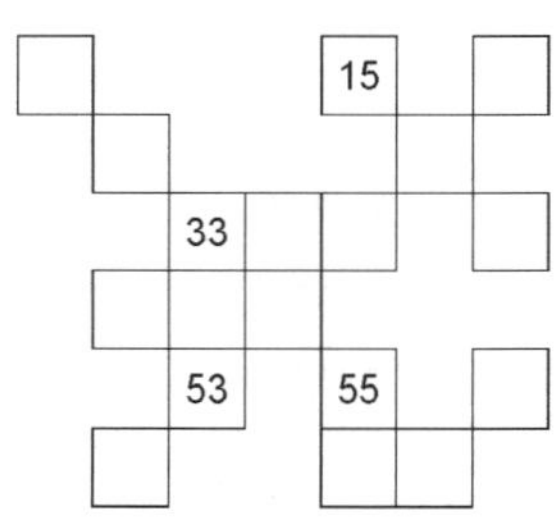

Variations

- Provide the children with fewer numbers already on the grid.
- Alter the activity for a 101–200 number square.
- Provide the children with one of the grids with no numbers on it and ask them to write four numbers on it to make their own 'Order the numbers' grid for a friend to solve.

Whole-class, group or individual activities

Across and up

Addition and subtraction

Notes for the teacher

- This activity is ideal for practising and consolidating the concepts of 1 or 10 more or less.
- For each grid write:
  - a number in the grey box
  - an operation (addition or subtraction symbol followed by a number) on each of the arrows
  - two or three answers in the other boxes on the grid.
- When children have completed the grids, discuss with them any patterns and relationships they notice.

Notes for the children

- Ensure children understand that to complete each grid they start with the number in the grey box and to this number they perform the operations given on the arrows, writing the answers in the appropriate boxes on the grid. They continue across and up the grid performing subsequent operations on the previous numbers written on the boxes, for example:

↑ +1

4	6	8	10
3	5	7	9
2	4	6	8
1	3	5	7

→ +2

Example of differentiation content

Challenge 1

↑ +1

			10
2			
1	3		

→ +2

↑ −2

		6	
10			
12	11		

→ −1

Variations

- Ensure that all answers are less than 20.
- Provide the children with more answers already on each grid.

Challenge 2

↑ +2

			17
6			
2	5		

→ +3

↑ −3

11			
			8
20		16	

→ −2

(continued)

Whole-class, group or individual activities

Challenge 3

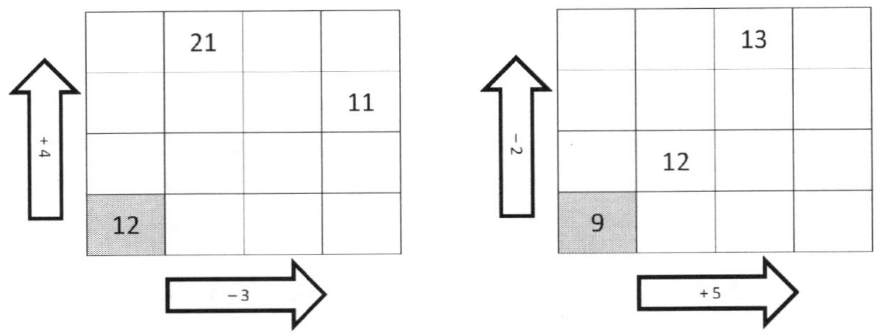

Variations

- Provide the children with fewer (or no) answers already on each grid.
- Include calculations that involve adding and subtracting combinations of 1-digit and 2-digit numbers.
- Provide the children with grids with operations written on them, but no numbers in the grey boxes. The children write in their own numbers in the grey boxes and then complete the grids.

Calculations grid (small)
Calculations grid (large)

Addition and subtraction
Multiplication

Notes for the teacher

- There are two versions of this activity. The three examples given below are for the 'Calculations grid (small)' version however, the same principles apply to the 'Calculations grid (large)' version.
- For each grid write:
  - either the addition or subtraction symbol in the grey box in the top left-hand corner of the grid
  - numbers in each of the boxes in the top row and the left-hand column of the grid
  - two or three of the answers on the grid.
- Note that for the Challenge 3 example provided on page 146, teachers need to complete the grid and then carefully delete some of the answers and numbers in the top row and left-hand column, ensuring that the numbers remaining are sufficient for the children to fill in all the missing numbers on the grid. This version helps children develop their understanding of the inverse relationship between addition and subtraction.
- When children have completed the grids, discuss with them any patterns and relationships they notice.

Notes for the children

- Ensure children understand that to complete each grid they start with the number in the left-hand column of the grid, perform the operation given in the grey box then add or subtract the number in the top row, writing the answer in the appropriate box on the grid.
- Although it makes no difference for grids involving addition (commutative law), for subtraction grids it is important that children get into the habit of always starting with the numbers down the left-hand column rather than the numbers in the top row.

–	6	2	9	4
17	11	15	8	13
20	14	18	11	16
11	5	9	2	7
14	8	12	5	10

Whole-class, group or individual activities

Example of differentiation content

Challenge 1

+	1	3	2	5
4	5			
10				
8			10	
6		9		

Variations

- Ensure that all answers are less than 20.
- Provide the children with more answers already on each grid.

Challenge 2

−	6	2	9	4
17		15		
20				
11			2	
14				

Variations

- The 'Calculation grids (small)' can also be used to practise and consolidate children's fluency in multiplication. However be aware that at this stage, it may involve the multiplication facts beyond the 2, 5 and 10 multiplication tables, for example:

×	8	6	12	9
5				
10	80			
2				
3			36	

Challenge 3

+	9			11
				29
12		16		
				20
15			21	

Variations

- Provide the children with fewer (or no) answers already on each grid.
- Include calculations that involve adding or subtracting combinations of 1-digit and 2-digit numbers.

Calculation boxes

Addition

Notes for the teacher

- For each grid write:
  - four numbers in the boxes as shown in the Challenge 1 and Challenge 2 examples below
  - the addition symbol (+) in the circle at the top.
- Note that for the Challenge 3 example, teachers need to complete the grid and then carefully delete some of the numbers, ensuring that the numbers remaining are sufficient for the children to fill in all the missing numbers on the grid. This version helps children develop their understanding of the inverse relationship between addition and subtraction.
- When children have completed the grids, discuss with them any patterns and relationships they notice.

Notes for the children

(+)

3	5	8
2	4	6
5	9	14

- Ensure children understand that to complete each grid they:
  - add pairs of numbers in each row, for example 3 + 5 = 8 and 2 + 4 = 6, writing the answers in the appropriate spaces
  - add pairs of numbers in each column, for example 3 + 2 = 5 and 5 + 4 = 9, writing the answers in the appropriate spaces
  - add the two answers in the right-hand column, i.e. 8 + 6 = 14 and write this answer in the grey box.
- If they are correct, this is also the answer to the sum of the two numbers in the bottom row, i.e. 5 + 9 = 14.
- Note that children can complete the final part of the activity by adding the two answers in the bottom row first, writing this answer in the grey box, and then adding the two answers in the right-hand column to check.

Example of differentiation content

Challenge 1

(+)

3	5	
2	4	

Variations

- Ensure that all answers are less than 20.
- Provide the children with the final total in the grey box.

(continued)

Whole-class, group or individual activities

Challenge 2

+

12	7	
5	9	

Challenge 3

+

	14	22
11		
	17	

Variations

- Include calculations that involve adding combinations of 1-digit and 2-digit numbers.

Whole-class, group or individual activities

Calculation strips

Addition and subtraction
Multiplication and division

Notes for the teacher

- For each strip write:
  - an operation (addition, subtraction or multiplication symbol followed by a number) in the circle
  - a number in each of the boxes down the left-hand side of the strip
  - one or two answers down the right-hand side of the strip.
- The star at the bottom of each strip can either be used for the children to write their score out of 10, or if you are timing the activity, the time it took them to complete it.
- Note that for the Challenge 3 example, teachers need to complete the strip and then delete one number from either the left- or right-hand side of the strip. This version helps children develop their understanding of the inverse relationship between addition and subtraction, or multiplication and division.
- When children have completed the strips, discuss with them any patterns and relationships they notice.

Notes for the children

- Ensure children understand that to complete each strip, they perform the operation given in the circle on each of the ten numbers down the left-hand side of the strip, writing each answer in the box to the right.

+5

6	11
2	7
10	15

Example of differentiation content

Challenge 1

+5

6	
2	
10	
4	
1	
7	
9	14
3	
8	13
5	

☆

Variations

- Ensure that all answers are less than 20.
- Provide the children with several answers down the right-hand side of the strip.

(continued)

Whole-class, group or individual activities

Challenge 2

−7

10	
15	
13	6
20	
17	
11	
14	
18	11
16	
12	

☆

Challenge 3

x 5

6	
3	
	35
	10
9	45
4	
	60
	25
11	
	40

☆

Variations

- Don't provide the children with any answers down the right-hand side of the strip.
- Include calculations that involve adding or subtracting combinations of 1-digit and 2-digit numbers.

Whole-class, group or individual activities

Calculation walls

Addition and subtraction

Notes for the teacher

- For each wall write:
  - three numbers in the 'bricks' as shown in the Challenge 1 and Challenge 2 examples below
  - the operation (+ or –) in the circle at the top.
- Note that for the Challenge 3 example, teachers need to complete the wall and then carefully delete some of the numbers, ensuring that the numbers remaining are sufficient for the children to fill in all the missing numbers on the wall. This version helps children develop their understanding of the inverse relationship between addition and subtraction.
- When children have completed the walls, discuss with them any patterns and relationships they notice.

Notes for the children

- Ensure children understand that to complete each wall they:
  - add adjacent pairs of numbers in the bottom row, for example: 3 + 5 = 8 and 5 + 2 = 7, writing the answers in the 'bricks' immediately above each pair of numbers
  - add adjacent pairs of numbers in the remaining row(s), for example: 8 + 7 = 15, writing the answer(s) in the 'brick(s)' immediately above this pair / each pairs of numbers
  - write the final answer in the 'brick' at the top of each wall.

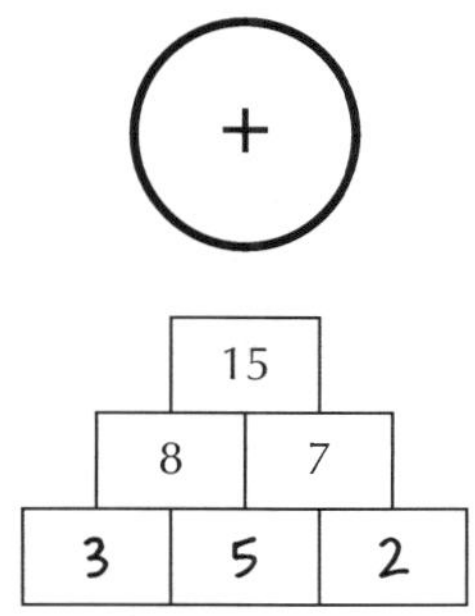

Example of differentiation content

Challenge 1

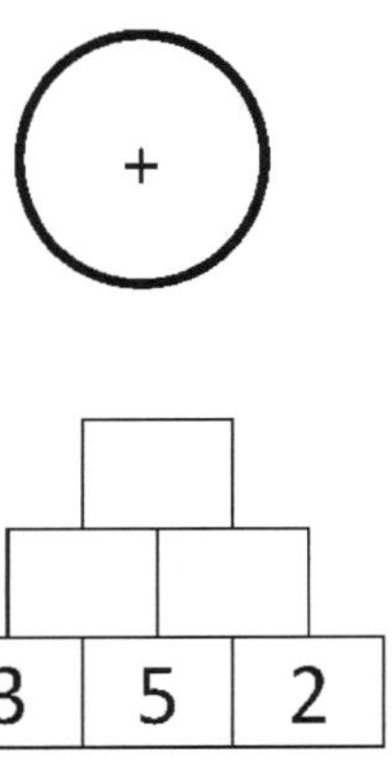

Variations

- Ensure that all answers are less than 20.
- Provide the children with the final total in the top 'brick'.

(*continued*)

Whole-class, group or individual activities

Challenge 2

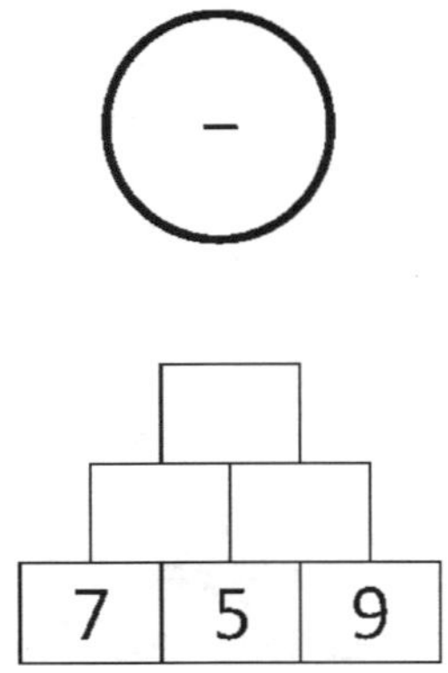

Variations

- The ‘Calculation walls’ can also be used to practise and consolidate children’s fluency in subtraction and, in particular, seeing subtraction as finding the difference, for example:

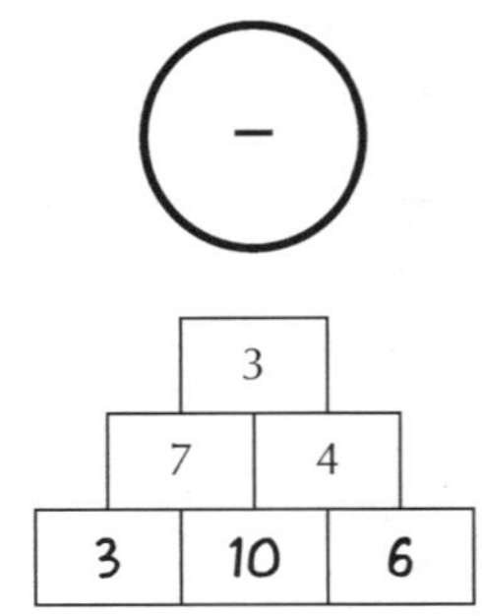

Challenge 3

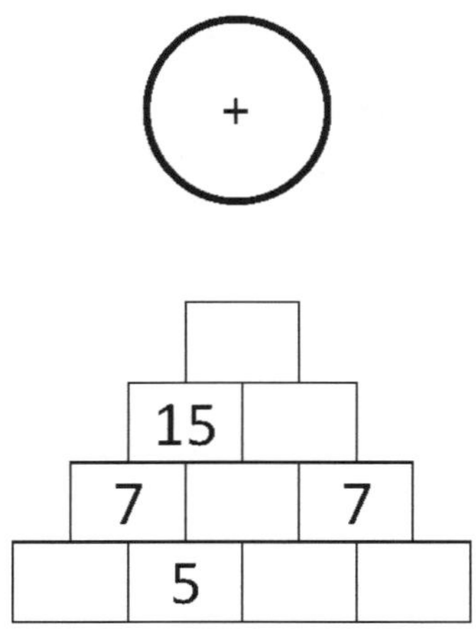

Variations

- Include calculations that involve adding or subtracting combinations of 1-digit and 2-digit numbers.

Whole-class, group or individual activities

Number chains

Addition and subtraction

Additional resources

- 1–6, 0–9, 1–12 or 1–20 dice (per child)

Notes for the teacher

- For each chain write a number in the grey box.
- This activity can be differentiated not only by the number you write in the grey box, but also by the dice you give the children to use.

Notes for the children

- Children roll the dice, write the number rolled on the line to the right of the grey box, add the dice number to the number in the grey box and write the answer in the first white box.

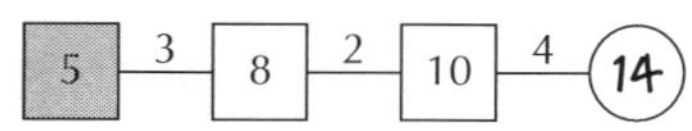

- The chain continues in this way, with the child rolling the dice, writing the number rolled on the line, adding the dice number to the number in the previous white box and writing the answer in the next white box.
- Each chain finishes when the child writes the final answer in the circle.

Example of differentiation content

Challenge 1

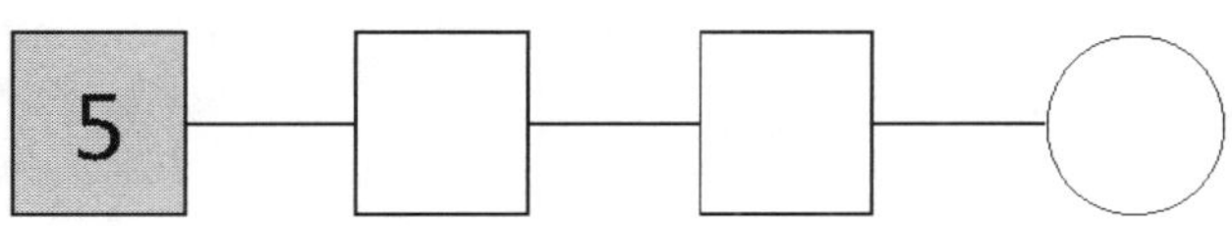

Challenge 2

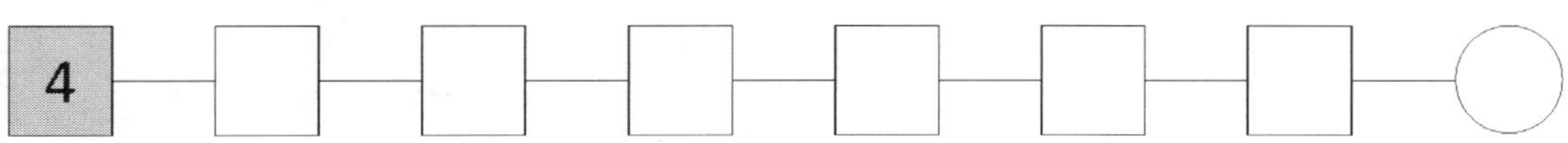

Challenge 3

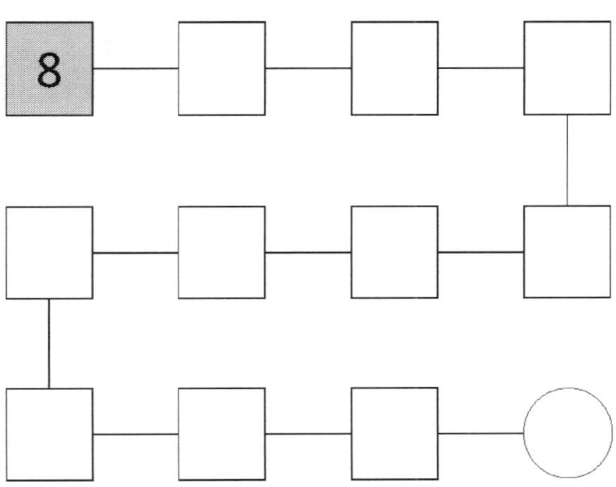

(continued)

Whole-class, group or individual activities

Variations

- Write a large number in the grey box. Children subtract the dice number from the numbers in the grey and white boxes. Ensure that the final answer in the circle will not be a negative number.
- Write a 'teens' number in the grey boxes and provide the children with a number dice and a six-sided addition and subtraction symbol dice. Children roll both dice and perform the operation generated. If the children reach a point along the chain where they cannot do the calculation, for example, the answer will give a negative number, the children roll both dice again.

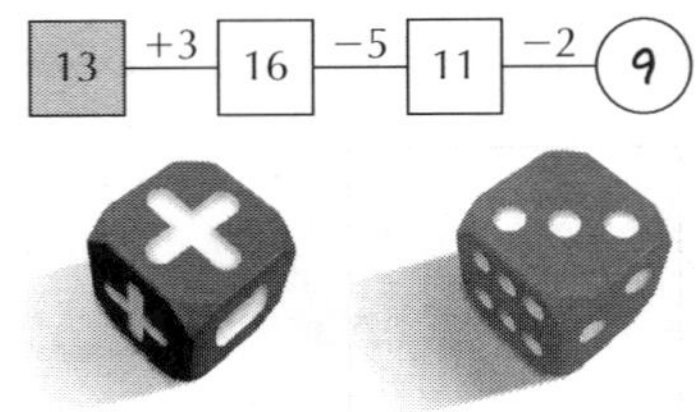

Add and subtract

Add and multiply

Subtract and multiply

Addition and subtraction

Multiplication and division

Notes for the teacher

- There are three versions of this activity. The three examples given below are for the 'Add and subtract' table, however the same principles apply to all three versions.
- These activities are introducing children, in an informal way, to the concept of algebra.
- For each table write:
  - a number in each of the eight boxes below the circle ○
  - a number in each of the eight boxes below the square □.
- Ensure that when using the 'Add and subtract', and 'Subtract and multiply' versions, for each row, you write the larger number in the circle column and the smaller number in the square column.
- The star to the right of each table can either be used for the children to write their score out of 16, or if you are timing the activity, the time it took them to complete it.
- Note that for the Challenge 3 example, teachers need to complete the table and then delete two numbers from each row of the table. This version helps children develop their understanding of the inverse relationship between addition and subtraction, or multiplication and division. Also note that the example given may prove difficult for many children. It is important that before presenting such a table to children that you spend time discussing it with them.
- When children have completed the table, discuss with them any patterns and relationships they notice.

Notes for the children

- Ensure children understand that to complete each table, they perform the operation given in the top row of the third and fourth columns in the table, writing each answer in the appropriate box.

○	□	○ + □	○ − □
3	1	4	3
5	2	7	3
8	5	13	3
2	1	3	1

(continued)

Whole-class, group or individual activities

Example of differentiation content

Challenge 1

○	□	○ + □	○ − □
3	1		
5	2		
8	5		
2	1		
4	3		
9	4		
6	2		
10	5		

Variations

- Ensure that all answers are less than 20.
- Provide the children with several of the answers written in the table.

Challenge 2

○	□	○ + □	○ − □
17	9		
12	6		
19	8		
14	7		
20	4		
16	5		
18	3		
15	6		

Challenge 3

○	□	○ + □	○ − □
12	7		
20	8		
	6	16	
	3		11
	6		7
18			13
17			5
		23	15

Variations

- Include calculations that involve adding or subtracting combinations of 1-digit and 2-digit numbers.
- Include multiplication and division facts for the 2, 3, 4, 5, 8 or 10 multiplication tables.

Dice calculations (addition)
Dice calculations (subtraction)
Dice calculations (multiplication)
Dice calculations (division)

Addition and subtraction

Multiplication and division

Additional resources

- two 1–6, 0–9, 1–12 or 1–20 dice, or any combination of two dice (per child)

Notes for the teacher

- There are four versions of this activity – one for each of the four operations. With some exceptions (see below), the same principles apply to all four versions.
- The dice you give the children differentiate this activity.

Notes for the children

- Children roll both dice, writing one number in the square and one number in the triangle. They then perform the operation and write the answer in the circle.
- Note the following:
  - For 'Dice calculations (subtraction)' children must write the larger number in the square and the smaller number in the triangle.
  - 'Dice calculations (multiplication)' may not be appropriate for most children at Key Stage 1 as given the random nature of this activity, depending on the dice used, the multiplication calculations that children generate will be ones that they are yet to learn, i.e. for two 1–6 dice: multiplication tables up to 6 × 6; for two 0–9 dice: multiplication tables up to 9 × 9 and for two 1–12 dice: multiplication tables up to 12 × 12 (see Variations below for an alternative).
  - For 'Dice calculations (division)' children must write the larger number in the square and the smaller number in the triangle. However, this version may not be appropriate for most children in Key Stage 1 as given the random nature of this activity, most of the division calculations that children will generate will result in the answer having a remainder.

(continued)

Whole-class, group or individual activities

Variations

- For 'Dice calculations (addition)':
  - Write a number in each of the ten squares. Provide each child with only one die. Children roll the die, write the number in the triangle, add the two numbers together and write the answer in the circle.
  - Write a number in each of the ten triangles. Provide each child with only one die. Children roll the die, write the number in the square, add the two numbers together and write the answer in the circle.
  - Write a number in each of the ten circles. Provide each child with only one die. Children roll the die and write the number in the square. They then work out what number they need to add to the number in the square to make the total in the circle. They write this number in the triangle. Note that the numbers you write in each of the circles must be larger than the largest number it is possible to roll on the die. Also note that this variation is ideal for practising and consolidating pairs of numbers that make a given total, such as 10, 20 or 100.
  - Write a number in each of the ten circles. Provide each child with only one die. Children roll the die and write the number in the triangle. They then work out what number they need to add to the number in the triangle to make the total in the circle. They write this number in the square. Note that the numbers you write in each of the circles must be larger than the largest number it is possible to roll on the die. Also note that this variation is ideal for practising and consolidating pairs of numbers that make a given total such as 10, 20 or 100.
- For 'Dice calculations (subtraction)':
  - Write a number in each of the ten squares. Provide each child with only one die. Children roll the die, write the number in the triangle, find the difference between the two numbers and write the answer in the circle. Note that the numbers you write in each of the squares must be larger than the largest number it is possible to roll on the die.
  - Write a number in each of the ten circles. Provide each child with only one die. Children roll the die and write the number in the triangle. They then work out the minuend and write this number in the square.
- For 'Dice calculations (multiplication)':
  - Write the number 2, 5 or 10 in each of the ten squares. Provide each child with one 1–12 die. Children roll the die, write the number in the triangle, multiply the two numbers together and write the product in the circle.
  - Write the number 2, 5 or 10 in each of the ten triangles. Provide each child with one 1–12 die. Children roll the die, write the number in the square, multiply the two numbers together and write the product in the circle.

Challenge 3

- Rolling two 0–9 dice will generate all of the 2-digit numbers.
- For 'Dice calculations (multiplication)' write the numbers 2, 3, 4, 5, 8 or 10 in the squares or triangles.

Whole-class, group or individual activities

16 / 49 / 100 calculations (1-digit numbers)
16 / 49 / 100 calculations (numbers 1–12)
16 / 49 / 100 calculations (2-digit numbers)
16 / 49 / 100 calculations (3-digit numbers)
16 / 49 / 100 calculations (multiples of 10)
16 calculations (multiples of 100)
49 / 100 calculations (multiples of 10 and 100)

Addition and subtraction
Multiplication and division

Notes for the teacher

- There are 18 versions of this activity:
  - six versions each requiring the children to perform 16 calculations
  - six versions each requiring the children to perform 49 calculations
  - six versions each requiring the children to perform 100 calculations.
- The same principles apply to all versions.
- It is recommended that, except for the most able children, at Key Stage 1 you use the six versions that require the children to perform 16 calculations.
- For each grid write an operation (addition, subtraction or multiplication symbol followed by a number) in the circle, for example: + 6.
- The operation you write in the circle differentiates this activity.
- The star at the bottom of each grid can either be used for the children to write their score, or if you are timing the activity, the time it took them to complete it.
- When children have completed the grid, discuss with them any patterns and relationships they notice.

(*continued*)

Whole-class, group or individual activities

Notes for the children

- Ensure children understand that to complete each grid, they perform the operation given in the circle on the number written in the top left-hand corner of each box, writing each answer in the appropriate box.

+6

8 14	1 7	4 10	6 12
5 11	3 9	7 13	2 8
6 12	7 13	3 9	8 14
2 8	4 10	5 11	9 15

- Note that for activities involving subtraction, for example, – 5, ensure children subtract the number in the circle from the number written in the top left-hand corner of each box.

−5

74 69	69 64	26 21	34 29
52 47	78 73	95 90	49 44
88 83	45 40	13 8	56 51
31 26	23 18	67 62	82 77

Whole-class, group or individual activities

Challenge 1

Challenge 2

Challenge 3

Fluency in Number Facts | Years 1 & 2

16 Calculations (One-digit numbers)

Name: Date:

8	1	4	6
5	3	7	2
6	7	3	8
2	4	5	9

16 Calculations (One-digit numbers)

Name: Date:

8	1	4	6
5	3	7	2
6	7	3	8
2	4	5	9

Variations

Below is a list of suggestions as to possible operations to write. However, this list must not in any way be seen as the limits which are possible with these activities.

- 1-digit numbers: (+ 1), (+ 2), (+ 3), (+ 4), (+ 5) … ; (− 1); (× 2), (× 5), (× 10)
- Numbers 1–12: (+ 1), (+ 2), (+ 3), (+ 4), (+ 5) … ; (− 1); (× 2), (× 5), (× 10)
- 2-digit numbers: (+ 1), (+ 2), (+ 3), (+ 4), (+ 5) … ; (+ 10), (+ 20), (+ 30), (+ 40) … (+ 100); (− 1), (− 2), (− 3), (− 4), (− 5) … (− 13)
- 3-digit numbers: (+ 1), (+ 2), (+ 3), (+ 4), (+ 5) … ; (+ 10), (+ 20), (+ 30), (+ 40) … (+ 100); (− 1), (− 2), (− 3), (− 4), (− 5) … (− 106); (− 10), (− 20), (− 30), (− 40) … (− 100)
- Multiples of 10: (+ 1), (+ 2), (+ 3), (+ 4), (+ 5) … ; (+ 10), (+ 20), (+ 30), (+ 40) … (+ 100); (− 1), (− 2), (− 3), (− 4), (− 5) … (− 10); (× 2), (× 5), (× 10)
- Multiples of 100 (16 calculations version only): (+ 1), (+ 2), (+ 3), (+ 4), (+ 5) … ; (+ 10), (+ 20), (+ 30), (+ 40) … (+ 100); (− 1), (− 2), (− 3), (− 4), (− 5) … (− 100); (− 10), (− 20), (− 30), (− 40) … (− 100)
- Multiples of 10 and 100 (49 and 100 calculations versions only): (+ 1), (+ 2), (+ 3), (+ 4), (+ 5) … ; (+ 10), (+ 20), (+ 30), (+ 40) … (+ 100); (+ 100), (+ 200), (+ 300), (+ 400) … (+ 1000); (− 1), (− 2), (− 3), (− 4), (− 5) … (− 10)

Challenge 3

- Provide children with the six versions that require them to perform 49, or if appropriate, 100 calculations.

Whole-class, group or individual activities

Addition and subtraction facts

Multiplication and division facts

Mental fluency challenges

Objectives

- Recall and use addition and subtraction facts to 20 fluently, and derive and use related facts up to 100
- Add and subtract numbers mentally, including a 2-digit number and ones, a 2-digit number and tens, two 2-digit numbers, adding three 1-digit numbers
- Recall and use multiplication and division facts for the 2, 5 and 10 multiplication tables

Teacher resources

→ Mental fluency challenges

- scissors

Pupil resources

- 'Mental fluency challenge' (per child)
- pencil (per child)

Introduction

Fluency in Number Facts: Facts and Games: Years 1 & 2 includes 36 graded 'Mental fluency challenges':

- 18 for Year 1: → Mental fluency challenges → Year 1
- 18 for Year 2: → Mental fluency challenges → Year 2

These challenges are aimed at providing children with further practice and consolidation and also at offering teachers a means of assessing individual children's proficiency in the mental recall of number facts. They can be used with the whole class, specific groups or individual children.

Each exercise covers the key addition, subtraction, multiplication and division number facts that children need to be able to recall instantly by the end of Key Stage 1.

Careful consideration has been given to the progression of the Key Stage 1 curriculum, and for each year group the 18 challenges have been arranged into three different ability levels, with six exercises at each level: Challenge 1 easy, Challenge 2 average and Challenge 3 challenging.

Mental fluency challenges

(continued)

It is recommended that children do the same exercise on two or three consecutive days. This way, the majority of children will see themselves making progress over the two or three days, thus providing greater encouragement and self-motivation.

It is envisaged that these exercises could be given to the children either where they take as long as they need to answer all ten questions, or as a timed exercises (for example: *I want you to answer as many of these questions as you can in eight minutes. Ready? Go!*). Alternatively, to encourage speed and recall, set the children to work and as they finish the exercise they raise their hand and you tell them how long it took them to complete it.

Both PDF and WORD versions of the 'Mental fluency challenges' are provided.

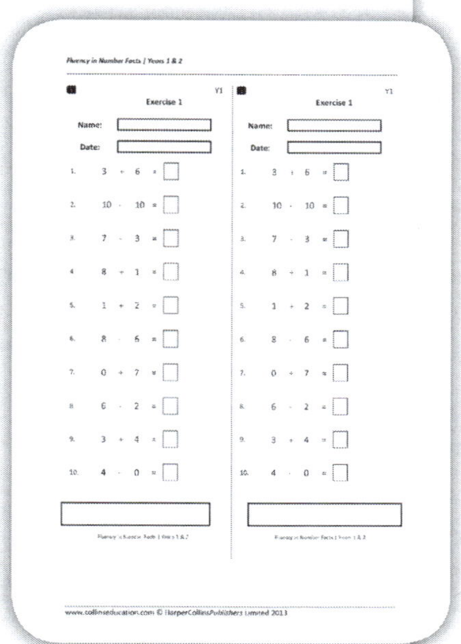
Fluency in Number Facts | Years 1 & 2

Y1

Exercise 1

Name:

Date:

1. 3 + 6 =
2. 10 - 10 =
3. 7 - 3 =
4. 8 + 1 =
5. 1 + 2 =
6. 8 - 6 =
7. 0 + 7 =
8. 6 - 2 =
9. 3 + 4 =
10. 4 - 0 =

www.collinseducation.com © HarperCollinsPublishers

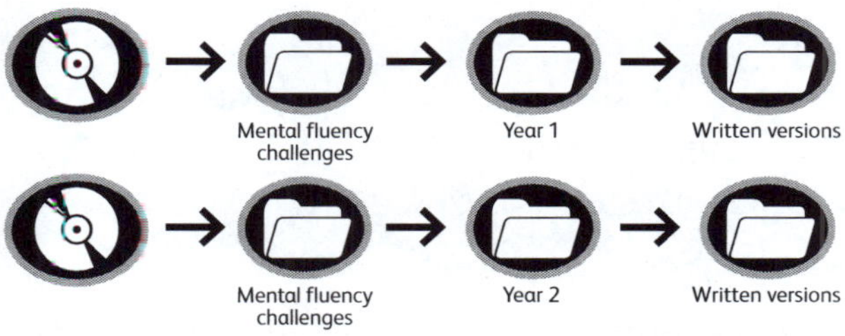

The WORD version is provided so that individual schools or classes can modify the content of the challenges to better suit the needs of their children. However, it is important to be aware that if changes are made to the content, the continuity and progression of the challenges will be affected.

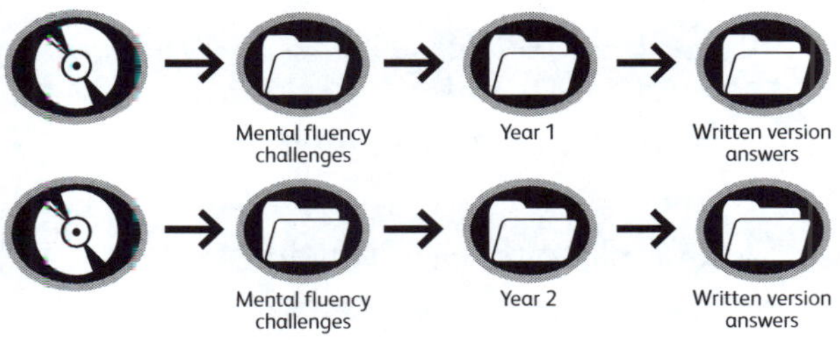

The answers to each of the challenges are provided as individual PDF files. Teachers may want to use these to display to the children when marking and discussing the challenges.

(continued)

Whole-class, group or individual activities

Mental fluency challenges

(continued)

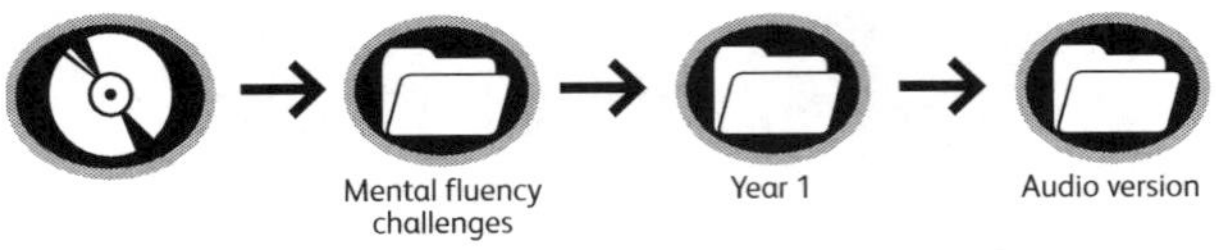

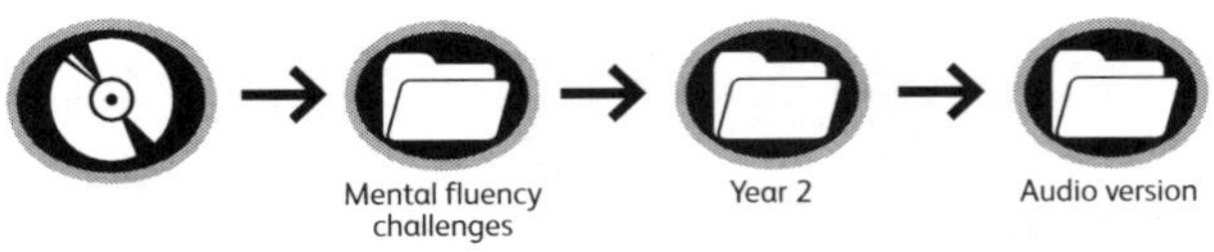

As well as the WORD and PDF versions of the 'Mental fluency challenges', there is also an audio file of each exercise.

A 'Mental fluency challenge answer sheet' is also provided for children to use to record their answers when using the auditory version of the exercises.

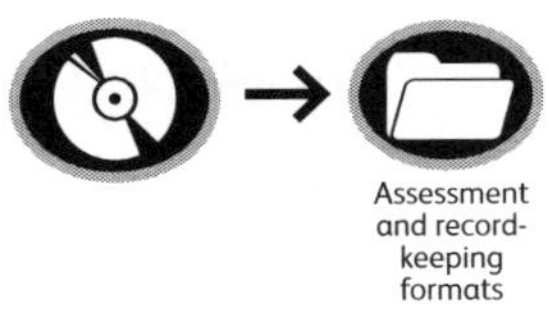

To assist with keeping a record of the different 'Mental fluency exercises' that individual children complete throughout the course of a year, a 'Record of mental fluency exercises chart' for Year 1 and Year 2 is also provided. These charts can also be used to record children's scores.

What to do

- Choose an appropriate exercise for the whole class, specific groups or individual children, taking careful consideration of the different needs and abilities of the children. If undertaking the activity with the whole class, you will probably use an exercise from two or three of the different levels: Challenge 1 easy, Challenge 2 average or Challenge 3 challenging.
- If using the WORD/PDF version, distribute the exercise(s) to the children. If using the audio version, ensure that each child has a copy of the 'Mental fluency exercise answer sheet'. Also ensure that each child has a sharpened pencil!
- Allow the children sufficient time to complete the exercise or set the exercise as a timed activity.
- Once the children have completed the exercise, immediately mark the exercise(s), using the relevant PDF answers sheet(s). You may want to mark the exercise(s) with the children's help, asking children to mark their own exercise or swapping and marking someone else's exercise.
- Be sure to discuss the results of the exercise(s) with the children, asking them which questions they found easy, which they found more difficult, and also referring to specific questions, asking them how they worked out the answer. This should provide some excellent data to help identify common errors or misconceptions that children may have. You can then either follow on with some brief impromptu teaching, assisting children to overcome the errors or misconceptions or, alternatively, keep this information in mind for some further teaching at a later date.
- You may want to use the appropriate 'Record of mental fluency exercises chart' to record the exercise that individual children have completed. You may also want to use the chart to record their score.
- And finally…remember to repeat the same exercise on two or three consecutive days.

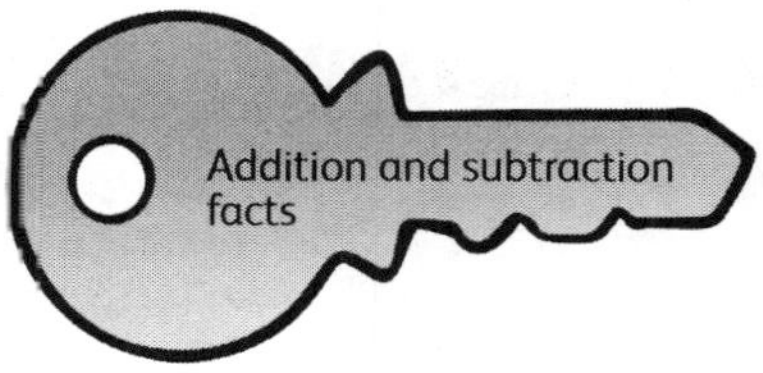

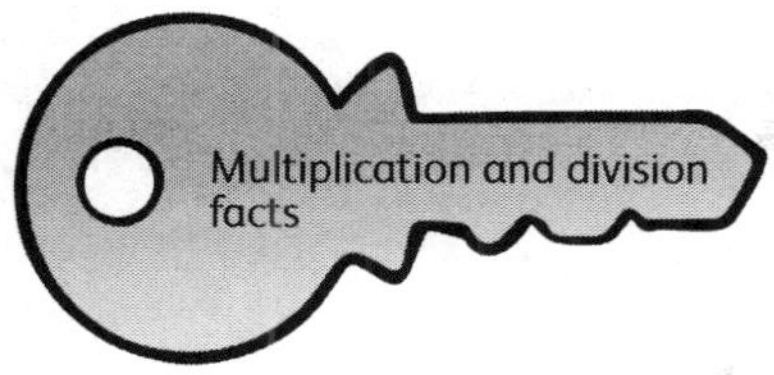

Paired calculations cards

Objectives

- Recall and use addition and subtraction facts to 20 fluently, and derive and use related facts up to 100
- Add and subtract numbers mentally, including a 2-digit number and ones, a 2-digit number and tens, two 2-digit numbers, adding three 1-digit numbers
- Recall and use multiplication and division facts for the 2, 5 and 10 multiplication tables

Teacher resources

- 'Paired calculation cards' (ideally printed onto card)

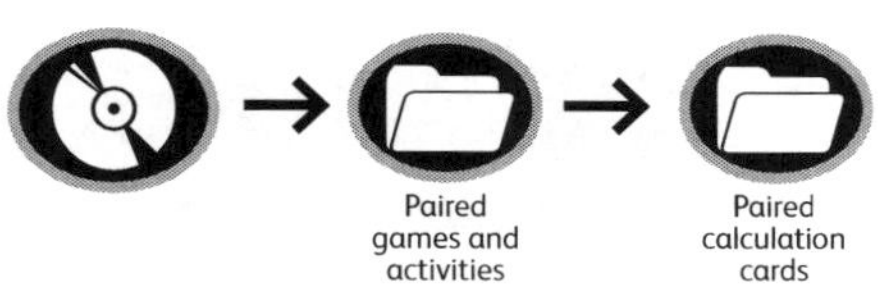

Pupil resources

- 'Paired calculations card' (per pair)

Introduction

Fluency in Number Facts: Facts and Games: Years 1 & 2 includes 36 graded 'Paired calculations cards':

- 18 for Year 1:

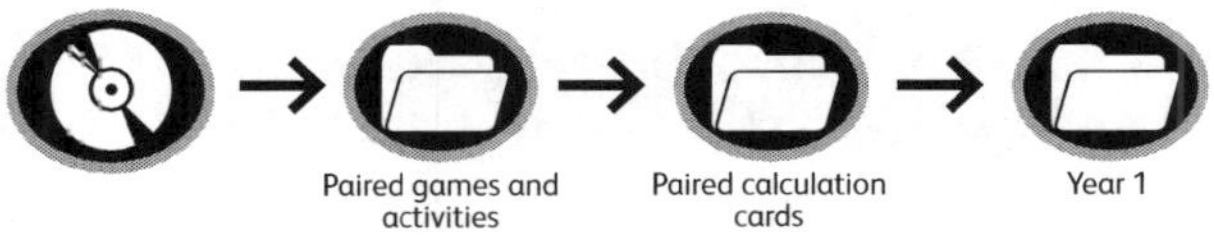

- 18 for Year 2:

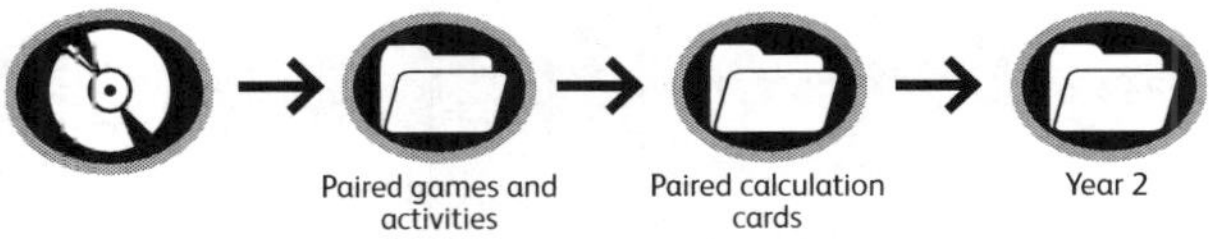

Each card covers the key addition, subtraction, multiplication and division number facts that children need to be able to recall instantly by the end of Key Stage 1.

Careful consideration has been given to the progression of the Key Stage 1 curriculum, and for each year group the 18 cards have been arranged into three different ability levels, with six cards at each level:

Challenge 1 easy, Challenge 2 average and Challenge 3 difficult.

It is recommended that pairs of children use the same card on two or three consecutive days. This way, the majority of children will see themselves making progress over the two or three days, thus providing greater encouragement and self-motivation.

(*continued*)

Paired games and activities

Assessment and record-keeping formats

To assist with keeping a record of the different 'Paired calculations cards' that individual children complete throughout the course of a year, a 'Record of paired calculations cards chart' for Year 1 and Year 2 is also provided.

What to do

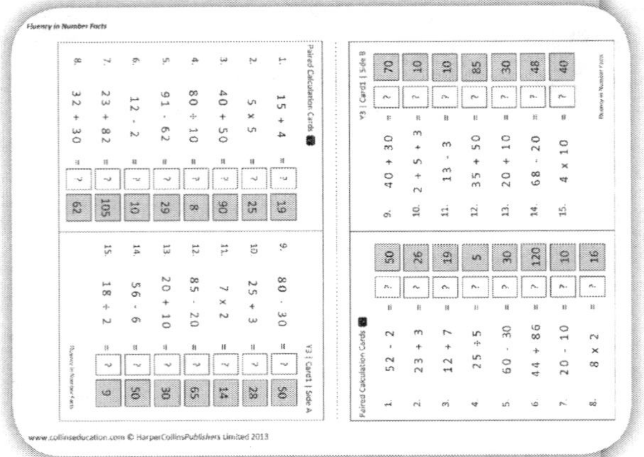

- Arrange the children into pairs of similar ability.
- Provide each pair with an appropriate card, taking careful consideration of the different needs and abilities of the children: Challenge 1 easy, Challenge 2 average or Challenge 3 difficult.
- Each pair positions the card between them, with one child having a clear view of Side A and the other child a clear view of Side B.
- Children take turns to ask their partner the ten questions on their side of the card. Ensure the children realise that they do *not* say the answer in the grey box.
- You may also need to demonstrate to the children how to phrase questions such as 12 + [?] = 30, i.e. *Twelve add what other number equals 30*, and [?] - 8 = 26, i.e. *What number, minus 8, equals 26*.
- As each child says an answer, their partner responds, saying whether the answer is correct or not.
- Once each child has asked their partner the ten questions on their side of the card, the children turn the card around and repeat.
- When pairs have finished be sure to discuss the results with the children, asking them which questions they found easy, which they found more difficult, and also referring to specific questions, asking them how they worked out the answer. This will probably provide some excellent data in helping identify common errors or misconceptions that children may have, which you can then either follow on with some brief impromptu teaching, assisting children to overcome the errors or misconceptions, or alternatively keeping this information in mind for some further teaching at a later date.
- You may want to use the appropriate 'Record of paired calculations cards chart' to record the card that pairs of children have completed.
- And finally…remember to ask pairs of children to use the same card on two or three consecutive days.

Addition and subtraction facts

Multiplication and division facts

Function machine strips

Objectives

- Recall and use addition and subtraction facts to 20 fluently, and derive and use related facts up to 100
- Add and subtract numbers mentally, including a 2-digit number and ones, a 2-digit number and tens, two 2-digit numbers, adding three 1-digit numbers
- Recall and use multiplication and division facts for the 2, 5 and 10 multiplication tables

Teacher resources

→ Individual activities → Function machine strips

- 'Function machine strips' (ideally printed onto card)
- scissors

Pupil resources

- 'Function machine strip' (per child)
- 'Function machine' ('My Little Maths Function Machine', B&W or colour version) printed onto card (per child)

Introduction

Fluency in Number Facts: Facts and Games: Years 1 & 2 includes 36 graded 'Function machine strips':

- 18 for Year 1: → Individual activities → Function machine strips → Year 1
- 18 for Year 2: → Individual activities → Function machine strips → Year 2

Each 'Function machine strip' covers the key addition, subtraction, multiplication and division number facts that children need to be able to recall instantly by the end of Key Stage 1.

Careful consideration has been given to the progression of the Key Stage 1 curriculum, and for each year group the 18 strips have been arranged into three different ability levels, with six strips at each level:

Challenge 1 easy, Challenge 2 average and Challenge 3 difficult.

It is recommended that children use the same strip on several consecutive days – perhaps even for a whole week. This way, the majority of children will see themselves making progress, thus providing greater encouragement and self-motivation.

(*continued*)

It is recommended that before children do the 'Function machine strip' activity for the first time, that you provide each child with a copy of the 'Function machine' ('My Little Maths Function Machine') which is printed onto card for the children to personalise.

Assessment & record-keeping formats

To assist with keeping a record of the different 'Function machine strips' that individual children complete throughout the course of a year, a 'Record of Function machine strips chart' for Year 1 and Year 2 is also provided.

What to do

- Provide each child with an appropriate strip, taking careful consideration of the different needs and abilities of the children: Challenge 1 easy, Challenge 2 average or Challenge 3 challenging.
- Children carefully feed the strip through their Function machine, only revealing one calculation at a time.
- The child works out the answer and then moves the strip on slightly to reveal the answer.
- Children continue in this way until they get to the end of the strip and the tenth answer is revealed.
- Encourage the children to use the same strip several times in one session – aiming to make fewer errors and/or to complete the strip in a shorter period of time.
- When individual children have finished, you may want to ask them which questions they found easy, which they found more difficult, and also referring to specific questions, asking them how they worked out the answer. This should provide some excellent data in helping identify common errors or misconceptions that children may have, which you can then either follow on with some brief impromptu teaching, assisting children to overcome the errors or misconceptions, or alternatively keeping this information in mind for some further teaching at a later date.
- You may want to use the appropriate 'Record of Function machine strips chart' to record the strips that individual children have completed.
- And finally…remember to ask the children to use the same strip on several consecutive days.